AUDITOR'S DICTIONARY

Terms, Concepts, Processes, and Regulations

David O'Regan

WILEY

John Wiley & Sons. Inc.

Library of Congress Cataloging-in-Publication Data:

O'Regan, David.
    Auditor's dictionary : terms, concepts, processes, and regulations / David O'Regan.
        p. cm.
    ISBN 0-471-53118-9 (cloth)
    1. Auditing—Dictionaries. I. Title.
    HF5667.O6728 2004
    657'.03—dc22

                                                                    2004003665

Printed in the United States of America

10 9 8 7 6 5 4 3 2 1

To Abhishikta and my parents

Acknowledgments

When this dictionary was under preparation a great deal of assistance, generosity, and razor-sharp comment came my way. I wish to acknowledge my gratitude to all those who helped me by answering queries, giving opinions, drawing attention to valuable sources, and supplying information and documents from private collections. All of this led to a better book.

I thank the following (with apologies for the inadvertent omission of any academic or professional titles): Lynne Alexander, Chris Allen, Rachel Alterator, Professor Urton Anderson, John Marnie Angeles, Dolores Argo, Susannah Bolton, Barbara Brady, Fergus Brown, Geordie Cassin, Professor Andrew Chambers, Chiba Kanan, Danielle Cohen, Dr. Robert Colson, Charlie Culkin, Shirley Davies, Stefan de Greling, Wendeline Dill, Aslam Dossa, Sheila Doyle, Kim Ellis, Professor Serge Evraert, Michael Feland, Professor Dale L. Flesher, Ndung'u Gathinji, Giam Siewhun, Damarys Gil, Deborah Harrington, Trish Harris, Ho Foong Chin, Midori Imhoof, Kathleen Kraemer, Lisa Krist, John Lamming, Professor Tom A. Lee, Brenda Lovell, Janet Maillard, Professor Keith Maunders, David McNamee, Christine Miller, Professor Belverd E. Needles Jr., George Ochido, Des O'Neil, Nicola Perry, Professor Michael Power, Professor Gary J. Previts, Professor Phil Reckers, Kathy Rice, Professor Jeffrey Ridley, Dr James Roth, Professor Prem Nath Sikka, Megan Spillane, Lesley Stephenson, Chuck Teeter, Geneviève Tremblay, Terry Trsar, Professor Curtis C. Verschoor, Professor Gerald Vinten, Margaret Walsh, Robert Whitaker, Jim Woehlke, Susan Wright, and Dan Zautis.

I also thank John Wiley & Sons, Inc., and Tim Burgard in particular, for taking on a project unprecedented in the field of auditing. I thank Karen Ludke, Petrina Kulek, and Louise Jacob at John Wiley & Sons, Inc., for their support in seeing the book through to publication.

My record of gratitude to all those who assisted me in my search for enlightenment does not imply any endorsement of my definitions. Indeed, individuals may on occasion dissent vigorously from my interpretations. This is not a dictionary created by a committee of consensus, and any errors are my responsibility alone. I invite readers' comments, corrections, and criticisms to help ensure the quality and accuracy of any future editions.

In his *Dictionary of the English Language* (1755), Samuel Johnson remarked that "to make dictionaries is dull work." I wouldn't necessarily agree with Dr. Johnson's view, but I can certainly confirm that dictionary-writing is a grueling task. I thank my wife, Abhishikta, for her encouragement, affection, and love, which greatly helped me in the preparation of this book.

David O'Regan
Oxford, U.K.
July 2004

About the Author

David O'Regan is Head of Audit at Oxford University Press in Oxford, England. He is a fellow of the Institute of Chartered Accountants in England and Wales. He is the author of *International Auditing—Practical Resource Guide* (Wiley, 2003) and two audit-related books for the Institute of Internal Auditors. His articles and essays have appeared in U.S. and British professional and academic journals, including *Internal Auditor* and *Managerial Auditing Journal*. Prior to joining Oxford University Press he worked for United Technologies Corporation and Price Waterhouse (the forerunner to PricewaterhouseCoopers). Further information on his writing is available at *www.davidoregan.com*.

Contents

Preface

What is meant by **Enronitis**, **facilitating payment**, **lapping**, **negative assurance**, and **phantom ticking**? This dictionary offers a measure of clarity to these and other terms in the complex and evolving language of auditing. Auditing has been in continuous development over the last century and a half, and words continue to jostle for prominence in the auditing lexicon: some auditing terms turn out to be intransient and fall away into obscurity, while others gather a solid basis of usage. With increasing trends toward systematic auditing practice and theory, there is now a pressing need for rigor in the discipline's terminology.[1]

Given the large number of auditing professionals today, and an ever-increasing level of public interest with auditing, it is perhaps surprising that no dictionary specifically dedicated to the subject has previously appeared.[2] This book aims to fill the gap, and it is therefore the first of its kind. Its target audience includes practitioners, students, and scholars of auditing. Indeed, it should be of use to anyone whose work demands familiarity with auditing and corporate governance, including individuals subjected to auditing processes and those whose duties involve the reading of audit reports. As well as serving as a reference tool, I also hope that the dictionary will act as a learning aid and as a complement to study.

As this dictionary has no precedent, an explanation of its aims may assist the reader in assessing its utility. My intention has been to define and clarify the meanings of essential auditing terms and concepts, to illustrate their usage, and to point toward further sources of information. In attempting to dispel some of the mists surrounding auditing terminology, I have attempted to combine a reasonable degree of academic rigor with brevity[3] and practical relevance. A book of this size cannot hope to provide in-depth treatment of every topic it mentions, and for this reason many of the entries have guidance to further reading and to more detailed sources of information. In areas of contention or dispute, I have tried to strike a neutral balance between differing standpoints. Although the dictionary's primary aim is to give up-to-date information, it also keeps an eye on the historical context in which the language of auditing has developed.

In addition to the terminology and concepts of auditing, the dictionary also covers the discipline's major international institutions, people, and publications. In all these cases, brief sketches are given, with suggested further reading and Web links, as appropriate. Some selectivity has been necessary. With institutions, I have tried to restrict entries to the auditing-related institutes of larger countries. For example, to include every single institute of chartered accountants seemed excessive; therefore, while I have listed the chartered accountants' institute of Bangladesh (population: 140 million), I have excluded that of neighboring Nepal (population: 25 million). With individuals, I have sought to include writers, theorists, and practitioners who have made important contributions to contemporary auditing thought or practice. I had to draw my lines somewhere, and the inclusion or exclusion of a publication, organization, or individual should not be interpreted as a definitive value judgment.

The terminology of auditing has a solid center, yet no discernable circumference. Its words are not simply lying around, ready to be picked up or harvested. In addition to what may be considered "core" auditing terminology, the dictionary also contains entries that derive from a number of disciplines: financial accounting, management accounting, corporate governance, economics, finance, information technology, law, and management science. Auditing borrows terminology in a promiscuous fashion, as it has emerged from complex interactions between all these contributory disciplines. However, auditing frequently modifies the meanings of the words it borrows. An auditor's definition of **cell**, for example, differs significantly from that of a biologist or a lawyer. A *chacun son métier*,[4] as the French would say.

For these reasons, no description, explanation, or portrayal of auditing can avoid encroaching on a range of disciplines. However, I have sought to strike a balance by selecting only the terms, concepts, and institutions from other disciplines that seemed most relevant to auditing,[5] and I have defined them with their auditing meanings prominent.

The first draft of this dictionary was written almost continuously, within one year, to encourage a broad consistency of style. I have taken a rather formulaic approach to the preparation of some categories of entry—the entries for auditing publications, for example, tend to contain similar types of information—but have attempted to make the narrative of entries sufficiently varied to avoid an overly mechanical feel.

Perhaps the atmosphere of Oxford University Press, home of the *Oxford English Dictionary*, provided the initial motivation and the subsequent inspiration for research into auditing lexicography. I soon discovered that the language of auditing shows no sign of losing its vigor, and it is to be expected that it will continue to evolve, redefine itself, and grow. As ground-breaking dictionary writers from Samuel Johnson in England to Pierre Larousse in France to Noah Webster in the United States have realized (and lamented), languages are unstable. In this sense, the language of auditing will never pause or come to rest, and it cannot be seized forever. As we have suggested, some words in current use may turn out to be ephemeral, while others may yet to have made their appearance. Dictionaries always carry inherent limitations and I am aware that this dictionary is a preliminary rather than a definitive work. A dictionary of auditing can be started, but in a sense it can never be completed.

It is to be expected, therefore, that an ambitious project such as this one cannot guarantee perfection. Further, this is not a dictionary by committee, but one individual's attempt to portray the languages, terms, institutions, and individuals of auditing—despite constant attempts at objectivity in compiling and describing this language inventory, an authorial voice is inevitably present. Regardless of help from a number of people who assisted me in various ways in the preparation of the dictionary (I list my gratitude in the acknowledgments), and the making of every effort to ensure the accuracy and completeness of the entries, any shortcomings in the dictionary are mine alone. It is a pioneering and innovative work, with all the strengths and weaknesses of an undertaking of this nature.

Not even the most zealous auditor or the most conscientious student always consults a dictionary out of a sense of duty. Reference to a dictionary often transcends the stern dictates of work: It can be a means of satisfying one's curiosity. Preparing this book was a labor of love, and I hope that it can be browsed—perhaps even read—as well as consulted. Extensive cross-references serve as a mechanism for meandering and browsing through the concepts, institutions, and personalities of auditing, while quotations and anecdotes are intended to enliven the text and to serve as memory-joggers. I hope the dictionary will be both a valuable contribution to the understanding and development of auditing, and an interesting gateway to an exploration of this complex, fascinating subject.

Notes

1. Some lexicographers may quibble with the use of the term "dictionary" to describe this book. "Alphabetical encyclopedia" and "encyclopedic dictionary" are among the terms commonly used to describe reference works that, like the present one, refer to things rather than to words (as coded linguistic units). A common rule of thumb used by linguists is that "an encyclopeadia can be translated, but a dictionary cannot" (Béjoint, 2000, 30). I believe this book could be translated, but I still prefer to use the term dictionary, as the word encyclopedia would suggest that this book contains all there is to know about auditing. But I shall leave the quibbling to the metalexicographical literature.

2. Although no dictionary of auditing has been published prior to this one, there have been limited attempts to describe aspects of auditing vocabulary. In 1975, for example, the Institute of Internal Auditors published James E. Smith's *Evaluation of Selected Internal Auditing Terms*. In addition, many auditing books contain glossaries of terminology that aim to define a selection of words. Otherwise, auditors have traditionally been obliged to consult the auditing-related entries of accounting dictionaries.

3. An example of brevity can be seen in entries for the Financial Accounting Standards Board, the International Accounting Standards Board, and other accounting standard-setting bodies. Individual accounting standards have not been listed, as that would have leaned too much toward the kind of information properly housed in an accounting reference source. In recompense, the entries have Web links to detailed accounting standards.

4. "Let each person do his or her own job."

5. I was guided in my selection of terms by the use of word frequency searches in auditing journals.

User Guide

Entries

Each dictionary entry begins with a head word or head phrase in bold type. Many head words and phrases are followed by additional information in parentheses, ranging from abbreviations and acronyms to the biographical dates of individuals. Entries are arranged alphabetically by the entry's entire heading. This letter-by-letter alphabetization ignores hyphens and spaces in compound word entries, so **bankruptcy** appears between **bank reconciliation** and **bank statement**, and **value-at-risk** between **value added tax** and **value-for-money auditing**. Numbers are listed before letters, so the entry *Head 2 Head* appears before **Head of Audit**.

Each entry contains an explanatory narrative. The first sentence within an entry provides a brief, basic definition, and the remainder of the entry gives further information and, where appropriate, examples of usage and sources of further information. Variants of definitions and meanings are listed under numerical subheadings—generally, primary (or most recent) meanings are listed before secondary (or archaic) meanings. The book's focus is naturally on the meanings of words most closely relevant to auditing. For example, the entry **population** considers the term from the point of view of sampling analysis, rather than from a human demographic perspective. Lists within entries are normally numbered with lower case Roman numerals, unless it is a direct quotation that uses another listing method, such as bullet points or Arabic numerals (as in the entry for **postulates of auditing**).

Spelling conventions

In general, the dictionary's spelling conventions follow those of American English, unless a reference is to another version of English—British, Australian, Indian, and so on. The context should make this clear. In quotations, spellings have on occasion been Americanized for consistency with the entry as a whole (e.g., the ending of some words have been changed from —ise to —ize). The use of upper case letters where there are no hard and fast rules (in examples like **Certified Internal Auditor** and **chartered accountant**) has been guided by general convention.

Grammar

All verbs listed as head words are indicated by the particle "to." Otherwise, the dictionary only specifies the grammatical functions of words in cases where different meanings are attributable to different grammatical uses. For example, the term **multinational** is listed as both a noun and an adjective. In these cases, the grammatical use is stated in square brackets.

Italics

Italics are used for the names of publications, for Web addresses, and for non-English words.

Abbreviations

Abbreviations are not generally listed as separate headings in the main body of the dictionary: They are stated instead after the relevant head word or head phrase, and are used thereafter within the narrative of the corresponding entry. For clarity, there is a separate list of abbreviations at the end of the dictionary that cross-references into the main body of the text. However, some entries are based on acronyms that serve as the standard name or term for a concept, institution, or publication: for example, **CSA Sentinel** and **KPMG International**.

Proper names

All names of individuals are listed in the sequence of family name followed by given names: for example, **Montgomery, Robert Hiester (1872–1953)**. This convention is followed for names from countries, such as Japan, where the order of names is usually the reverse of that in the English-speaking world.

Cross-references

An asterisk denotes a cross-reference to another dictionary entry, such as a synonym, antonym, or related item. The asterisk appears immediately before the cross-referenced word, phrase, or name. When a cross-reference is to an entry with several definitions, the number of the definition is specified where there is a risk of confusion. With individuals' names, the asterisk precedes the entire name, but the corresponding dictionary entry occurs with the surname only—for example, ***Prem Nath Sikka** indicates a cross-reference to the entry **Sikka, Prem Nath (born 1951)**. The cross-referencing system ignores grammatical differences, so that **fraudulent** cross-references to **fraud, materiality** to **material**, and **reconcile** to **reconciliation**. Cross-references also ignore inflections of words, including differences between singular and plural forms. A cross-reference given in a quotation does not suggest the presence of an asterisk in the original, cited text.

Cross-references occur only when a major connection is at issue, but they are nonetheless relatively extensive in the dictionary. However, while there are innumerable instances where it is worthwhile to prompt the reader to look elsewhere to shed light on a series of intellectual links, measures have been taken to avoid overburdening the text with too many asterisks. First, asterisks appear only with the first appearance of a word within an entry (or within a numbered section of an entry). Second, a number of commonly occurring words and phrases have generally not been cross-referenced, including **accounting**, **audit(ing)**, **external audit(ing)**, **internal audit(ing)**, and **management**, unless they form part of a compound word entry like **audit shop** or **management accounting**.

Quotations and examples of usage

Quotations and examples of usage are placed within quotation marks. An abbreviated reference in parentheses links a quotation to a work listed in full in the bibliography. For example, the reference "Power, 1997" corresponds to the bibliography's full format of "Power, Michael (1997) *The Audit Society: Rituals of Verification* (Oxford and New York: Oxford University Press)." Where more than one text is listed for an individual author in a specific year, the publications are numbered with lower case letters—for example, 1997a, 1997b, and so on. Where more than one author shares a surname, an initial is used to distinguish them. For example, **Andrew Chambers** and **Raymond John Chambers** are referred to as **Chambers, A.** and **Chambers, R. J.**, respectively.

An edited quotation uses three dots to indicate an omission, while the use of square brackets within a quotation identifies an item inserted to ease the grammatical flow of the text. Unless stated otherwise, all references to books, articles, and Web resources are to English-language items.

Where no reference is given, phrases in quotation marks are illustrative examples of usage devised by the author. Examples of usage are given liberally throughout the dictionary, especially to distinguish alternative meanings of a word.

Etymologies

The dictionary does not generally give the etymologies of words, unless they are unusual or of particular interest—for example, **acid test**, **blue chip**, and **boycott**. Etymologies are also discussed where they add to an understanding of a term. For example, the etymology of the word **audit** adds to an understanding of auditing's history and development. Quotations of words and phrases are not usually the first example of usage, but rather illustrative examples of the use of the term or concept under discussion.

Registered trademarks

Evidence of trademarks and registered brands has been identified in the dictionary by use of the symbols ®, TM, and SM. Every effort has been made to verify the existence of trademarks. Many professional organizations and publications have trademark protection yet choose to avoid the overt use of trademark symbols. Where there was any doubt, the potential trademark holder was contacted during the preparation of this dictionary to clarify trademark status—most replied, but some did not. The reader should not therefore consider either the presence or absence of a trademark designation as a judgment on its legal status, and should take appropriate legal and professional advice before using any name or term with potential proprietary status. Reference in the dictionary to a trademark can refer to a name, an acronym, or the design of an acronym embedded in a logo or symbol.

"'When *I* use a word,' Humpty Dumpty said in a
rather scornful tone, 'it means just what I choose it to mean—
neither more nor less.'"

—Lewis Carroll, *Through the Looking Glass* (1872)

"What a comfort a Dictionary is!"

—Lewis Carroll, *Sylvie and Bruno Concluded* (1893)

abacus An archaic calculating contraption. Various forms of abacus have existed throughout the ages in many of the world's cultures, from ancient China to premodern Central Asia.

Abacus: A Journal of Accounting, Finance and Business Studies An Australian scholarly accounting journal. Established by *Raymond John Chambers in 1965, *Abacus* is published in three issues annually by Blackwell Publishing, on behalf of the University of Sydney's *Accounting Foundation. It is available in print and online formats. The journal's notes (available at its Web link) state that it provides "a vehicle for the expression of independent and critical thought on matters of current academic and professional interest in accounting, finance and business. The journal reports current research; critically evaluates current developments in theory and practice; analyses the effects of the regulatory framework of accounting, finance and business; and explores alternatives to, and explanations of, past and current practices." Although primarily geared toward accounting, it also has extensive coverage of auditing. Its coverage is international.

Web link: *www.blackwellpublishing.com/journals/ABACUS*

abnormal spoilage Avoidable waste, scrap, and defective goods arising from manufacturing processes. In contrast to *normal spoilage, abnormal *spoilage is not considered to be an inherent part of a manufacturing process, and it tends to be expensed as incurred.

ABO Reporter, The A U.S. accounting newsletter. Published twice a year by the Accounting, Behavior and Organizations (ABO) Section of the *American Accounting Association, the newsletter is available in both print and online formats. It includes announcements and calls for papers for publication in the ABO journal *Behavioral Research in Accounting*.

Web link: *http://business.baylor.edu/Charles_Davis//abo/rptr_home.htm*

above the line In a position in an *income statement that directly affects *net income. The "line" is the point in the income statement that separates items that determine net income from items that determine *funding and the *distribution of net income. Traditionally, *Generally Accepted Accounting Principles

(GAAP) around the world have distinguished between *exceptional items, treated above the line, and *extraordinary items, treated *below the line. In recent years, however, GAAP has tended to move toward encouraging both these categories of unusual expenses to appear above the line, and thereby to directly affect *earnings per share.

absolute risk A *risk unaffected or unmitigated by *internal controls.

absorption costing A costing method that allocates all *manufacturing costs to *units of *inventory or other measures of output. Normally required by most systems of *Generally Accepted Accounting Principles, absorption costing takes account of both *direct (or *variable) costs and manufacturing *overheads. The overheads are typically allocated to *cost centers and then absorbed into units of inventory at predetermined rates. Nonmanufacturing costs (both fixed and variable) are expensed as incurred and are not absorbed into inventory valuation.

Academy of Accounting Historians A U.S. organization dedicated to accounting history. Established in 1973, the academy's activities include conferences, research programs, and the publication of monographs, newsletters (or "notebooks"), and the *Accounting Historians Journal*. Although primarily geared toward accounting, the academy's work frequently covers auditing. Membership is internationally based.

Web site: *accounting.rutgers.edu/raw/aah*

ACCA Internal Audit Bulletin A British internal auditing newsletter. Published online by the *Association of Chartered Certified Accountants (ACCA), the quarterly bulletin covers internal auditing news and events in an international context.

Web link: *www.accaglobal.com/publications/audit*

accelerated method A cost allocation method that provides for larger amounts in earlier time periods. The rationale for using an accelerated method is that the economic activity of the underlying assets or circumstances occurs most intensively in the earliest time periods. For example, under accelerated *amortization the cost of a *long-term asset is expensed more heavily in the early years of its *useful economic life, on the grounds that the asset is characterized by rapidly diminishing efficiency, or is subject to a high risk of early *obsolescence. Where amortization costs are deductible for tax purposes, accelerated methods of depreciation offer accelerated tax benefits.

Accenture® An international management consulting, technology services, and *outsourcing organization. Formerly known as Andersen Consulting, Accenture broke away from the now-defunct *Big Five accounting firm *Arthur Andersen in 2000, after an acrimonious corporate divorce. Accenture has a huge global presence, with more than 75,000 employees around the world.

Web site: *www.accenture.com*

account **1.** A record of financial *transactions within a *general ledger for an individual *asset or *liability, or for an area of *revenue or *expenditure. Normally expressed in monetary terms, accounts are the recording mechanisms through which the transactions of *double entry bookkeeping are effected. Accounts are summarized into a *trial balance en route to the preparation of *financial statements. Some accounts, known as *memorandum accounts, are designed to be maintained separately from the double entry bookkeeping process. **2.** A summary of the financial transactions between two parties. For example, relations between a bank and its customers are normally controlled through individually numbered accounts. Accounts of this nature are normally summarized in formal, periodic statements between the two parties: the *bank statement is the classic example.

accountability The condition of being responsible for an action, *asset, *entity, *procedure, or *process. Individuals with accountability are usually required to justify their actions or decisions in the areas they monitor or safeguard. Modern *corporate governance is dedicated to defining organizational accountability, and to establishing suitable mechanisms for its enforcement and reporting. A *board of directors effects a large part of its accountability for *stewardship of a corporation to *investors and other *stakeholders through the mechanism of published *financial statements. It is sometimes noted that chains of accountability generally run upward through organizational structures, in contrast to chains of delegation of authority, which tend to run downward.

*Audits are often depicted as central to accountability: auditing has been described as a means of "securing the accountability of individuals and organisations" (Flint, 1988, 3), and it has been claimed that "Without audit, no accountability; without accountability, no *control; and if there is no control, where is the seat of power?... great issues often come to light only because of scrupulous *verification of details" (W. J .M MacKenzie, foreword to Normanton, 1966). See also *agency theory.

AccountAbility An international *not-for-profit organization dedicated to the promotion of *sustainability and corporate *accountability. Based in London, and founded in 1986, AccountAbility's full name is the Institute of Social and Ethical Accountability. Its activities include publications, research, public policy initiatives, and the promulgation of formal assurance standards for sustainability reporting. The standards, known as the AA1000 framework, are intended to encourage *stakeholder participation in corporate activities.

Web site: *www.accountability.org.uk*

accountancy A British term for *accounting.

Accountancy A British professional accounting magazine. The monthly magazine of the *Institute of Chartered Accountants in England and Wales, *Accountancy* is available in print and online formats. The magazine focuses on professional developments and news in the fields of accounting, auditing, and taxation, with particular focus on the United Kingdom.

Web site: *www.accountancymag.co.uk*

Accountancy, Business, and the Public Interest A British scholarly accounting journal. Established in 2002, the journal's founding editors were Christine Cooper of the University of Strathclyde, Glasgow, and *Prem Nath Sikka of the University of Essex. Published twice a year in online format by the *Association for Accountancy and Business Affairs, the journal is available free of charge. It follows the objectives of its parent organization by providing a forum for critical analysis of auditing and accounting practices. Reformist in tone, and reflecting many concerns of the *critical accounting movement, its coverage focuses on the United Kingdom.

Web site: *http://visar.csustan.edu/aaba/aabajournalpage.htm*

Accountancy Foundation An accounting regulatory authority in the United Kingdom. Established in 2000, the Foundation is headquartered in London. Its Web site states that its "overriding objective is to maintain and enhance the standards of work and of conduct of accountants working in the United Kingdom and the Republic of Ireland." Its structure of subsidiary bodies—the *Auditing Practices Board (APB), the Ethics Standards Board, and the Investigation and Discipline Board—is overseen by a Review Board. At the time of writing, the Financial Reporting Council was taking over the duties of the Accountancy Foundation.

Web site: *www.accountancyfoundation.com*

Accountancy Ireland An Irish accounting magazine. Published bimonthly by the *Institute of Chartered Accountants in Ireland, the magazine is available in both print and online formats. It focuses on professional developments and news in the fields of accounting, auditing, and taxation, with emphasis on Ireland and (to a lesser degree) the European Union.

Web link: *www.icai.ie/Publications/lp-accire.cfm*

Accountancy S.A. A South African accounting magazine. Published monthly by the *South African Institute of Chartered Accountants, it is available in both print and online formats. The magazine focuses on professional developments and news in accounting, auditing, and taxation, with particular focus on South Africa (and, to a lesser extent, Africa more widely).

Web site: *www.accountancysa.org.za*

accountant An individual who performs *accounting duties. Some of the accountant's responsibilities may overlap with those of the *bookkeeper, in terms of the recording of individual financial *transactions, but the accountant's terms of reference tend to be the wider of the two. Among other things, the accountant may prepare, audit, or analyze *financial statements; analyze *costs; prepare *taxation schedules; or perform operational *consulting services. Most accountants derive their authority from membership of *professional organizations such as the *American Institute of Certified Public Accountants and the *Institute of Management Accountants. Membership of professional accounting bodies tends to require examination success, periods of relevant experience, or a combination of both.

Accountant, The A British accounting newsletter. Published monthly by Lafferty Publications, the newsletter claims to be the world's oldest accounting serial. It is available in both print and online formats. The newsletter's Web page states that it "reports on the development of accounting standards and corporate reporting practices world-wide, auditor liability, increasing competition, the policies and politics of *professional bodies and all the major issues which face accountants in today's complex marketplace." Its coverage is international, and the auditing content tends to focus on external auditing.

Web link: *www.lafferty.com/newsletter/newsletter_02_publication.asp?PubID=TA*

accounting A broad term that encompasses the preparation, analysis, and audit of financial information. The many specialisms of accounting include auditing, *consulting, *cost accounting, *financial accounting, *management accounting, *public accounting, *public sector accounting, and *taxation. Although accounting covers many disciplines, professional accounting retains a rather dull image—an old joke (quoted in Fox, 2003, 181) has defined an "extroverted accountant" as "one who stared at the client's shoes while speaking instead of staring at his own shoes."

Accounting & Business A British professional accounting magazine. Published monthly by the *Association of Chartered Certified Accountants, the magazine is available in both print and online formats. It covers a range of business and accounting topics, with frequent articles on auditing. Its coverage is international, but with emphasis on the United Kingdom.

Web link: *www.acca.co.uk/publications/accountingandbusiness*

Accounting and Auditing Organization for Islamic Financial Institutions (AAOIFI) An accounting and auditing body dedicated to the promotion of Islamic principles for financial institutions. Established in 1991 and headquartered in Bahrain, the AAOIFI is an affiliated member of the *International Federation of Accountants. Its Web site describes its primary focus as the preparation of "accounting, auditing, governance, ethics and Shari'a standards for Islamic financial institutions." Its membership is internationally based, and includes investment banks and accounting organizations. To meet the requirements of Shari'a law and the traditions of *Islamic finance, the AAOIFI issues English-language accounting and auditing standards, details of which are available from the AAOIFI Web site.

Web site: *www.aaoifi.com*

Accounting and Business Research A British scholarly accounting journal. Established in 1970, the journal is published quarterly by the *Institute of Chartered Accountants in England and Wales. It is available in print format only. The journal focuses on research into aspects of accounting and auditing, with the latter's emphasis on external auditing. Its coverage is international, but with special focus on the United Kingdom.

Web site: *www.icaew.co.uk*

Accounting, Auditing and Accountability Journal A British scholarly accounting and auditing journal. Established in 1988, the journal is published in five issues a year by MCB University Press in Bradford, England. It is available in print and online formats. The journal's notes declare its focus to be research into "the interaction between accounting/auditing and their socio-economic and political environments," and claim that the journal "challenges conventional wisdom, explores alternatives and offers new perspectives." Its coverage is international.

Web site: *www.mcb.co.uk*

Accounting, Business, and Financial History A British scholarly accounting history journal. Established in 1990, the journal is published in three issues a year by Routledge. It is available in print and online formats. The journal focuses on accounting history, and includes regular coverage of auditing history. Its notes state that its focus includes investigation of "the inter-relationship between accounting practices, financial markets and economic development." Its coverage is international.

Web link: *www.tandf.co.uk/journals/routledge/09585206.html*

Accounting Education: An International Journal A British scholarly accounting journal. Established in 1992, the journal is published quarterly by

Routledge. It is available in print and online formats. The journal's notes describe it as "devoted to publishing research-based papers and other information on key aspects of accounting education and training of relevance to practitioners, academics, trainers, students and professional bodies." The journal's coverage includes auditing, and it is international in scope.

Web link: *www.tandf.co.uk/journals/routledge/09639284.html*

accounting equation, the *Assets = *liabilities + *capital. Under the conventions of *double entry bookkeeping, each accounting transaction has at least one *debit entry and at least one *credit entry of equal value. At any moment, the mathematical integrity of bookkeeping can be established by reference to the accuracy of the accounting (or *balance sheet) equation. In the balance sheet, assets are recorded through debit entries, and liabilities and capital (or *equity) through credit entries. While the accounting equation shows that a balance sheet balances, it does not indicate whether individual transactions have been booked to the appropriate *accounts.

Accounting Foundation An Australian accounting organization housed within the University of Sydney. Established in 1982, the foundation oversees the publication of the journal *Abacus, manages the activities of the *Pacioli Society, and funds accounting-related research and scholarships. Its Web site states that its objectives include cooperation between "industry, commerce and the accounting profession to promote excellence in all fields of accounting and financial management in Australia." Its activities are wider than this would suggest, however, and it encourages international academic links.

Web link: *www.econ.usyd.edu.au/content.php?pageid=567*

Accounting Hall of Fame An institution that honors contributions to accounting and auditing. Established by Ohio State University in 1950, the Accounting Hall of Fame is located in the university's Fisher College of Business, and its Web site describes its purpose as follows: To be "honoring accountants who have made or are making significant contributions to the advancement of accounting since the beginning of the twentieth century." It describes the types of services to accounting expected of its inductees: "[C]ontributions to accounting research and literature, significant service to professional accounting organizations, wide recognition as an authority in some field of accounting, advancement of accounting education, and public service." The Ohio State University Press also publishes works of some of the Hall of Fame members. The nominating board is international in character, and individuals honored in the Hall of Fame include *Raymond John Chambers and *Robert Kuhn Mautz.

Web link: *http://fisher.osu.edu/hall*

Accounting Historians Journal A U.S. referred accounting history journal. Established in 1974 and published semi-annually by the *Academy of Accounting Historians, the journal is available in print format only. Its editorship changes annually. This highly scholarly journal disseminates research into aspects of accounting history, including a significant emphasis on auditing history. The journal's notes declare its aim of embracing "all subject matter related to accounting history, including but not limited to research that provides an historical perspective on contemporary accounting issues." Its coverage is international.

Web link: *http://accounting.rutgers.edu/raw/aah*

Accounting History An Australian referred accounting history journal. Established in 1996 and published semi-annually by the Accounting History Special Interest Group of the Accounting and Finance Association of Australia and New Zealand, it is available in print format only. The journal's coverage is international, and it frequently covers the history of auditing.

Web site: *www.aaanz.org*

Accounting Horizons A U.S. scholarly accounting journal. Established in 1987, the journal is published quarterly by the *American Accounting Association. It is available in both print and online formats. The journal's notes state that it focuses on the "scholarship of integration and application," with emphasis on the practical implications of accounting research. The journal focuses mainly on accounting, though there is some coverage of auditing topics.

Web link: *http://aaahq.org/ic/browse.htm*

Accounting, Organizations and Society A British scholarly accounting journal. Established in 1976, it is published in eight issues a year by Elsevier Science in both print and online formats. The journal's notes describe its concern "with all aspects of the relationship between accounting and human behaviour, organizational structures and processes, and the changing social and political environment of the enterprise," and its areas of focus include "the social role of accounting" and "behavioural aspects of budgeting, planning and investment appraisal." Its coverage is international, and it frequently contains auditing topics.

Web link: *www.elsevier.nl/inca/publications/store/4/8/6*

Accounting Principles Board (APB) The forerunner to the *Financial Accounting Standards Board (FASB). Established in 1959 by the *American Institute of Certified Public Accountants, the APB functioned until 1973. (It replaced the Committee on Accounting Procedure, which had operated from 1936 to 1959.) The APB issued accounting standards in the form of *Opinions and*

Statements. On its creation in 1973, the FASB adopted the APB's pronounce-ments, and has gradually revised or replaced them with its own standards.

Accounting Review, The A U.S. scholarly accounting journal. Established in 1926, the journal is published quarterly by the *American Accounting Association, in both print and online formats. The journal is a forum for research into aspects of accounting, and auditing topics are frequently covered. Its scope is international, but with focus on the United States.
   Web link: *http://raw.rutgers.edu/raw/aaa/pubs/acctrev.htm*

accounting standard Rules and guidance on accounting practice. Along with *legislation and custom, accounting standards are the foundation of *Generally Accepted Accounting Principles. In recent years, the term accounting standard has been largely superseded by *financial reporting standard. The latter term is intended to cover not only accounting rules for the recognition, measurement, and disclosure of *financial statement items, but also the *disclosure of addi-tional information like *earnings per share and *executive remuneration.

Accounting Technology® A U.S. accounting magazine. Founded in 1987, *Accounting Technology* is published in 11 issues a year by the Accountants Media Group, a division of Thomson, as part of the *WebCPA* framework. Its focus is on developments in accounting-related software and technology, with particular emphasis on technologies to support *public accounting.
   Web site: *www.webcpa.com/accountingTechnology*

Accounting Today® A U.S. accounting magazine. Founded in 1987, *Accounting Today* is published biweekly by the Accountants Media Group, a division of Thomson, as part of the *WebCPA* framework. Its coverage focuses on accounting, tax, and external auditing in the United States.
   Web site: *www.webcpa.com/accountingtoday*

accounts payable *Short-term, invoiced *liabilities owed for the supply of goods or services. Accounts payable balances are classified as a *current lia-bility in the *balance sheet.
   Further reading: Banks (2001)

accounts receivable *Short-term, invoiced amounts due from *customers for the supply of goods or services. Accounts receivable are classified as a *current asset in the balance sheet—when their recoverability becomes doubtful, an *allowance for bad debts is created.

accruals basis The matching of *revenues and *expenses to the periods in which they are earned or incurred. In contrast to a *cash basis approach, which *recognizes revenues and expenses in line with the receipt or payment of cash, an accruals basis of accounting is based on the timing of the underlying transaction. For example, when *interest payable to a bank is incurred evenly over a year, but payment falls due only at the year-end, the accruals basis of accounting requires recognition of the interest expense on a monthly basis. Most systems of *Generally Accepted Accounting Principles require an accruals basis of accounting.

The accruals basis operates through the mechanisms of *accrued revenue, *unearned revenue, *accrued expenses, and *prepaid expenses. Deliberate bending or circumvention of the accruals concept is a common *creative accounting technique.

accrued assets An alternative term for *accrued revenue.

accrued expense An unpaid expense incurred and *recognized in a *financial reporting period, and recorded as a *liability at the end of that period. In line with the *accruals basis of accounting, accrued expenses are matched with the accounting periods to which they relate, and are held within either *current or *long-term liabilities until the related cash payment is made. For example, an unpaid, long-term rental cost would be expensed over the periods to which it related, and an appropriate, accumulated balance would be recorded on the balance sheet within *accrued expenses until the item was fully settled in cash.

accrued liabilities An alternative term for *accrued expenses.

accrued revenue Revenue earned and *recognized in a *financial reporting period, for which the related cash has yet to be received. The accrued revenue is recorded as either a *current or *long-term asset at the end of the financial reporting period, in line with the *accruals basis of accounting. For example, revenue on a contract to supply goods or services over several years would be recognized in progression with completion of the contract, and an appropriate, accumulated accrued revenue balance recorded on the balance sheet until the amounts were settled in cash.

acid test **1.** The ratio of *current assets to *current liabilities. The acid test ratio is a quick means of assessing an entity's *liquidity, and its alternative names include the "quick" ratio and the "liquid" ratio. Only liquid current assets are used in the ratio—normally *cash, cash equivalents (such as marketable *securities), and *accounts receivable. *Inventory is usually excluded from current assets, owing to the time delay typically required to convert inventories into cash. *Prepaid expenses are also typically excluded from liquid current assets in the ratio calculation. **2.** Any critically important test. The term "acid test" derives from the use of nitric acid to test for gold. By extension, it has come to refer to the testing of any important activity.

acquisition **1.** The purchase of an asset, service, or legal right. **2.** The purchase of an organization, or the obtaining of operational or legal control of an organization. In contrast to the generally voluntary nature of *mergers, acquisitions are often made against the wishes of the *management of the acquired organization. Under most forms of *Generally Accepted Accounting Principles (GAAP), the accounting treatment of corporate acquisitions normally gives rise to *goodwill, which is the difference between the *consideration paid by the acquiring company and the *fair value of the net assets acquired. Acquired entities are *consolidated into the group *financial statements of the *parent organization. Most forms of GAAP tend to strictly differentiate between mergers and *acquisitions, owing to the vastly different accounting treatment for both categories of *business combination. In most jurisdictions, large corporate acquisitions that concentrate market power and reduce *competition are frequently reviewed by regulatory authorities.

Further reading: Davison (2001); Selim et al. (2002)

acquisition cost The purchase *price of an asset, service, legal right, or *entity.

activity based budgeting (ABB) A budgeting methodology that focuses on an organization's cost-incurring activities and operations. See *activity based costing.

activity based costing (ABC) A costing method that uses an organization's activities and operations to allocate costs to *products. In contrast to *absorption costing methodologies, which use production volumes as a *cost driver, activity based costing (ABC) uses activities as cost drivers. Cost drivers typically used in ABC costing to charge costs to products include the number of machine hours used, or the quantity of weight handled in a production process. Major aspects of ABC philosophy are the notions that (i) activities drive costs and (ii) product markets drive activities.

Further reading: Gunasekaran (1999); Keller (1997)

actuary An individual who undertakes mathematical and statistical analysis of the *risks and *probability estimates that underlie *insurance schemes and *pension plans. Actuarial estimates are used to establish pension plan contributions, funding requirements, insurance *premiums, and related matters.

add value, to **1.** To increase the *value (excluding *raw material costs) of a good or service as it passes through incremental stages of *production and distribution processes. **2.** In a general sense, to add *either quantitative or *qualitative *worth to an activity, item, or organization. Auditors frequently claim that their services "add value" to an organization. The value added by an *internal auditing department, for example, may be quantitative (e.g., the cost savings arising from audit reviews) or qualitative (assumed enhancements to an organization's *corporate governance processes). The value added by an external audit may extend beyond *assurance given on the *fair presentation of *financial statements to supplementary information like *benchmarking and *risk assessment information.

Further reading: Roth (2000); Roth (2002); Roth (2003)

adjustment A change or modification to an *account, *transaction, or *financial statement. Adjustments may be made to correct *errors, or to *allocate revenues or expenses in line with the *accruals basis of accounting. Adjustments to financial statements may arise as a result of *errors discovered during an external audit, or as a result of an *event after the balance sheet date.

***ad valorem* tax** An *indirect tax whose rate is based on a proportion of the *value of the item taxed. The Latin term *ad valorem* means "in proportion to the value," and *ad valorem* principles are often used in property taxes and *customs duties.

advance **1.** A prepayment toward the purchase of goods or services, or toward the costs of expenses like *salaries. The *accruals basis of accounting requires the matching of advances to appropriate accounting periods through the mechanisms of *prepaid expenses and *unearned revenue. **2.** A *loan.

Advances in Accounting A collection of scholarly accounting essays. Founded in 1983, *Advances in Accounting* is published annually by Elsevier Science in print format only. Its notes describe its mission in the following terms: "[T]o provide a forum for discourse among and between academic and practicing accountants on issues of significance to the future of the discipline." It frequently covers external auditing topics.

Web link: *www.elsevier.com/inca/tree/?key=B1AA*

Advances in International Accounting A collection of scholarly accounting essays. Founded in 1988, the journal is the international counterpart of **Advances in Accounting*. It is published annually by Elsevier Science in print format only, and it frequently examines external auditing.

Web link: *www.elsevier.com/inca/publications/store/6/2/0/9/7/2*

adverse opinion An external auditor's opinion that an entity's financial statements do not conform with *Generally Accepted Accounting Principles, or do not offer a *fair presentation of the entity's financial position, the results of its operations, or changes in cash flows. Under most systems of *Generally

Accepted Auditing Standards, external auditors are obliged to explain the reasons for an adverse opinion, which applies only to *material items that could mislead financial statement users. An adverse external audit opinion can damage a corporation's public image by sending shock waves through its *stockholders and the wider investing community. For this reason, adverse opinions are relatively rare for large corporations, and external auditors tend to prefer to persuade an organization's management to amend financial statements to avoid an adverse opinion. Compare *disclaimer, *qualified opinion, and *unqualified opinion.

adverse variance An alternative term for *unfavorable variance.

affiliate **1.** An organization in which another entity holds a significant but not controlling interest. An affiliate contrasts with a *subsidiary, as the latter is *consolidated into the *financial statements of a controlling *holding company or *parent organization. **2.** An organization related to another through their common control by a *holding company or *parent organization.

African Development Bank Group (ADBG) An international financial institution dedicated to economic development in Africa. Established in 1964, the ADBG is headquartered in Abidjan in the Ivory Coast. (At the time of writing, political instability in the Ivory Coast has forced the ADBG to temporarily relocate its administrative functions to Tunisia.) The ADBG comprises three institutions—the African Development Bank, the African Development Fund, and the Nigeria Trust Fund. It fulfills its mission of economic development in Africa through financial and technical assistance to *developing countries, and in 2003 it was supported by 77 countries from around the world.
   Web site: *www.afdb.org*

agency **1.** An alternative term for *agency theory. **2.** An organization that performs intermediary services, such as hiring personnel or providing security services.

agency costs The negative effects described in *agency theory of an *agent acting in self-interest to the detriment of a *principal. For example, managers in a corporation may seek to enhance their own status and remuneration in defiance of the corporation's best interests. Inefficiencies arising from discrepancies between the self-interests of *principals and *agents may be qualitative or quantitative.

agency theory The relationship between two parties, a *principal and an *agent, in which the latter represents or acts on behalf of the former. *Agency costs may arise if the goals of a principal and agent are not congruent: an agent, in other words, may be tempted to act in self-interest to the detriment of the principal. The relationship between a corporation's *investors and its *management is often described in terms of principal and agent, in so far as a corporation's managers act as agents on behalf of investors. The monitoring of the proper functioning of this relationship between investors and management is frequently portrayed as the main purpose of external auditing: the audit fee is often viewed as "the cheapest form of insurance against defaults in the principal-agent relationship in corporate activity" (Lee, 1993, 125). However, the notion of the role of the modern external auditor as an impartial referee in corporate agency relationships has been challenged by the *critical accounting movement, and by advocates of *stakeholder theory who bring more players into the web of relations and responsibilities created by corporations.

Some commentators on *corporate governance suggest that a company's *board of directors acts as the main monitoring body of the agency relationships between investors and managers, and that the appointment of external auditors is simply one means of supporting the agency function carried out by the board of directors. However, other commentators bracket the board of directors with an organization's management as agents who act on behalf of investors.

Further reading: Berle and Means (1932); Chwastiak (1999); Jensen and Meckling (1976)

agent An individual who, in *agency theory, accepts responsibilities to represent or act on behalf of a *principal.

aging of balances The stratification of a balance sheet amount by either *transaction or cash *settlement date. Balances for which aged analyses are prepared typically include *accounts receivable, *inventory, and long-term *loans. Aging is often used for management information purposes. For example, an aged analysis of accounts receivable facilitates *credit control procedures by identifying overdue customer balances. Aging can also be required for *disclosure of items in financial statements.

aid Government assistance in the form of cash, goods, or services. Government aid to a country's industrial sectors or geographical regions ranges from *grants to *tax breaks to *technical assistance. International aid includes the transfer of resources from *developed to *developing countries, which can also take a number of forms, such as cash transfers, or technical and military assistance.

Allied Crude Vegetable Oil Refining Corporation See the *great salad oil swindle.

allocation The identification of costs or revenues with specific activities, assets, liabilities, or time periods. An example of the time allocation of costs is the recognition of *amortization expenses over an asset's *useful life. An example of the allocation of costs to activities is the identification of production *overheads to manufactured products in *absorption costing methodologies. The term allocation is frequently used to refer to the identification of an entire cost or revenue with a single, corresponding activity, asset, liability, or time period—in contrast, the term *apportionment can be used to refer to the division of costs and revenues between various items. However, the two words are often used interchangeably.

allowance for bad debts A reduction in the value of *accounts receivable. One or more *general ledger accounts are used to record allowances for bad debts, which represent the value of accounts receivable whose ultimate collection is in doubt. The allowance may be for specific accounts receivable balances, or it can be a general allowance based on a percentage of accounts receivable. In the latter case, an *aging of balances allows different allowance rates to be applied on the basis of receivables' overdue dates. The allowance for bad debts is *offset against accounts receivable in the *balance sheet, and movements on the allowance are reflected in the *income statement.

The creation of an allowance suggests that the corresponding customer balance may ultimately be received (i.e., the receivable is doubtful rather than irrecoverable). Allowances for bad debts are reversed when initially doubtful balances are subsequently collected. Where a receivable is known with certainty to be irrecoverable (e.g., if a customer is *bankrupt), the balance is normally eliminated by a *write-off.

alternative procedures The adoption of additional *audit tests when planned audit procedures prove impossible or ineffective. For example, external auditors frequently *circularize an organization's customers to obtain documentary evidence of the existence and accuracy of *accounts receivable balances. If the responses to a circularization are disappointing, the auditor may adopt alternative auditing tests to verify accounts receivable balances. These additional tests may include (i) the tracing of transactions recorded in sales invoices to *inventory delivery documentation and (ii) the matching of cash subsequently received to receivable balances at a specific date.

American Accounting Association (AAA) A U.S. scholarly accounting organization. Headquartered in Sarasota, FL, the AAA was established in 1916 as the American Association of University Instructors in Accounting. It has used its current name since 1936. Its Web site states that its mission is "to foster world-wide excellence in the creation, dissemination and application of accounting knowledge and skills." Its activities include the promotion of accounting research and teaching, and a vigorous publication program that includes monographs and scholarly journals. See the entries for the *Accounting Review*, *Accounting Horizons*, *Auditing: A Journal of Practice and Theory*, and *Behavioral Research in Accounting*. The AAA also publishes newsletters, including the *ABO Reporter* and the *Auditor's Report*.

Web site: *www.aaahq.org*

American Institute of Certified Public Accountants (AICPA) The principal professional accounting organization in the United States. The AICPA was established in 1887, and it is headquartered in New York, with offices in New Jersey and Washington, DC. Individual U.S. states license *Certified Public Accountants (CPAs), but the AICPA is the *public accountants' national association. The AICPA's Web site states that its mission is "to provide members with the resources, information, and leadership that enable them to provide valuable services in the highest professional manner to benefit the public as well as employers and clients." It is a highly influential organization and its activities include the provision of technical guidance to its members and contributions to national and international accounting issues. It also sets the uniform CPA examination, runs an Anti*fraud and Corporate Responsibility Center, and maintains an active publishing program. Its publications include a number of journals, magazines, and newsletters: the *CPA Letter*, *In Our Opinion*, the *Journal of Accountancy*, and *The Practicing CPA*.

Prior to 1973 the AICPA set U.S. *accounting standards through the Committee on Accounting Procedure (1936 to 1959) and the *Accounting Principles Board (from 1959 to 1973). Accounting standards are now the responsibility of the *Financial Accounting Standards Board (FASB) and, for the public sector, of the *Governmental Accounting Standards Board. U.S. *auditing standards are set by the *Auditing Standards Board, which is an AICPA committee, supported by the *Audit and Attest Standards Team.

Web site: *www.aicpa.org*

American National Standards Institute (ANSI)® The U.S. body for voluntary standardization and conformity assessment. Headquartered in Washington, DC, ANSI has used its current name since 1969, but it traces its origins through predecessor bodies to the early twentieth century. The ANSI mission, as described on its Web site, is "to enhance both the global competitiveness of U.S. business and the U.S. quality of life by promoting and facilitating voluntary consensus standards and conformity assessment systems, and safeguarding their integrity." ANSI has facilitated the issuing of at least 10,000

American National Standards, and it is a member of the *International Organization for Standardization.

Web site: *www.ansi.org*

American Society of Women Accountants (ASWA) A U.S. professional accounting organization for women. Formed in 1938, the ASWA aims to promote the interests of women in the accounting profession. On its Web site, the ASWA states its mission to be as follows: "To enable women in all accounting and related fields to achieve their full personal, professional and economic potential and to contribute to the future development of their profession." The ASWA had more than 4,000 members in 2003.

Web site: *www.aswa.org*

American Standard Code for Information Interchange (ASCII) A standardized code that facilitates communication between different *brands and types of computer.

amortization A cost *allocation method used to record the reduction in value of an asset over time. The classic case of amortization is the matching of the cost of an item of *property, plant, and equipment to its *useful life. Assets generally lose value as a result of *wear and tear, damage, and *obsolescence, and *amortization methodology is based on the matching of an asset's cost to the periods of time in which the asset generates economic benefits. The term *depreciation is often used when referring to *tangible assets, and the term amortization when referring to *intangible assets, but in practice the terms are often used synonymously.

Amortization accounting can be on a *straight-line basis, with regular fixed expenses, or on a reducing balance or *accelerated method in which larger amortization charges occur in earlier time periods. Accelerated amortization is often justified on the grounds of an asset's intensive use in the early years of its life—a *sum of the digits methodology is sometimes used for this purpose. There are also other, sophisticated amortization accounting methods that attempt to closely match an asset's costs to fluctuations in economic value over its life. These include *revaluations of an asset's *historic cost.

Amortization can be calculated on the full cost of an asset, but the costs of many assets are adjusted to reflect any resale or *residual value. To take a simple example, an asset that costs $100,000 with a useful life of 10 years, and no residual value, would be amortized at a rate of $10,000 a year on a straight-line basis. In many countries, amortization rates are fixed by legislation, but *Generally Accepted Accounting Principles in most English-speaking countries allow a corporation's management to base amortization rates on reasonable estimates of assets' useful lives.

analytical review An auditing technique that focuses on analysis of the movements in *account balances over time, and on assessing the *reasonableness of
financial statement items. At the level of financial statements, an auditor's
analytical review typically focuses on changes over time in high-level balances
and ratios. It also includes assessments of the interrelationships between items
in financial statements. For example, if an organization's *revenues double in
size from one *financial reporting period to the next, then (all things being
equal) one would expect the level of *accounts receivable to increase significantly between the two time periods. If accounts receivable did not follow the
trend of revenues, analytical review might highlight this apparent inconsistency as an area for further investigation. The analytical review of financial
statements may also comprise comparisons with the financial data of similar
organizations—for example, an industry average of payroll cost per employee
is a common *benchmark to assess the reasonableness of payroll costs. At the
level of the *general ledger, analytical review procedures typically involve a
scanning of entries in an account for evidence of unusual items, and the analysis
of *variances between actual and budgeted balances.

Auditors' analytical review procedures are intended to highlight potential,
*material *misstatements in the general ledger or in financial statements. As
a high-level audit technique, analytical review usually raises (rather than
answers) questions, and therefore tends to be a means of identifying areas for
further review. For this reason, analytical review is often a key element in the
*audit planning process, though it is considered a valuable *substantive auditing
test in its own right.

Further reading: Glover et al. (2000); Lin et al. (2003)

Anderson, Urton L. (born 1951) A U.S. academic, author, and internal
auditing specialist. Professor of Accounting at the University of Texas at
Austin, Anderson has authored several authoritative internal auditing texts
and has participated in the professional developments of the *Institute of
Internal Auditors (IIA). His writings include a contribution to the IIA's
Research Opportunities in Internal Auditing (Anderson, 2003) and the IIA
research report *Quality Assurance for Internal Auditing* (1983). Anderson
chaired the *Internal Auditing Standards Board in 2003.

Further reading: Anderson (1983); Anderson (2003)

Web link: *www.mccombs.utexas.edu/dept/accounting/faculty/ua.html*

annualization The restatement of an item to reflect a 12-month period.
Annualization is common in financial planning and taxation calculations,
which often require extrapolation of costs and revenues to cover a full *fiscal
year. Annualization calculations are normally performed on a simple, straight-

line basis, in which costs or income are deemed to accrue evenly. For example, if an expense of $10,000 occurs in one month, it may be annualized to $120,000 simply by multiplying by 12. Compare *calendarization.

annuity Periodic payments of a constant amount that continue until a specified *maturity date. Compare *perpetuity.

antitrust laws Legislation designed to encourage an *efficient market. Antitrust laws are intended to combat the activities of *monopolies and *cartels, and to enhance *competition in a market. Antitrust laws originated in the United States: The *Sherman Antitrust Act* of 1890 was landmark legislation that made monopoly or the restraint of trade illegal. The 1890 Act reflected growing public opinion in the late nineteenth century that legislation could be used to control the imperfections of *free-market economies. The term antitrust was adopted because "trust" was a common term for monopoly in the nineteenth century. Other landmark U.S. antitrust laws include the *Clayton Act* of 1914, the *Robinson-Patman Act* of 1936, and the *Celler-Kefauver Act* of 1950. Antitrust laws have spread around the world: The concept has been introduced into Italy, for example, where the term "antitrust" has been directly adopted from English into the Italian language.

application control A control over an aspect of a computer program. Application controls may be either programmed or manual, and they are designed to ensure the accuracy and completeness of data and transactions. Examples of application controls include the validation of data input and the verification of batch totals. Auditors test the correct functioning of application controls through the use of representative *test data.

apportionment See *allocation.

appraisal **1.** The *quantitative evaluation of an *investment (or potential investment), or of any asset or liability. Appraisals are often central to decision-making processes: A *due diligence appraisal process, for example, usually proceeds a corporate *acquisition. **2.** The evaluation—*qualitative or *quantitative—of an activity, control, procedure, or employee. Many manufacturing operations have product appraisal procedures embedded in their *quality control processes, while employee appraisals form part of most modern *human resources practices.

appreciation The increase in value of an asset. Most systems of *Generally Accepted Accounting Principles set out strict rules for the *recognition in financial statements of the amounts by which assets—typically land, property, and *securities—may appreciate. Contrast *depreciation.

approval **1.** An alternative term for *authorization. **2.** Acceptance. In commerce, goods sent to a customer on approval are sent for examiniation without an obligation to purchase.

Arab Society for Certified Accountants (ASCA) A regional, Arabic-language accounting organization. The ASCA was formed in 1984 in London. Its Web site states that its main objective is "to advance the science of accountancy, financial management and associated or connected subjects as applied to all or any of the professional services provided by accountants…throughout the Arab world." The ASCA's activities include a certification program, and accounting and auditing publications in Arabic.

Web site: *www.ascasociety.org*

arbitrage The exploitation of *price differentials on an *asset traded in two or more *markets. One benefit often claimed of arbitrage is its role in bringing about price *equilibrium between markets. For example, the opportunities given to consumers in the European Union to purchase goods throughout Europe has tended to narrow price differentials for many consumer goods between individual European countries. *Prices are known with certainty in arbitrage, and it is therefore a less *risky activity than *speculation. Assets typically subject to arbitrage include *currencies and *commodities.

arbitration Quasi-judicial recourse to an independent individual or organization to settle a dispute between two or more parties. Arbitration is often used to settle commercial, labor, and political disputes, and it is an alternative to civil law proceedings. Arbitration has a long history—it was used extensively in classical Rome. Arbitration decisions can be either binding or nonbinding, depending on the terms of reference agreed to by the parties.

arithmetic progression A sequential pattern of numbers with differences of equal size between consecutive numbers. An example is 1, 3, 5, 7, and so on. Contrast *geometric progression.

arm's length transaction A transaction at *fair market value between unrelated parties, or a transaction made as if it were between unrelated parties— for example, "All the sales between the corporation's overseas branches are made at arm's length."

arrears Overdue liabilities or payments.

Arthur Andersen (AA) A former member of the *Big Five accounting firms. Arthur Andersen collapsed in 2002 following the *Enron corporate scandal. Founded in Chicago in 1913 as Andersen, DeLany & Company, the firm adopted the name Arthur Andersen in 1928. It enjoyed incredible growth, success, and prestige in the twentieth century. Ironically, given the circumstances of its demise, AA was initially noted for its principled stand on the correctness of accounting methodology, even at the risk of losing clients. The firm was also famous for the sophistication of its *consulting and *management advisory services. Amid the rather faceless world of the large accounting firms, the AA culture was perceived as uniquely differentiated. The culture was reinforced by a strong internal training program that inculcated intense organizational loyalty and conformity. Skeptical or jealous outsiders were known, tongue-in-cheek, to refer to the stereotyped image of the clean-cut, white-shirted, earnest Arthur Andersen employee as an "Android."

Following decades of phenomenal growth, the last few years of the firm were troubled ones, and its once-proud image became increasingly tarnished. First, a power struggle that led to a bitter divorce between the firm's profitable consulting division and the auditing-driven remainder of the business was played out in full media glare: The result was the independence in 2000 of Andersen Consulting, later to become *Accenture. More seriously, and fatally, one insider identified a corrosion of values at the heart of the firm. From its status as "a great and venerable American institution" and "a global symbol of strength and solidity" with over 80,000 employees worldwide, AA allegedly became an organization that placed fee maximization ahead of professional integrity, to the extent that some of its auditing employees "forgot that the true purpose of their job was to protect the investing public" (Toffler and Reingold, 2003, 7).

To an extent, the questions raised over AA's approach to auditing reflect a more general malaise in the external auditing profession in the early twenty-first century. However, a series of accounting scandals that engulfed AA clients seemed to point to particular problems at the firm: Severe problems at the operations of the Baptist Foundation of Arizona, Sunbeam, Delorean, and Waste Management were forerunners to the massive accounting scams at Enron and *WorldCom. The Enron affair led to a criminal indictment for AA, and in June 2002 a federal grand jury found the firm guilty of obstructing justice in official investigations of Enron. The shredding of thousands of Enron-related documents played a major part in the jury's decision-making process. The firm's reputation was seriously undermined: Even the U.S. President is reported to have joked (in relation to weapons inspections prior to the second Gulf War of 2003): "The good news is that [Saddam Hussein is] willing to have his nuclear, biological, and chemical weapons counted. The bad news is he wants Arthur Andersen to do it" (quoted in Fox, 2003, 294).

Amid allegations of *conflicts of interest between auditing and the supply of management advisory services (not to mention accusations of poor auditing and the large-scale destruction of auditing records) Arthur Andersen collapsed in 2002. The Enron and AA scandals prompted U.S. legislators to pass the *Sarbanes-Oxley Act* in 2002, in an attempt to reform *corporate governance and thereby restore investor confidence.

Further reading: Jeter (2003); 207-212; Schwartz and Watkins (2003); Spacek (1989); Toffler and Reingold (2003)

articles of incorporation Legal documents required for the establishment of a U.S. corporation. The articles form part of a corporation's charter, and they set out its mission and range of activities.

Asian Development Bank (ADB) An international financial institution dedicated to economic development in Asia. Established in 1966 and headquartered in Manila in the Philippines, the ADB's activities focus on financial and technical assistance to Asian *developing countries. In 2003 the ADB was supported by 61 countries from around the world.

Web site: *www.adb.org*

AS/NZS Joint Standard 4360: Risk Management A *risk assessment standard issued by the joint Standards Australia/Standards New Zealand Committee. The standard first appeared in 1995 and was revised in 1999. It has had a major international impact on risk management methodology and theory.

Further reading: *AS/NZS 4360* (1999)

assessment **1.** The financial *appraisal of an existing or potential *investment. **2.** A nonquantitative evaluation of an activity, control, process, or procedure. **3.** A formal *tax calculation.

asset A resource expected to provide future economic benefits. Assets possess a number of characteristics: (i) they provide economic benefits; (ii) they are under the control of an individual or organization; (iii) their existence is certain, although they can be *intangible (like *goodwill or *intellectual capital); and (iv) they tend to be quantifiable (although the valuation of intangible assets can be problematic). *Generally Accepted Accounting Principles around the world usually set strict criteria for the *recognition and valuation of assets. In particular, the recognition of many intangible assets, such as *brands, are severely restricted. An asset is recorded as a *debit entry under the conventions of *double entry bookkeeping, and *short-term assets are usually referred to as *current assets. Contrast *liability.

asset stripping A pejorative term for the deliberate depletion of *assets in an organization. Asset stripping often occurs following an *acquisition (definition 2), when an acquirer believes that the breakup of a purchased organization's assets can enhance their overall value. This may be the case when the value of a corporation's *common stock has fallen below the value of its separate, *tangible assets. Less commonly, the term asset stripping may also be a tactical (or even malicious) means of avoiding a corporate takeover. An organization that is the target of an unwelcome *acquisition bid, for example, may take the extreme measure of depleting its assets to make it less attractive to a potential acquirer. See also *poison pill.

Association for Accountancy and Business Affairs (AABA) A British reformist organization that focuses on accounting and auditing. The AABA's Web site states its objectives to include the following: To "advance the public interest by facilitating critical scrutiny of commercial and non-commercial organisations... to facilitate critical scrutiny of professional bodies... and to campaign for such reforms as will help to secure greater openness and democracy, protect and further the rights of stakeholders and to make disclosures where necessary." The organization's activities include the publication of monographs. It also has an online journal, *Accountancy, Business, and the Public Interest*. AABA trustees include Professor *Prem Nath Sikka and the British Member of Parliament *Austin Mitchell, both leading figures in the *critical accounting movement.

The AABA is a fearless critic of auditing practices, especially those of external auditing, as can be gained by the titles of some of its monographs: *Auditors: Holding the Public to Ransom* (Cousins et al., 1998), and *Dirty Business: The Unchecked Power of Major Accountancy Firms* (Mitchell and Sikka, 2002).

Web site: *visar.csustan.edu/aaba/aaba.htm*

Further reading: Cousins et al. (1998); Mitchell and Sikka (2002); Mitchell et al. (1998)

Association for Investment Management and Research (AIMR®) A U.S.-based professional association for investment practitioners and educators. Established in 1990 by the merger of the Financial Analysts Federation (originally founded in 1947) and the Institute of Chartered Financial Analysts (founded in 1959), the AIMR is headquartered in Charlottesville, VA. Its Web site describes its mission as follows: To "serve its members and investors as a global leader in educating and examining investment managers and analysts and sustaining high standards of professional conduct." The AIMR's international membership exceeded 50,000 in 2003. The association's Financial Accounting Policy Committee contributes to debates on the development of *accounting standards, and it publishes on the AIMR Web site formal comments on the initiatives of organizations like the *Financial Accounting Standards Board.

Web site: *www.aimr.org*

Association Francophone de Comptabilité (AFC) A French-language academic accounting association. Based in Paris, and founded in 1980, the AFC provides a French-language forum for international researchers and educators of accounting, auditing, and related areas. Its activities include conferences, study workshops, and publication of the journal *Comptabilité, Contrôle, Audit.*
   Web site (French only): *www.afc-cca.com*

Association of Accounting Technicians (AAT) A British professional accounting organization. The AAT was established in 1980 by combining two previously existing associations: The Association of Technicians in Finance and Accounting, and the Institute of Accounting Staff. The AAT's Web site states that its vision is "to be a strong, visible and respected body for accounting technicians; to offer internationally recognised membership and qualifications, which are valued by the public, employers and the business world." Most of the AAT's members work in industry, and after AAT certification many members proceed to the examinations of the *Association of Chartered Certified Accountants or other members of the United Kingdom's *Consultative Committee of Accountancy Bodies. The AAT has over 100,000 international members, including students, and it is an associate member of the *International Federation of Accountants.
   Web site: *www.aat.co.uk*

Association of Certified Fraud Examiners (ACFE) An international professional body dedicated to combating *fraud. Based in Austin, TX, and founded in 1988 by Joseph T. Wells, the ACFE had approximately 28,000 members in 2003. The ACFE mission, as stated on its Web site, is "to reduce the incidence of fraud and *white-collar crime and to assist the Membership in its detection and deterrence." The association's activities include education, publications, and a certification program.
   Web site: *www.cfenet.com*

Association of Chartered Accountants in the United States (ACAUS) A professional organization for U.S.-based *chartered accountants. ACAUS was founded in 1985, and in 2003 it had approximately 5,000 members. Headquartered in New York, ACAUS groups together accountants from the United Kingdom, Australia, Canada, Ireland, New Zealand, and South Africa.
   Web site: *www.acaus.org*

Association of Chartered Certified Accountants (ACCA) A British professional accounting organization. The ACCA has existed in a variety of forms and under a series of names since the early 1900s: It obtained a royal charter in 1974, and took its current name in 1996. Headquartered in London, the ACCA's members have traditionally been accountants in business, with a focus on cost and management accounting, though the association's members also work in a wide range of accounting and auditing roles. The ACCA is one of the United Kingdom's five *Recognised Qualifying Bodies for external auditors. Many British internal auditors are ACCA members.

The ACCA's Web site states that its mission is, among other things, to "provide quality professional opportunities to people of ability and application throughout their working careers" and to "promote the highest ethical and governance standards." The association's publications range from magazines and newsletters—the *ACCA Internal Audit Bulletin* and *Accounting & Business*—to a respected series of research monographs. The ACCA's certification program has a high international profile, and it attracts a large number of students around the world, especially in the former British colonies of Hong Kong and Malaysia. Members carry the designatory letters ACCA or FCCA, the latter representing fellowship and determined by seniority. The ACCA's international membership (including students) exceeded 300,000 in 2003.

Web site: *www.acca.co.uk*

Association of College and University Auditors (ACUA) A U.S.-based, international organization dedicated to internal auditing in the higher education sector. Founded in 1958 and headquartered in West Hartford, CT, the ACUA's activities include professional guidance, conferences, and networking.

Web site: *www.acua.org*

Association of Government Accountants (AGA®) A U.S. professional *public sector accounting organization. Founded in 1950 as the Federal Government Accountants Association, the association adopted its current name in 1975. It is headquartered in Alexandria, VA. The AGA's Web site states that it "serves government accountability professionals by providing quality education, fostering professional development and certification, and supporting standards and research to advance government accountability." Its activities include publication of the quarterly *Journal of Government Financial Management* and a monthly newsletter, *Government Financial Management TOPICS*. The AGA membership stood at approximately 18,000 in 2003.

Web site: *www.agacgfm.org*

Association of International Accountants (AIA) A British-based professional accounting organization. Headquartered in Newcastle, England, the AIA was founded in 1928 and incorporated four years later, in 1932. The AIA was recognized in 1994 as a *Recognised Qualifying Body for external auditors in the United Kingdom, and it registered its first company auditor in 1998.

Most AIA members, however, work outside *public accounting. The association's Web site states that it "promotes and supports the advancement of the accounting profession both in the UK and internationally." The AIA's magazine *International Accountant* appears quarterly. The AIA membership totalled 14,500 (including 10,000 students) in 2003, with a strong international dimension, as its name suggests.

Web site: *www.aia.org.uk*

Association of News Media Internal Auditors (NMIA) An internal auditing specialty organization. The NMIA was established in 1977 by internal auditors employed by major news media corporations. Its activities include networking, newsletters, and an annual conference.

Web site: *www.nmianews.org*

assurance **1.** A positive declaration on an *audit objective. Assurance can cover a wide range of matters, from the *fair presentation of *financial statements to the effective operation of *internal controls. Assurance does not offer the certainty of a *guarantee; indeed, to offer absolute assurance in an auditing context is generally unfeasible, owing to the existence of *risk. It has been observed that auditors "can never be 100 per cent certain of the information on which their opinion or report is based" (Flint, 1988, 112). Auditors therefore tend to form their judgments on the results of a mixture of *sample testing of large *audit populations and *compliance testing of procedures and internal controls. Neither of these categories of *audit testing offers absolute assurance. Auditors, in consequence, tend to prefer to use the term "reasonable assurance." The term assurance has become increasingly popular following its use in the *American Institute of Certified Public Accountants' 1997 report *Serving the Public Interest: A New Conceptual Framework for Auditor Independence* (AICPA, 1997). The report identified various means of improving the quality of *financial reporting and related information. **2.** In the United Kingdom, a branch of the *insurance industry in which policies compensate the death of the policy holder.

Further reading: AICPA (1997); Gray and Gray (2000)

asymmetric information A mismatch of the depth and quality of information between two or more parties to a *transaction or *contractual arrangement. A classic example of asymmetric information frequently discussed in economic literature is that found in markets for secondhand automobiles. The purchaser of a used car is normally at a significant information disadvantage in comparison to the seller. The concept of *caveat emptor* is of particular relevance in such circumstances. Between a *principal and an *agent, *agency costs can be exacerbated by asymmetries of information, as an agent may be tempted to exploit detailed knowledge of a transaction or organization to the disadvantage of a principal.

attest, to 1. To declare that *financial statements offer a *fair presentation of an organization's financial position, results of operations, and cash flows. Attestation is a form of audit *assurance and it is normally formalized in the form of an *audit report. **2.** To sign a legal document, as a witness to the genuineness of the signatures of the party or parties to a transaction.

attorney's letter In external auditing, a letter addressed to the attorney of a client to request details of litigation and other legal matters. The external auditor uses an attorney letter to obtain *audit evidence of the existence and *materiality of *contingent liabilities.

attribute sampling A statistical method that analyzes the occurrence of a *qualitative characteristic in a *population. For example, an auditor may analyze an organization's *disbursements to assess the occurrence of non-*authorized items: The attribute in this case is the nonauthorization of individual disbursements. The occurrence rate of authorization in a sample can be extrapolated to the entire population of disbursements, subject to precision errors inherent in *sampling methodologies. Attribute sampling is common in *compliance testing.

auction The sale of an item by competitive bidding.

audit An independent review of an asset, liability, activity, organization, or set of *financial statements. Audits are usually performed to support or refute defined *audit objectives, and normally result in an *audit opinion on the matter under review. There is no single, satisfactory definition of auditing, but the following examples illustrate widely held interpretations of the term: (i) "Auditing is a systematic process of objectively obtaining and *evaluating evidence regarding assertions about economic actions and events to ascertain the degree of correspondence between those assertions and established criteria and communicating the results to interested parties" (American Accounting Association, 1973). (ii) "Auditing is a human evaluation process to establish the adherence to certain norms, resulting in an opinion (or judgment)" (Schandl, 1978, 4). (iii) "The purpose of the audit is to investigate and review the actions (or inaction), decisions, achievements, statements or reports of specified persons with defined responsibilities, to compare these actions, etc. with some norm, and to form and express an opinion on the result of that investigation, review or comparison" (Flint, 1988, 20). (iv) An audit is a means of "monitoring the behavior of *agents" in the context of *agency theory" (Lee, 1993, 23).

The term audit is used widely, and it includes the following: (i) *external audit, (ii) *internal audit, (iii) *environmental audit, (iv) *financial audit, (v) *operational audit, (vi) *clinical audit, (vii) *management audit, and (viii) *social audit.

It has been claimed that auditing is "an old science with well-established principles" (Ridley and Chambers, 1998, xx). There is evidence of auditing practices that date from classical empires of Rome and China, which created elaborate civil services to monitor and report on government finances. Some commentators even claim that auditing practices date from the very dawn of literate civilization: "According to earliest Mesopotamian records dating back to 3600 BC, scribes used to prepare summaries of financial transactions. These were separate from the lists of amounts handled and which others had prepared.... Tiny marks, dots, and circles indicated the painstaking comparison of one record with another—marks that have survived the centuries and that auditors still use to *tick off their *verification of records. Thus were born two control devices still used around the world: *division of duties, and provision for the review of another's work" (Sawyer and Vinten, 1996, 23). In England in the Middle Ages, many of the parties interested in manorial audits were illiterate and audits were usually presented orally. As a result, the modern English word "audit" came into use, derived from the Latin verb *audire* ("to hear").

Despite auditing's long history, the discipline's dramatic and apparently inexorable rise since World War II has been met with disapproval by some commentators, who see it as a symptom of a decline in trust between individuals and organizations. The external audit, for example, has been described as "the principal means by which *accountability is attempted when trust in relationships disappears" (Lee, 1998, 219). Others have portrayed auditing as a parasitical activity: "The "*audit society is a symptom of the times, coincidentally a *fin de siècle*, in which a gulf has opened up between poorly rewarded 'doing' and highly rewarded 'observing'" (Power, 1997, 147). Some commentators have also drawn attention to an alleged obscurity at the heart of auditing theory—for example, auditing has been described as "paradoxical, tense and subjective" (Frecknall Hughes et al., 1998, 98). Concerns over the substance of auditing theory may reflect discomfort with the sheer variety of social practices that have adopted the term "audit." However, notwithstanding the frequency of criticisms of auditing's social and political functions (e.g., in the writings of the *critical accounting movement), auditing practices have been adopted by most *private and *public sector organizations.

Further reading: American Accounting Association (1973); Flint (1988); Lee (1993); Power (1997); Schandl (1978); Wolnizer (1987)

auditability The feasibility of undertaking auditing procedures. Auditability is the first of the *postulates of auditing elaborated by *Robert Khun Mautz and Hussein A. Sharaf: It is, in effect, the prerequisite to auditing. If all the records of a transaction-intensive organization were irrecoverably lost in a fire, for example, the organization would in all likelihood be unauditable. *Alternative procedures may be undertaken by the auditor in such circumstances (including the reconstruction of *transactions by memory, or the confirmation of transactions by third parties), but it is highly unlikely that alternative procedures would lead to an *unqualified opinion in the context of complete destruction of records. In a less extreme scenario, questions of auditability can arise from (i) inadequate cooperation from *auditees and (ii) inadequate systems of *internal control.

auditable unit An organization, operation, individual, or other discrete entity that can be subjected to an audit. During *audit planning, an auditor determines an *audit universe of auditable units, and dedicates appropriate levels of auditing resources to each unit. For example, the auditor of a *multinational corporation may define individual overseas branches as auditable units. Within each overseas branch, the auditor may proceed to define a series of further auditable units along the lines of the *purchasing and *revenue cycles and other operational activities.

audit agenda **1.** An alternative term for *audit program. **2.** An alternative term for *audit schedule.

Audit and Attest Standards Team A group within the *American Institute of Certified Public Accountants (AICPA). The AICPA Web site states that the team "directs and supports the development of auditing, attestation, accounting and review services, and quality control standards." The team supports the work of the AICPA's *Auditing Standards Board, and it produces nonauthoritative interpretative and implementation guidance for U.S. *auditing standards.

Web link: *www.aicpa.org/members/div/auditstd/about1.htm*

audit approach The strategy for an audit, or the manner of conducting an audit. Deciding a suitable audit approach is an essential part of the *audit planning process, and a common decision is the balance to be adopted between *compliance and *substantive testing. An audit approach is often determined by, among other factors, (i) the nature of the *auditee, (ii) the time available for the audit, (iii) the level of cooperation of the *auditee, and (iv) the sophistication of systems of *internal control. See also *"black box" audit approach.

audit assignment A discrete, separately identifiable audit. Compare *special assignment.

audit assumption A presumption or judgment that underpins an audit or an *audit test. Unlike *postulates of auditing, which are of general validity, an audit assumption is specific to an auditing assignment. Examples of audit assumptions include the judgment that an *auditee is telling the truth, and the judgment that (from the findings of *compliance testing) the vast majority of an organization's *disbursements are appropriately authorized.

audit charter See *internal audit charter.

Audit Command Language™ (ACL™) Audit-related software produced by ACL Services Ltd. This software ranges from *data accuracy tools to data extraction and analysis mechanisms.
Web link: *www.acl.com*

audit committee A committee of a *board of directors (or similar governing body) that oversees an organization's auditing and *financial reporting. Under most systems of corporate governance, audit committees tend to be comprised of *outside directors to encourage *independence and to minimize potential *conflicts of interest. Typical activities of audit committees include reporting to the board of directors on the oversight of (i) *financial reporting, (ii) the *internal control environment, (iii) the work of external and internal auditors, (iv) external audit fees, (v) the appropriateness of accounting policies, and (vi) *risk management procedures.
Further reading: AICPA (2000); Klein (2002); Raghunandan et al. (2001); Rezaee et al. (2003); Spira (2002); Verschoor (2000); Verschoor (2002)

audit competence The ability and credentials of an individual who aspires to undertake auditing. It has been written that "the first requirement for the authority of auditors is competence. Audit competence requires both knowledge and skill, which are the products of education, training and experience" (Flint, 1998, 48). The auditing *professional bodies seek to define and monitor their members' audit competence.

audit cycle The process of conducting an audit or a series of audits over time. In external auditing, the audit cycle tends to be scheduled in several important phases: (i) interim visits to perform *analytical and *compliance reviews; (ii) attendance at *physical inventory counts; (iii) visits at (or shortly after) financial period-ends to perform detailed *substantive testing; and (iv) the finalization of the audit. From year to year, the audit cycle may envision different areas of focus. For example, in one year the audit team may focus on the *revenue cycle, while in the following year it may skew its tests toward the *purchasing cycle.

An *internal audit function's overall agenda may envision coverage of the *audit universe within a recurring cycle of periodic audits, with different areas of focus in different time periods.

audit department An alternative term for *internal audit function.

auditee An individual or organization subject to an audit. Contrast *auditor.

audit engagement **1.** An alternative term for *audit assignment. **2.** The process of agreeing to a *contract for the services of an external auditor.

audit evidence Information that supports or refutes an *audit objective. Lee (1993, 172) distinguishes between "evidence (the overall basis for audit reporting) and evidential material (the various means by which auditors construct their evidence to support their conclusions)," but in general usage the term audit evidence is used in both contexts. Audit evidence can be gathered from a wide variety of sources, ranging from documentary information to oral testimony to the *observation of procedures. For example, an auditor wishing to substantiate the existence and accuracy of an organization's *accounts receivable balances at a specific date may turn to the following sources of evidence, among others: (i) detailed *general ledger transactions; (ii) original sales invoices; (iii) *inventory dispatch information; (iv) *confirmation letters from customers; (v) the matching of cash received to specific accounts receivable balances; and (vi) discussions with management and employees. The interpretation of evidence is a fundamental aspect of auditing, and it has been suggested that "Deductive reasoning is by far the most important and also the most difficult source of audit evidence" (Flint, 1988, 113–114). Auditors tend to record the evidence used to support their judgments and opinions in formal *working papers.

Further reading: Maroney and Bedard (1997); Ratliff and Johnson (1998)

audit guide **1.** An alternative term for *audit program. **2.** An alternative term for *auditing standard or the interpretative literature of *Generally Accepted Auditing Standards.

auditing The process or action of undertaking an *audit. Although the gerund auditing places greater emphasis on action than the simple noun audit, the two terms are largely interchangeable.

Auditing: A Journal of Practice and Theory A U.S. scholarly auditing journal. Established in 1981, it is published quarterly in print and online formats by the *American Accounting Association. The journal is scholarly in tone and focuses mainly on external auditing.

Web link: *http://accounting.rutgers.edu/raw/aaa/audit/pubs.htm*

Auditing Practices Board (APB) The external auditing standards-setter in the United Kingdom. A subsidiary board of the *Accountancy Foundation, the APB issues *Statements of Auditing Standards* and interpretative bulletins, which together comprise British *Generally Accepted Auditing Standards. The APB in its current form was established in 2002, when it took over the responsibilities of a preceding organization of the same name.

Web link: *www.accountancyfoundation.com/auditing_practices_board/ index.cfm*

Auditing Roundtable A U.S. organization for *environmental and health and safety auditing. Founded in 1972 and headquartered in Scottsdale, AZ, the Roundtable's activities include publications and the issuing of *Standards for the Performance of Environmental Audits*. With the *Institute of Internal Auditors, the Roundtable founded the *Board of Environmental, Health & Safety Auditor Certifications in 1997.

Web site: *www.auditear.org*

auditing standard 1. Formal rules and guidance for external auditing. In the United States the *Auditing Standards Board issues *Statements on Auditing Standards*, while the *International Auditing and Assurance Standards Board of the *International Federation of Accountants issues *International Standards on Auditing*. Formal auditing standards of this nature are the main component (in addition to legislation and custom) of *Generally Accepted Auditing Standards. **2.** The *Standards for the Professional Practice of Internal Auditing* of the *Institute of Internal Auditors.

Auditing Standards Board (ASB) The external auditing standards-setter in the United States. A technical committee of the *American Institute of Certified Public Accountants (AICPA), the ASB's standards take the form of *Statements on Auditing Standards* (SAS). (It also issues *Statements on Standards for Attestation Engagements*, and *Statements on Quality Control Standards*.) The SAS are issued after public consultation and are binding on AICPA members who conduct external audits. In addition to promulgating standards in this way, the ASB also issues comments on and interpretations of SAS. See also *Generally Accepted Auditing Standards.

Web link: *www.aicpa.org/members/div/auditstd/index.htm*

AuditNet® A Web-based auditing resource center. Established by Jim Kaplan, the AuditNet Web site describes itself as a "communications network for auditors and professional associations" and describes its mission as follows: To "develop a complete 'utility' on the World Wide Web for audit related information, products, and services." AuditNet offers many services to its users, including online *standard audit programs, job recruitment listings, and travel resources.

Web site: *www.auditnet.org*

Audit News A British external auditing newsletter. Issued by the Professional Standards Directorate of the *Institute of Chartered Accountants in England and Wales, the newsletter is published in two or three issues a year. It is available online, and it focuses on external auditing developments and regulations in the United Kingdom.

Web link: *www.icaew.co.uk/index.cfm?AUB=TB2I_3321*

audit objective **1.** The purpose of an audit. Audits are normally performed to support or refute specific objectives. The external audit of an organization, for example, typically has the following main objectives: "To obtain evidence that the organization's financial statements conform with *Generally Accepted Accounting Principles, and offer a *fair representation of the entity's financial position, the results of its operations, and changes in cash flows." If sufficient *audit evidence is gathered to confirm these objectives, the external auditor can issue an *unqualified opinion. (Secondary objectives of an external audit may include the identification of *material *fraud, or serious weaknesses in *internal controls.) The objectives of internal auditing tend to be more varied than those of external auditing: This reflects the wide remit of internal auditing, through *financial and *operational audits to *compliance and *consulting reviews. **2.** The purpose of a specific *audit test. It is generally considered best practice to state an objective (or objectives) for each individual audit test, and to conclude on the objectives after sufficient *audit evidence has been gathered to perform the test. For example, an audit *work paper may start as follows: "To obtain evidence that bank balances are accurately stated and correctly classified in the *general ledger." It may finish as follows: "objectives achieved." The formal stating of objectives for each audit test encourages the focus of auditing work in contributing to the overall objective of the audit. If the objectives of a specific test are not met, then alternative tests may be required.

audit opinion An auditor's conclusion on the extent to which *audit evidence refutes or confirms an *audit objective. *Independence is considered to be central to the credibility of audit opinions, especially in the context of an external audit: "An auditor's opinion is no more than an opinion, but it must be believed to be an informed opinion honestly held" (Flint, 1988, 47). For external auditing, see *unqualified opinion, *qualified opinion, *adverse opinion, *disclaimer, and *negative assurance.

auditor An individual or organization that performs an audit. Contrast *auditee.

auditor independence See *independence.

auditor's luck A semi-ironic term that refers to the inclusion in an auditor's *sample of an awkward or discomforting item. For example, an auditor may select a *judgmental sample of twenty sales invoices taken from an *accounts receivable ledger and discover a sale that exceeds a customer's *credit limit without appropriate internal authorization. The *auditee may claim that the auditor has stumbled by chance across a rare exception, and dismiss the finding as the auditor's allegedly uncanny ability to hit on unrepresentative items that cause *auditee discomfiture.

Auditor's Report, The A U.S. auditing newsletter. Published quarterly by the *American Accounting Association, the newsletter focuses on academic and professional developments in auditing.
   Web link: *http://accounting.rutgers.edu/raw/aaa/audit/auditorsreport.htm*

audit plan **1.** An alternative term for *audit program. **2.** An alternative term for *audit schedule (definition 1).

audit planning The steps taken to prepare for an audit. Planning is tailored to the circumstances of individual audits, but typically includes some or all of the following: (i) information gathering to establish the background and circumstances of an entity or activity to be audited; (ii) discussions with an *auditee to ascertain *material facts; (iii) a *risk assessment of the area under audit; (iv) logistical arrangements for visiting the location of an audit; and (v) *analytical review of an organization's *financial statements and *trial balance. The *professional standards of both external and internal auditors requires careful planning, and the audit planning process normally results in a formal *audit program that sets out the scope of audit work.

audit point A section of an *audit report that comprises one or more *audit recommendations.

audit program A document that sets out *audit tests. It is generally considered best practice to conclude an *audit planning process with a formal, written program of audit tests, but in practice audit programs vary significantly in detail and sophistication. At one extreme, an audit program may simply be a bullet-point list of audit tests. At the other extreme, an audit program may give extensive guidance on the performance of sequential audit tests, including the names of individual auditors responsible for each test.

audit quality The good performance and positive characteristics of an audit. It has been suggested that audit quality "depends on both technical competence and *independence" (Beattie et al., 2001, 14), and external auditing quality is often assessed by *peer review. Compare *quality audit.

audit recommendation In an *audit report, a proposed action to remedy a problem or potential problem. Audit recommendations addressed to *auditees normally form the basis of *internal auditors' reports, while external auditors tend to communicate their recommendations for improvements in procedures and *internal controls in the form of a *management letter.

audit report A document that summarizes the findings of an audit. An external audit report sets out an *audit opinion. Most systems of *Generally Accepted Auditing Standards have standardized formats for external audit reports and require explanations of any *unqualified opinion (such as an *adverse opinion, a *disclaimer, or a *qualified opinion). The content and style of internal audit reports are largely at the discretion of individual *internal audit functions. All audit reports, however, should follow basic criteria of "clarity, precision, unambiguity, and comprehensiveness in disposal of the [audit's] terms of reference" (Flint, 1988, 121).

Public skepticism over the usefulness of the *boilerplate language used in external audit reports has a long history. It is reflected, for example, in this humorous and poetic audit report spoof of the 1950s (quoted in Chambers, R. J., 1995, 91):

> We have audited the balance sheet and here is our report:
> The cash is overstated, the cashier being short;
> The customers' receivables are very much past due,
> If there are any good ones, they are very, very, few;
> The inventories are out of date and practically junk,
> And the method of their pricing is very largely bunk;
> According to our figure the enterprise is wrecked...
> But subject to these comments, the balance sheet's correct.

Further reading: Walker (1997)

audit risk **1.** In external auditing, the *risk of giving an inappropriate *audit opinion on the *fair presentation of an organization's *financial statements. The *sampling of transactions and the *compliance testing of controls cannot offer cast-iron guarantees that all *irregularities have been identified, though external audit risk can be mitigated by (i) careful *audit planning, (ii) *representation letters from management, and (iii) adequate *malpractice insurance. External audit risk is sometimes analyzed into three components—*inherent risk, *control risk, and *detection risk—that can be quantified and multiplied together. Audit risk is assessed in order to direct *audit tests at the areas of highest risk: "Generally, the higher the assumed risk, the more stringent the audit action" (Lee, 1993, 177). **2.** In internal auditing, the *risk of overlooking or misinterpreting *material matters of concern. The matters under consideration may be quantitative or qualitative.

audit rotation The periodic changing of external auditors. Some countries—Italy and Spain, for example—have traditions of requiring listed corporations to rotate auditors after a defined time period (typically five or seven years) in an attempt to encourage external auditor *independence. Rotation of auditors can be costly, however, in terms of the disruption and inefficiencies arising from the *learning curve of a newly appointed auditor unfamiliar with an organization's activities. Audit rotation can refer to changes of audit firms or changes of audit partners from a single firm.

audit schedule **1.** A formal list of auditing assignments determined by an *internal audit function's planning process. The audit schedule's coverage may extend to *long-term planning of three, five, or more years. **2.** An alternative term for *work paper.

audit shop An alternative term for *internal audit function.

audit society A term coined by *Michael Power to denote allegedly pervasive and negative influences of auditing practices in modern life. Power has elaborated the concept in, among other writings, *The Audit Society: Rituals of Verification* (1997), and has offered further reflections in the essay "The audit society—second thoughts" (Power, 2000). The notion of the audit society has links to the polemical theories of the *critical accounting movement, and it is notable for disputing "official" justifications of the utility of auditing practices offered by the discipline's *professional associations.

The concept of the audit society is complex and multifaceted, and only a handful of characteristics are summarized here. Michael Power casts doubt on the theoretical validity of standard auditing philosophies, suggesting that auditing is more a social construct rather than a scientific practice: "Auditability cannot be defined; it is negotiated" (1997, 81). He is also suspicious of many of the claims made of the utility of auditing, like the *operational auditing notion of the *Three E's of economy, efficiency, and effectiveness. He suggests instead that auditing is often more parasitical than useful: The "audit society is a symptom of the times, coincidentally a *fin de siècle*, in which a gulf has opened up between poorly rewarded 'doing' and highly rewarded 'observing'" (1997, 147). Power also claims that auditing fails frequently to live up to its own promises, descending instead into a hollow, self-serving activity of limited value to organizations: "At worst auditing tends to become an organizational ritual, a dramaturgical performance" (1997, 141). He also interprets the expansion of auditing as an indication of institutional and cultural decline, writing that the audit society "can be understood as a label for a loss of confidence in the central steering institutions of society, particularly politics. So it may be that a loss of faith in intellectual, political and economic leadership has led to the creation of industries of checking which satisfy a demand for signals of order" (2000, 188).

Power's depiction of the audit society is an articulate challenge to conventional wisdom of the utility of auditing, and it has been debated in great detail in the academic auditing literature. A special issue of the *International Journal of Auditing* (Vol. 4, No. 1, 2000) was devoted to its analysis. For many, Power's arguments explain some of the roots of external auditing's *expectations gap.

Further reading: Power (1994b); Power (1994c); Power (1997); Power (2000)

audit software **1.** Computer software programs used to gather and evaluate *audit evidence. Audit software can be used in several evidence-gathering ways, including (i) data sorting, (ii) *sampling analysis, (iii) the performance of *walk-through tests, (iv) the production of *exception reports of nonstandard transactions, and (v) the generation of *confirmation letters. See also *computer assisted audit techniques. **2.** Computer software programs used to document an audit. Audit software for this purpose includes the following standardized tools: (i) *work papers, (ii) *audit planning templates, (iii) *flowcharting software, and (iv) *audit report formats.

audit step **1.** An alternative term for *audit test. **2.** An individual measure or action within an *audit test. For example, the performance of a *circularization of customers is a step within an audit test to establish the existence and accuracy of an organization's *accounts receivable balances.

audit test An action or procedure to gather and evaluate *audit evidence. Audit tests are normally formalized in *audit programs, and they may be classified into (i) *substantive and (ii) *compliance testing. *Analytical review procedures are normally classified within substantive testing, and *walk-through tests within compliance testing. The auditing of *populations of transactions or other items is normally performed through the use of *sampling techniques. See also *inspection and *observation.

audit trail An information flow that allows an auditor to trace the evolution of a *transaction. The chronological evolution of a transaction originates in its underlying activity (e.g., an inventory movement, or a sale to a customer), and a satisfactory audit trail is in place if the *audit evidence of the transaction can be viewed in its entirety through to the *general ledger. The verification of audit trails is important in both *substantive and *compliance testing. *Walk-through tests (a form of compliance testing) specifically focus on the adequacy of audit trails.

AuditTrends® A U.S. internal auditing consulting organization. Established in 1992 by *James Roth, AuditTrends undertakes consulting services and seminars in internal auditing and *corporate governance.

Web site: *www.audittrends.com*

audit universe The total potential scope of work within an auditor's remit. *Audit planning involves the allocation of resources to individual *auditable units within an audit universe, normally on the basis of a combination of the following: (i) *materiality, (ii) *risk assessment, (iii) a cyclical or rotational factor to ensure periodic coverage of every auditable unit, and (iv) requests from *auditees. The audit universe of a *multinational corporation, for example, may include the operational and financial activities of the individual overseas branches: An *internal audit function may determine the frequency of audit assignments at individual branches from a balanced assessment of the four factors listed above.

Audit Vision A U.S. information technology auditing newsletter. Published monthly by Audit Serve Inc., and distributed by e-mail, *Audit Vision* offers news and guidance on computer security and related areas.

Web link: *www.auditserve.com/forms/newsletter*

Auditwire A U.S. auditing newsletter. Published bimonthly by the *Institute of Internal Auditors (IIA), *Auditwire* alternates with the months of publication of the IIA magazine *Internal Auditor*. It is available online. The newsletter's Web page states that it offers "perspectives on current and emerging issues and delivers news about the IIA and the people, events, and issues that shape the [internal auditing] profession."

Web link: *www.theiia.org/ecm/newsletters.cfm?doc_id=757*

authorization The giving of approval or permission. Authorization is central to many of the *internal controls found in modern organizations, from the making of *disbursements to the hiring of employees. Authorization can be effected through written signatures or *password-controlled access to *transactions in a computerized information system. Authorization rights derive from the status of an individual in an organization, and are normally restrained by *accountability for the exercise of the rights.

average A single number calculated to represent a set of numbers. The term average is popularly used as a synonym for *mean, but it also covers the *median and the *mode. See also *weighted average.

avoidable cost An item of expenditure incurred at the discretion of the management of an organization. In contrast to a *sunk cost, an avoidable cost can be incurred or avoided on the basis of a management decision. For example, potential rental fees for warehousing space can be avoided if management decides not to occupy the warehouse, or the *raw material costs of a manufacturing process can be avoided if management decides not to produce the item in question. Avoidable costs can be *variable or fixed in nature. See also *unavoidable cost and *controllable cost.

B

backflush costing A costing method in which *costs are allocated to products when a manufacturing process is finished, or when a sale is made. Backflush costing is normally associated with *just-in-time (JIT) manufacturing and delivery practices, and it offers the advantage of avoiding cumbersome and expensive cost tracking mechanisms. It is particularly suited to the typically low *inventory levels of JIT environments.

back office The administrative functions of a *brokerage operation that trades in *securities, *commodities, and *currencies. Compare *front office.

backup 1. The periodic copying of accounting and other data in case of loss of information. The backup of computerized information systems permits data recovery and is normal practice in modern organizations. The frequency and storage arrangements of backup copies are driven by the importance and difficulty of replacement of the information, though adequate backup procedures are often required for *business continuity *insurance purposes. 2. Moral, financial, or administrative support given to an individual or organization.

bad debt An *accounts receivable balance whose collection is doubtful. Under most systems of *Generally Accepted Accounting Principles, an *allowance for bad debts is raised to acknowledge the reduced likelihood of recoverability of a customer balance. When an item is known with certainty to be irrecoverable, it is usually subjected to a *write-off to expenses. The term "bad debt" is sometimes distinguished from "doubtful debt" in that the former designates a customer balance known to be irrecoverable, while the latter indicates a customer balance of potential, if unlikely, recoverability. However, the two terms are frequently used synonymously.

balance 1. The net total of *debit and *credit entries in a *general ledger *account. 2. The equalizing effect of the total *debit and *credit entries in a *general ledger. An assessment of the integrity of the mechanics of *double entry bookkeeping can be effected through preparation of a *trial balance. 3. The net total of *debit and *credit entries in a bank or loan account, or in an *accounts payable or *accounts receivable account.

balance of payments The record of a country's economic *transactions with other countries and with international institutions. The balance of payments is normally analyzed into a current account that records trading transactions and a capital account that records transactions relating to *long-term assets and liabilities.

balance sheet An accounting summary of the financial position of an organization or individual at a specific date. A balance sheet offers a snapshot of *assets, *liabilities, and *equity, and it sets out the results of the *accounting equation of *double entry bookkeeping. Under most systems of *Generally Accepted Accounting Principles, balance sheets are based on *historical costs and, therefore, are unlikely to reflect the *fair market value of an organization's assets. Along with an *income statement, the balance sheet is prepared from a *trial balance: The balance sheet and income statement are the primary elements of *financial statements.

balance sheet equation, the An alternative term for the *accounting equation.

balancing figure An item inserted into a *general ledger account, a *trial balance, or a *balance sheet in order to make the totals of *debit and *credit entries agree with each other. The inclusion of a balancing figure in a trial balance is sometimes used to correct mistakes in computations of the *accounting equation.

bank float See *float (definition 2).

bank reconciliation A periodic *internal control procedure to identify differences between *bank statements and corresponding bank *balances stated in *general ledger *accounts. Errors and timing differences may arise between the accounting of *transactions by a bank and its customers. To ensure the accuracy of both bank balances and the general ledger, an organization or individual periodically *reconciles bank statements with related general ledger accounts. Typical differences include *checks not yet processed through the bank, and items in transit.

bankruptcy The legal status of an organization or individual unable to settle its *liabilities. Bankruptcy tends to mean the end of a business as a *going concern, though bankruptcy laws in most jurisdictions include allowance for attempts to rescue all or part of the business. In the United States, for example, *Chapter 11 of the 1978 *U.S. Bankruptcy Reform Act* provides for the financial reorganization of a business while it continues to operate under defined restrictions. Bankruptcy law relating to individuals tends to be markedly different from corporate bankruptcy law in most jurisdictions.

bank statement A summary of *transactions in a bank account prepared for a bank customer. Bank statements are usually prepared at regular intervals, and they increasingly have *real-time availability. *Bank reconciliations—the agreeing of bank statement amounts to corresponding *general ledger accounts—are a fundamental *internal control procedure.

barriers to entry Restrictions on the entry of new competitors into a *market. Barriers to entry may result from technical and economic factors. For example, the large-scale investment in machinery needed for some production processes may be beyond the economic means of many potential entrants to a market, or a firm may hold an exclusive *patent right that gives it a technical advantage in manufacturing a product. Barriers can also derive from *monopolistic and restrictive trade practices, or from *tariffs and other *protectionist measures. Compare *barriers to exit.

barriers to exit Restrictions on the ability of participants in a *market to withdraw from an activity or to deploy resources elsewhere. A common barrier to exit is the existence of a law or regulation that forces an organization to produce goods or provide services deemed to be for the public good. Another barrier to exit is the impact of *sunk costs: An organization that makes massive investments in machinery may find it impractical to abandon the activity for which the machinery was purchased.

barter The acquisition of goods or services through exchange for other goods or services, without the intermediary of *money. Although barter systems tend to be cumbersome and inefficient, and have largely been replaced by money systems, individual barter transactions are still common. For example, some *developing countries frequently exchange *raw materials for food or manufactured goods. The accounting treatment of the elements of barter transactions normally values them at *fair market values.

base document 1. A document that serves as *audit evidence. Examples include *bank statements, *vendor invoices, and *general ledger extracts. 2. A document that includes the *population of data from which a *sample can be extracted for audit purposes.

base period 1. A period of time that serves as a framework or starting point for financial or operational analysis. 2. A specific date from which an index is calculated. Comparisons of *inflation rates and the *market values of *securities are often calculated in this manner.

base rate 1. An *interest rate used for reference or comparative purposes. 2. A term used in the United Kingdom (and in some other countries with strong

British influence) for the *interest lending rate set by a *central bank. Base rates are used as a control mechanism for a national economy, and commercial banks calculate their lending rates in line with national base rates.

base stock The minimum level of *inventory required for day-to-day operational purposes. The base stock level is a critical measurement, and inventory falling below it can adversely affect an organization's operations.

bear **1.** [noun] An individual who believes that *prices in a *securities or *commodities market will fall. Contrast *bull. **2.** [adjective] A *securities or *commodities market in which there are general expectations of falling market *prices. Contrast *bull.

Behavioral Research in Accounting A U.S. scholarly accounting journal. Established in 1989, it is published annually in both print and online formats by the Accounting, Behavior and Organizations (ABO) Section of the *American Accounting Association. It frequently includes analysis of behavioral aspects of auditing.
Web link: *business.baylor.edu/Charles_Davis//abo/briainfo_home.htm*

bell curve See *normal distribution.

below the line In a position in an *income statement that does not directly affect *net income. The "line" is the point in the income statement that separates items that determine net income from items that determine *funding and the *distribution of net income. If an item is below the line, it is excluded from net income. Traditionally, *extraordinary items were treated below the line, but in recent years *Generally Accepted Accounting Principles around the world have moved toward encouraging such items to appear *above the line, and thereby to directly affect *earnings per share.

benchmarking The comparison of data or operations against those of similar organizations. Benchmarking, whether *quantitative or *qualitative, is often performed with the intention of seeking ways to improve an organization's operations. Auditors also frequently use benchmarking as part of their *analytical review procedures. For example, an industry average of payroll cost per employee is a common benchmark to assess the reasonableness of payroll costs in a specific organization. The *Global Auditing Information Network of the *Institute of Internal Auditors offers benchmarking information at the level of the *internal audit function.

best practices Policies, procedures, or *internal controls held by general consensus to represent optimal conduct. An example of voluntary adherence to auditing best practices can be observed in the following by many internal auditors, even non-members of the Institute of Internal Auditors (IIA), of the Professional Practices Framework of the (IIA).

beta **1.** A measure of the degree to which the *returns on a *security track the rest of a market. A beta coefficient is a measurement of the volatility of a *security's *systematic risk, which under *portfolio theory cannot be reduced through *diversification. A beta of one suggests that a security's returns follow the movements of the rest of the market, and that it therefore has an average risk. A beta of more than one indicates that a security moves in the same direction as a market, but to a greater degree. A beta of less than one denotes that a security moves in the same direction as a market, but is less responsive than the market as a whole. A negative beta indicates that a security's returns follow a market inversely. **2.** The second letter of the Greek alphabet, used extensively in statistics and financial economics.

Beta Alpha Psi (BAP) A U.S. national accounting fraternity. BAP was founded in 1919, and its Web site states that it "recognizes academic excellence and complements members' formal education by providing interaction among students, faculty and professionals, and fosters lifelong growth, service and ethical conduct."

Web site: *www.bap.org*

beta coefficient See *beta (definition 1).

betterment The enhancement of the condition and operational functionality of a *fixed asset. Betterment costs are normally *capitalized in a *balance sheet. Contrast *maintenance.

big bath reserves *Reserves created for charges arising from *acquisitions or *restructuring. Many systems of *Generally Accepted Accounting Principles restrict the use of big bath reserves, owing to their rather tainted reputation as a potential means of *cooking the books. The creation of inflated reserves can be exploited to release the reserves (and thereby inflate *net income) during periods of weak financial performance. Such misuse of big bath reserves is a subversion of the *accruals basis of accounting. See also *cookie jar reserves.

Big Five, the The name given to the largest global accounting and professional services firms prior to the demise of *Arthur Andersen in 2002. Now known as the *Big Four.

Big Four, the **1.** The Big Four accounting firms are *Deloitte Touche Tohmatsu, *Ernst & Young, *KPMG, and *PricewaterhouseCoopers. These firms are more than merely global accountants and auditors: External auditing is their core activity but they also provide a range of professional services, from tax advice to business *consulting. The *outsourcing of internal auditing has been an important area of Big Four activity in recent years. However, regulators throughout the world have raised concerns about the levels of the Big Four's often-lucrative *management advisory services (MAS), and the extent to which MAS can allegedly compromise the *independence of external *audit opinions. These concerns have intensified following the *Enron corporate scandal, and have crystallized in the United States' *Sarbanes-Oxley Act of 2002, part of which addresses the topic of external auditors' provision of MAS. Nonetheless, the Big Four remain the first-choice external auditors for large, *multinational corporations, for whom they offer a common auditing approach around the world.

Other than Ernst & Young, the origins of the current Big Four can be traced back to the United Kingdom in the nineteenth century, but their center of gravity has long shifted to the United States. Decades of cut-throat competition has led to consolidation among the international accounting firms: The Big Eight of the 1980s were halved in number by 2002, with the demise of *Arthur Andersen following the *Enron corporate scandal. **2.** In Japan, the term "Big Four" has traditionally referred to the country's four main investment banks. **3.** In the United Kingdom, the term "Big Four" is commonly used to refer to the country's four largest high-street, commercial banks.

Further reading: Matthews et al. (1998)

Big "R," the A U.S. educational novel that expounds *internal auditing principles. Coauthored by Larry D. Crumbley, Douglas E. Ziegenfuss, and John J. O'Shaughnessy, the novel uses the plot of a murder mystery set in the world of baseball to illustrate internal auditing theory. As the authors write in their preface: "This instructional novel mixes baseball, auditing, serial killers, *fraud, *risks, anthrax, and scuba diving to help students learn the principles of internal auditing." This original and entertaining approach of using a fictional narrative to expound auditing principles is rare. Another example is K. H. Spencer Pickett's *Internal Control—A Manager's Journey* (Pickett, 2001).

Further reading: Crumbley et al. (2000)

billion 1. One thousand million. **2.** An archaic, British term for one million million. Modern British usage normally means one thousand million, but the visitor to the United Kingdom should be wary of the term's potential ambiguity.

bill of exchange A written payment order used in international commerce. A bill of exchange is raised by an exporter and addressed to an importer (or an importer's *agent), to request payment of a specific amount at a specific date. It is similar to a *post-dated check.

bill of lading A document that serves as evidence of the delivery of goods in accordance with contractually agreed terms. Legal title for the goods is often linked to the physical transfer of the bill from vendor to purchaser.

bill of materials (BOM) A summary of the *raw materials and other elements of a manufactured product. A BOM can serve as (i) a record of the components of a product and (ii) a control document for the manufacturing process. The term can also be used in reference to the construction of a *fixed asset.

bill of sale A document that summarizes the contractual terms of a sale. The bill of sale confirms legal title to goods, rather than the possession of goods.

black, in the To achieve *income (definition 2) or to have positive *cash flow. Contrast the phrase "in the *red."

"black box" audit approach An *audit approach that sidesteps the technical complexities of a computerized processing system. A "black box" refers to a computer system ignored by an auditor, who focuses instead on a comparison of inputs with outputs. For example, an auditor may compare transactions entered into a computerized accounting system with *general ledger account balances printed from the system, without reviewing the detail of the manner in which the system processed the transactions. A "black box" approach is often adopted in the context of an auditor's inadequate technical knowledge of computerized systems, or in cases of restricted time or resources. It can produce worthwhile *audit evidence, but it is essentially *substantive and historical in nature, and it does not offer any ongoing *assurance for *internal controls.

black economy An alternative term for *underground economy.

black market An alternative term for activity in an *underground economy.

blind entry A *general ledger *transaction or *journal entry that lacks narrative explanation.

blue chip A corporation or its *common stock with a history of impressive *returns to investors and which is perceived as low *risk. The term derives from the color of chips used to place high-value bets in casinos.

Blue Ribbon Commissions *Corporate governance review panels established by the *National Association of Corporate Directors (NACD). The NACD Web site describes the reports of its Blue Ribbon Committees as "thought-leadership publications compiled by a commission of seasoned *directors and governance experts." In recent years areas investigated by commissions include *audit committees and *executive remuneration. In 2000, for example, the NACD published its *Report of the NACD Blue Ribbon Commission on Audit Committees*, which reviewed ways in which audit committees can function effectively, and the types of director that should be considered for audit committee service.

Further reading: NACD (2000); NACD (2001)

Web site: *www.nacdonline.org*

board of directors A group of *directors with ultimate responsibility for the *stewardship of an organization. Boards of directors have been described as "inescapably, the centre of the [corporate] governance system" (Cadbury, 2002, 33). Boards exercise their governance duties in several ways: they (i) elaborate strategies and plans for an organization, (ii) define *internal control strategies, (iii) oversee and report on *external control, (iv) provide leadership to an organization, and (v) address the concerns of *stakeholders. A main board of directors (or "top table") may delegate some of its authority to subordinate boards (e.g., in operational divisions and overseas *subsidiaries), but it retains overall responsibility for an organization's stewardship.

The responsibilities of a board of directors can be distinguished from those of an organization's *managers—a board has a strategic oversight role, while management takes charge of day-to-day operations. This difference has been summarized by the *National Association of Corporate Directors in the acronym NIFO—"nose in, fingers out" (NACD, 1996). Individual *inside directors, however, may have to juggle the potentially conflicting responsibilities of directing and managing an organization.

In English-speaking countries, a board of directors tends to have a unitary (or single-tier or monistic) structure. In contrast, two-tier (or dualistic) boards are the norm in continental Europe and some other parts of the world. In Germany, for example, a corporation's supervisory board (made up of representatives of *stockholders and employees) appoints a management board to run the corporation's day-to-day business. This arrangement is intended to promote social partnership between various parties interested in an organization's stewardship, and to avoid an excessive concentration of power within the board structure. Although there is little evidence of moves toward a two-tier structure in the English-speaking world, the increasing importance of *outside directors may be interpreted as an enhancement of independent oversight within the unitary board structure.

See also *audit committee, *remuneration committee, and *tone at the top.

Board of Environmental, Health & Safety Auditor Certifications (BEAC) A U.S. *environmental auditing organization. Founded in 1997 by the *Institute of Internal Auditors (IIA) and the *Auditing Roundtable, the BEAC is based at the IIA's headquarters in Altamonte Springs, FL. Its certification programs cover environmental and health and safety auditing, and include the *Certified Professional Environmental Auditor (CPEA) designation. The BEAC also issues environmental *auditing standards and a competency framework for auditors in this specialized field.

Web site: *www.beac.org*

boilerplate Standardized language used in *audit reports, legal contracts, and other documents. Boilerplate language is often used to minimize legal *risks. The term is frequently used in a pejorative sense to indicate the allegedly unimaginative, uninformative, and clichéd content of external auditors' reports and corporate statements on *internal control and *risk management.

bond A *financial instrument issued by a *public or *private sector institution. There are many varieties of bonds: (i) secured (by *collateral) or unsecured, (ii) short- or *long-term, and (iii) with fixed or variable *interest. The issuer of a bond commits to paying the bond's owner its *face value at a specific *maturity date, and often also periodic *interest payments. Unlike *common stock, a corporation's bonds do not normally carry voting rights.

book 1. [plural noun] The *financial statements, *general ledger, and other accounting records and *ledgers of an organization or individual. The term is used in a range of expressions from *book value to *cooking the books. 2. [verb] To record an *entry in a *general ledger account or in a *subsidiary ledger. See also *posting.

bookkeeper An individual responsible for recording *general ledger *transactions and preparing a *trial balance. The duties of bookkeepers vary between organizations, but there is a commonly understood distinction between the supporting functions of a bookkeeper and the more complex activities of an accountant.

bookkeeping audit An audit of *general ledger *transactions that focuses on the detection of *bookkeeping errors or *fraud.

books of account See *book (definition 1).

books of prime entry A rather archaic term for accounting records used to summarize information before the information is transferred to a *general ledger. A *petty cash register is an example of a book of prime entry. Compare *subsidiary ledger.

book value 1. The historical cost of an asset recorded in a *general ledger. Book values do not take account of *revaluations and, in financial statements, they are normally stated net of any *amortization. Contrast *fair market value. **2.** An alternative term for *carrying value.

bottleneck A stage of a process or activity subjected to congestion or obstruction. In production processes, a bottleneck indicates that manufacturing capacity has been exceeded.

bottom line 1. *Net income as recorded in an *income statement. The net income figure is used in *earnings per share calculations. **2.** The outcome of an activity or campaign in activities as diverse as advertising and employee recruitment (e.g., "The bottom line is that this recruitment campaign must bring results"). **3.** The crux of an argument.

box-ticking approach An approach to auditing or *compliance testing characterized by a superficial or unimaginative use of *checklists and *questionnaires. The term is used pejoratively, to imply a focus on the formalities of auditing or compliance over a true understanding and appreciation of underlying issues. A common theme in *corporate governance is the desirability of proactive compliance in a spirit of understanding, rather than a box-ticking approach that fails to address the true areas of concern.

boycott The withdrawal of economic relations with an individual, organization, or country. Boycotts arise from economic or political disputes, and examples include the actions of pressure groups to discourage the purchasing of the goods and services of corporations of whose actions they disapprove. The term derives from the name of a nineteenth century British land agent in colonial Ireland, who was the subject of economic protests against excessively high rents. Compare *embargo and *sanction.

brainstorming The spontaneous suggestion of ideas by an individual or a group of individuals. Brainstorming is often advocated by modern management theory as a means of tossing out a large number of ideas to solve a problem, or to enhance the so-called *Three E's in an organization's operations. Generally, the large number of suggestions generated by a brainstorming session are gradually pruned and narrowed to produce focused recommendations for action.

branch An operational or administrative unit of an organization. Many *multinational corporations have branches around the world, and *control over remote operating units of this nature present particular challenges to auditors. Organizational *risks are magnified for branches separated from their head offices by (i) large geographical distances, (ii) cultural dissonance, (iii) linguistic differences, (iv) variations in local laws, regulations, and taxation, (v) differences in *Generally Accepted Accounting Principles, and (vi) differences in *Generally Accepted Auditing Standards. The degree of *decentralization and the level of autonomy granted to the managers of individual branches can also complicate an organization's *internal control environment. Control over branches is sometimes effected by the supervisory role of *divisional groups.

Further reading: O'Regan (2003a)

brand The value of the attraction to *consumers of the name or logo of a product or service. Brands are *intangible assets, and are notoriously difficult to quantify. The value of brands is often evident during corporate *acquisitions, when it is reflected in *goodwill figures.

break-even point A level of activity at which total *costs equal total *revenues. Break-even analysis can be applied to individual products or services, or to an entire organization. At a break-even point, no profit or loss is made.

bribe An improper or illegal inducement made with the intention of gaining influence over an individual or organization. Bribes can take the form of cash, assets, or services. Most legal and ethical systems forbid bribes, owing to their *corrupting effects, though in practice the dividing lines between bribes and acceptable *gifts and entertaining can often be fuzzy. In some cultures, the offering of expensive gifts is commonplace. The *Foreign Corrupt Practices Act forbids U.S. organizations and individuals from engaging in international bribery. Compare *facilitating payment.

Further reading: Pacini et al. (2002)

Brink, Victor Z. (1906–1992) A pioneering U.S. *internal auditing author, educator, and practitioner. With experience straddling both academic life (at Columbia University) and professional life (at Ford Motor Company and the Pure Oil Company), Brink has been described as "the most influential individual in the history of internal auditing" (Flesher and McIntosh, 2002, 149). He was one of three main cofounders of the *Institute of Internal Auditors (IIA), along with *Robert B. Milne and *John B. Thurston. Brink authored the pioneering text *Internal Auditing* in 1941, which was based on a doctoral thesis and is considered by many to be the first major text on the subject. Still in print today, the book has been updated by other authors under the eponymous title *Brink's Modern Internal Auditing* (Brink et al., 1999). Brink's 1941 book acted as a major catalyst in the creation of the IIA, as it brought its author to the attention of Milne and Thurston.

Brink made many contributions to the IIA: He held senior positions in the organization's hierarchy (e.g., the IIA's first research director) and he also wrote the IIA's first history, *Foundations for Unlimited Horizons* (1977). The IIA awarded him with its first Lifetime Achievement Reward in 1991.

Further reading: Brink (1941); Brink (1977); Brink and Dittenhofer (1994); Brink et al. (1999); Flesher (1991); Flesher and McIntosh (2002)

British Accounting Association (BAA) A British scholarly accounting organization. The British equivalent of the *American Accounting Association, the BAA was established in 1947. It is administered from Sheffield University, in the north of England. The BAA Web site states its main objective to be "the advancement of knowledge and understanding of accounting," and its activities focus on the encouragement of accounting research and teaching. It also publishes the *British Accounting Review*, a scholarly journal.

Web site: *www.shef.ac.uk/~baa*

British Accounting Review A British scholarly accounting journal. Established in 1984, the journal is published quarterly by Elsevier Science on behalf of the *British Accounting Association. It is available in both print and online formats, and its notes describe it as "a forum for communication throughout the world between members of the academic and professional community concerned with the research and teaching, at degree level and above, of accounting, finance, and cognate disciplines." Its coverage is more internationally focused than its title might imply, and it frequently addresses auditing subjects. (Before becoming a fully fledged academic journal in 1984 the magazine existed in several forms. It traces its history back to the *Association of University Teachers of Accounting Newsletter* that first appeared in 1948.)

Web link: *www.elsevier.com/locate/issn/0890-8389*

broker An intermediary in financial transactions. Brokers typically act as *agents to purchase and sell assets on behalf of others, and they operate in *markets for *securities, *commodities, *currencies, and *insurance policies. Brokers are normally rewarded by *commission fees.

budget A quantitative plan for the future activities of an organization or individual. The preparation of budgets is common in most *private and *public sector organizations, and budgets normally fulfill one or more of the following purposes: They act as (i) a record of planned activities, (ii) a standard against which to compare *variances with actual performance, (iii) a means of communicating an organization's plans to employees, (iv) an *accountability mechanism for activities and assets, (v) a means of motivating and rewarding individuals for performance against budget, and (vi) an *internal control over operations. The sophistication and methodology of budgets varies widely. Budgets can be limited to high-level data on assets, revenues, and expenses, or they can consist of detailed financial statements, *cash flows, and operational statistics for individual areas of an organization. Budgeting methodologies tend to follow the costing methodologies adopted by an organization, like *activity based costing or a *just-in-time philosophy.

While budgets can have a motivational effect on individuals, they can also have dysfunctional consequences. For example, employees may be tempted to incur inappropriate expenses to fully use a budget, in order to ensure they are allocated a similar budgetary level in future years. More generally, organizational turf wars can erupt over the allocation of budgeted resources, and it has been perceptively noted that "it is a rare organization in which budgets do not create a framework for conflict" (Sawyer and Vinten, 1996, 245). Compare *forecast.

budget committee A group of individuals responsible for *authorizing budgets. Budget committees tend to comprise (i) an organization's senior operational managers, (ii) the *Chief Financial Officer, and sometimes also (iii) the *Chief Executive Officer.

bug 1. An error or flaw in a computer software program. 2. An error in the operation of computer hardware. 3. [less commonly] An alternative term for *virus (both definitions).

bull 1. [noun] An individual who believes that *prices in a *securities or *commodities market will rise. Contrast *bear. 2. [adjective] A *securities or *commodities market in which there are general expectations of rising *prices. Contrast *bear.

business combination The amalgamation of one or more organizations to form a new economic unit. Most business combinations take the form of *acquisitions or *mergers, and give rise to *consolidated financial statements.

business continuity planning Policies and procedures designed to ensure the survival of an organization following a disaster. Continuity planning addresses potential disasters like (i) the loss of accounting data, (ii) the destruction of buildings and inventory by fire, and (iii) the disruption of distribution networks by adverse weather conditions.

Typical components of business continuity planning include (i) adequate *backup of accounting information, (ii) procedures for the rapid replacement of key employees who may be injured or killed, and (iii) guidelines for conducting press relations to explain *material disruption to operations.

business process re-engineering (BPR) Radical changes to an organization's *processes and *procedures aimed at reducing costs or enhancing the *Three E's of operations.

Further reading: Frigo et al. (1995)

by-product An incidental product emerging from a *production process. By-products typically have significantly less value than main production items, and are often unavoidable: for example, paraffin and lubricants are frequent by-products of oil refining processes. Depending on *materiality, a by-product can be accounted as a separate unit of *inventory, or revenues from its sale can simply be offset against the production costs of the principal manufactured items. Compare *joint product.

C

Cadbury Report A British *corporate governance report of 1992. The influence of the *Cadbury Report* has been international in its impact. Prepared by a committee chaired by *Sir Adrian Cadbury, the formal title of the report was the *Report of the Committee on the Financial Aspects of Corporate Governance*. Adrian Cadbury is a member of the Cadbury chocolate manufacturing dynasty, and he held the post of chairperson of Cadbury Schweppes Plc, a British listed corporation with Quaker (Society of Friends) origins, from 1975 to 1989. He was also a director of the Bank of England from 1970 to 1994.

The Committee on the Financial Aspects of Corporate Governance was established in 1991 by the London Stock Exchange and the British accounting profession following a series of corporate accounting scandals in the United Kingdom. *The Cadbury Report* focused on the importance of a culture of openness, integrity, and *accountability as prerequisites for effective corporate governance, and it resulted in a *Code of Best Practice* that is commonly referred to as the *Cadbury Code*. The Cadbury Committee requested that its work be reviewed and updated after several years: This led to the *Hampel Report* of 1998.

Further reading: *Cadbury Report* (1992); Cadbury (2002); Chapman (2003)

Cadmus, Bradford (d. 1964) An *internal auditing practitioner, researcher, and leading member of the *Institute of Internal Auditors (IIA) in its early years. Cadmus was the first paid managing director of the IIA, appointed in 1947, and he contributed to internal auditing literature with research reports and his *Operational Auditing Handbook* of 1964. His influence on the IIA was so significant that he was known as "Mr. Internal Auditing" (Flesher, 1991, 149). In 1966 the IIA honored Cadmus with the establishment of the Bradford Cadmus Memorial Award, for extraordinary contributions to the internal auditing profession.

Further reading: Cadmus (1962); Cadmus (1964); Flesher (1991)

CAE Bulletin A U.S. internal auditing newsletter. Linked to the *Chief Audit Executive (CAE) Services Program of the *Institute of Internal Auditors, the newsletter is published at least monthly. Its Web page describes its aim to be the provision of "news and guidance" for heads of internal audit, and it is available online.

Web link: *www.theiia.org/ecm/newsletters.cfm?doc_id=756*

CAGC Guidelines   See the *Commonwealth Association for Corporate Governance.

calendarization   The recording of the monthly distribution of an item. To take a simple example, a yearly expense totalling $120,000 may be calendarized over 12 months by simply dividing by 12, unless the pattern in which the cost is incurred falls unevenly between individual months. Calendarization is common in *budgeting calculations. Compare *annualization.

California Public Employees' Retirement System (CalPERS)   A major *institutional investor. Based in Sacramento, CA, CalPERS is the largest public pension fund and retirement system in the United States. Founded in 1932 as the State Employees' Retirement System, it adopted its current name in 1967. The CalPERS Web site stated in 2003 that it provided "retirement and health benefit services to more than 1.3 million members and nearly 2,500 employers." CalPERS is no passive investor; it has made significant contributions to *corporate governance debates. For example, its 1998 *Corporate Governance Core Principles and Guidelines* address the foundations of *accountability between a *corporation's managers and owners. The CalPERS Shareowner Forum is intended to "provide an education and communication resource for those interested in the field [of corporate governance]."
   Further reading: CalPERS (1998)
   Web site (CalPERS): *www.calpers.ca.gov*
   Web site (CalPERS Shareowner Forum): *www.calpers-governance.org*

call option   The right to purchase an *asset or *security at a specific *price within a defined time period. Contrast *put option.

CalPERS   See *California Public Employees' Retirement System.

CA Magazine   **1.** A British professional accounting magazine. Published monthly by the *Institute of Chartered Accountants of Scotland, the magazine is available in print format, though some sections (mainly editorials) are also published online. The magazine focuses on professional developments and news in the fields of accounting, auditing, and taxation, with focus on the United Kingdom. Its Web pages describe it as "Scotland's largest circulating business magazine." **2.** A Canadian professional accounting magazine. Published monthly by the *Canadian Institute of Chartered Accountants, the magazine is available in both print and online formats. It focuses on professional developments and news in accounting, auditing, and taxation, with emphasis on the Canadian environment.
   Web link (Scotland): *www.icas.org.uk/cms/sectionView.asp?section=74*
   Web link (Canada): *www.camagazine.com/index.cfm/ci_id/287/la_id/1.htm*

Canadian Academic Accounting Association (CAAA) A Canadian scholarly accounting organization. The Toronto-based CAAA was established in 1976, and its Web site states its main objective to be as follows: To "promote excellence" in Canadian accounting education and research. Its activities include research programs, conferences, and publications. The latter include monographs and the journal *Contemporary Accounting Research*.

Web site: *www.caaa.ca/home.html*

Canadian Institute of Chartered Accountants (CICA) Canada's main professional accounting organization. Established by royal charter in 1902, the CICA is Canada's main body for accounting and external auditing, and it enjoys significant international prestige and influence. The work of its *Criteria for Control (CoCo) Board, renamed the Risk Management and Governance Board in 2001, has been recognized globally. The CICA's Accounting Standards Board sets Canadian *accounting standards, and its Assurance Standards Board sets the country's external *auditing standards. The *CICA Handbook* is the institute's main reference source. The CICA also publishes the monthly *CA Magazine*.

CICA membership was approximately 75,000 in 2003, including student members. This makes it significantly larger than Canada's two other accounting organizations, CMA Canada and the Certified General Accountants Association of Canada, which have approximately 45,000 and 55,000 members respectively (including students), working mainly as management accountants in industry. Following British traditions, CICA members are designated *chartered accountants.

Web site: *www.cica.ca*

capacity 1. The maximum amount of *production that a *manufacturing process can handle. Typical limiting factors on production capacity include restrictions arising from (i) space, (ii) *labor, (iii) plant and machinery, (iv) the supply of *raw materials, and (v) financing. 2. The maximum storage space offered by a *warehousing facility.

capex A popular abbreviation for *capital expenditure.

capital 1. Ownership interest in the *equity (definition 1) of an organization. Under the conventions of *double entry bookkeeping and the *accounting equation, *stockholders' capital is calculated as total *assets less total *liabilities. For corporations, stockholders' equity consists of the *par value of *common stock plus *retained earnings. 2. An individual's *wealth as measured by his or her total * assets less total *liabilities. 3. *Fixed assets with wealth-generating potential. (For *current assets, see *working capital.) 4. In economic theory, one of the three (of four) *factors of production, representing either *cash or *tangible assets.

capital asset pricing model (CAPM) A theoretical framework in financial economics for analysis of the relationships between the *risks and *returns of securities. CAPM suggests that securities' *prices tend to adjust to ensure that securities' returns adequately reward investors who bear the risk of holding them within a perfectly *diversified *portfolio. CAPM makes a number of assumptions, including the following: (i) all the investors in a market hold a diversified portfolio of securities, so the activity of any single security will not materially affect the market; (ii) the risk of a particular security can be assessed only in terms of its performance to the rest of the portfolio; and (iii) the price of a security whose returns follow market trends will tend to be low. CAPM states that a security's risk can be analyzed into *systematic and *unsystematic risk. The former is nondiversifiable risk and it is measured by the use of *beta (definition 1); the latter is a diversifiable risk.

capital expenditure The purchase or *betterment of *long-term assets like *property, plant, and equipment. The term is often abbreviated to capex. Contrast *revenue expenditure.

capitalization 1. The inclusion or reclassification of a cost to an *asset account. Most systems of *Generally Accepted Accounting Principles permit the capitalization of assets of a *long-term nature in the *balance sheet. For example, the costs of renovating a piece of production machinery to extend its life by more than one year can usually be capitalized into the cost of the asset. See also *betterment. 2. The market value of a corporation's total issued *common stock.

capital lease A *lease whose contractual terms and economic effects involve the transfer of the *risks and *rewards of a leased asset. Under most systems of *Generally Accepted Accounting Principles, a *lessee *capitalizes in its *balance sheet an asset obtained though a capital lease. Contrast *operating lease.

carrying value Amounts shown in financial statements for assets and liabilities, net of any *offsetting items. For example, the carrying value of a *fixed asset is normally calculated after deduction of *amortization charges, and the carrying value of *accounts receivable is typically shown net of an *allowance for bad debts.

cartel An arrangement among *suppliers of a good or service to influence *prices. Cartels are illegal in most countries, through *antitrust laws and regulations to enhance *competition. Some cartels operate internationally. An example frequently given in economic literature is the Organization of Petroleum

Exporting Countries (OPEC), which attempts to influence world oil prices, but OPEC itself states that it merely seeks to establish "fair and reasonable" prices for both suppliers and consumers. Compare *monopoly and *oligopoly.

cash 1. Tangible units of *money. In this sense, cash is restricted to bank notes and coins. Small quantities of cash held in an organization for day-to-day expenses are referred to as *petty cash. **2.** *Money deposited at a bank, and other highly *liquid assets like *checks and *matured financial instruments. Restrictions on the *liquidity of any of these items may not permit their classification as cash. For example, *post-dated checks and bank deposits with restricted access may not have sufficient liquidity to qualify as cash.

cash basis accounting The *recognition of *revenues and *expenses in line with related *cash movements. Cash basis accounting is not permissible for large organizations under most systems of *Generally Accepted Accounting Principles, which prefers an *accruals basis that recognizes items in an *income statement as they are earned or incurred.

cash cow An activity, product, or organization that regularly and reliably generates a healthy *cash flow. Cash cows are typically characterized by low growth and activity in mature markets.

cash equivalent value The amount of *cash that can be received in an *arm's length transaction for the sale of an asset. See also *fair market value.

cash float See *float (definition 1).

cash flow forecast A quantifiable estimate of future *cash movements arising from the operations of an organization or individual. Many *budgets include cash flow forecasts to accompany estimates of accounting costs and revenues.

cash flow statement An accounting summary of *cash movements arising from the operations of an organization or individual. Most systems of *Generally Accepted Accounting Principles require the inclusion of a cash flow statement in a corporation's *financial statements. Cash flow statements show cash inflows (e.g., from sales) and outflows (e.g., in the form of operating expenses and investments).

casting A British term for *footing.

caveat emptor A Latin expression meaning "let the buyer beware." The phrase is common in legal literature in the *common law systems of English-speaking countries. It emphasizes the *risks inherent in commercial transactions. The expression implies that a purchaser has a responsibility to carefully examine an article before acquiring it: In the absence of misrepresentation by the seller, the purchaser must bear the consequences of the decision to buy. In modern times, the imperatives of *caveat emptor* have been significantly diminished by the development of consumer protection legislation.

cell 1. An individual element of a *spreadsheet grid that contains numbers, mathematical formulae, or text. Cells occur at intersection points between a spreadsheet's rows and columns, from which they derive specific grid references. **2.** In manufacturing, an operational unit of machines, personnel, or other resources dedicated to a discrete task or series of tasks. Production cells are often used to control operational flows in *just-in-time environments.

central bank A national bank that regulates a country's economic system and acts as a lender of last resort to commercial banks. Central banks normally establish a country's short-term *base rate. The level of political influence over central bank policies varies from country to country.

centralization The concentration of activities, powers, and decision-making authority within an organization. Centralization can occur (i) in geographical terms (e.g., in the centralization of powers at a *multinational corporation's head office), (ii) in organizational terms (with power concentrated in the hands of a small number of individuals), or (iii) in a combination of geographical or organizational terms. The antonym of centralization is *decentralization.

central limit theorem See *normal distribution.

certainty With 100 percent *probability of occurrence. Contrast *uncertainty.

Certification in Control Self-Assessment (CCSA)® A specialty certification program of the *Institute of Internal Auditors that covers *Control Self-Assessment. The program was established in 1999.
Web link: *www.theiia.org/ecm/certification.cfm?doc_id=12#ccsa*

Certified Financial Services Auditor (CFSA)™ A specialty certification program of the *Institute of Internal Auditors (IIA) that focuses on the financial services sector. The IIA took over the CFSA program in 2002, as a result of a merger that year with the National Association of Financial Services Auditors, which had originally established the CFSA certification.
Web link: *www.theiia.org/ecm/certification.cfm?doc_id=12#cfsa*

Certified Government Auditing Professional (CGAP)® A specialty certification program of the *Institute of Internal Auditors (IIA) that focuses on *public sector auditing.
Web link: *www.theiia.org/ecm/certification.cfm?doc_id=12#cgap*

Certified Information Systems Auditor™ (CISA®) The certification program of the *Information Systems Audit and Control Association. Founded in 1978, the CISA certification covers the auditing of the control and security of information systems. By 2003 it was estimated that at least 30,000 individuals had obtained the CISA qualification.

Web link: *www.isaca.org/cisa*

Certified Internal Auditor (CIA®) The designation of successful candidates of the main certification program of the *Institute of Internal Auditors (IIA). The IIA Web site claims the CIA qualification to be "the only internationally accepted designation for internal auditors." The CIA examination was first given in 1974, and by 2003 nearly 40,000 individuals had obtained the qualification. Interestingly, the acronym CIA is identical to that of the U.S. Central Intelligence Agency, and there have been instances of internal auditors being mistaken for Central Intelligence Agency officials by political activists and guerrilla forces who have misinterpreted the CIA designation printed on business cards. Lives have even been put at risk—the IIA considered a name change in the 1980s but decided to retain the CIA acronym (Flesher, 1991, 50–51).

Further reading: Myers and Gramling (1997)

Web link: *www.theiia.org/ecm/certification.cfm?doc_id=12*

Certified Professional Environmental Auditor (CPEA) The certification program of the *Board of Environmental, Health & Safety Auditor Certifications (BEAC).

Web link: *www.beac.org/certification.html*

Certified Public Accountant (CPA) The designation of U.S. *public accountants who meet professional criteria in examination success and length of relevant experience. The Certified Public Accountant carries the designatory letters CPA, and is licensed to practice as a *public accountant and thereby to give external *audit opinions. The uniform CPA examination is set nationally by the *American Institute of Certified Public Accountants, while the experience criteria for licensure are established by individual states' boards of accountancy. The national umbrella organization for the latter is the *National Association of State Boards of Accountancy. A CPA-qualified individual may be permitted to practice in another state, but this frequently entails the accumulation of further professional experience to meet the requirements of local CPA licensing authorities.

A number of other countries have also adopted the term CPA to designate their public accountants (at least in the English translations of the names of their professional organizations). These include Israel (the *Institute of Certified Public Accountants in Israel), Japan (the *Japanese Institute of

Certified Public Accountants), and Kenya (the *Institute of Certified Public Accountants of Kenya). Many English-speaking countries refer to public accountants as *chartered accountants. In some countries competing organizations use the different terms to distinguish themselves: Ireland, for example, has an *Institute of Certified Public Accountants in Ireland and an *Institute of Chartered Accountants in Ireland.

chain of command A term derived from military planning to denote the flow of *authority and *accountability within an activity or organization. In a chain of command, an individual takes orders from another individual at the next hierarchical level—for example, A commands B, who in turn commands C, who in turn commands D, and so on. Within a chain of command environment, departures from established *policies and *procedures are usually met with *sanctions (definition 2). Most organizations exhibit chain of command features that offer the advantages of discipline and clarity of purpose. However, chain of command arrangements can be inflexible, and *management theory in recent years has advocated increasing *empowerment of individuals throughout all levels of an organization.

Chambers, Andrew (born 1943) A British academic, author, and editor of the *Internal Control Newsletter* and the *International Journal of Auditing*. A Professor Emeritus at City University, London, Andrew Chambers also heads *Management Audit Ltd., a British consultancy, education provider, and publishing house. He is a prolific author in the field of internal auditing and *corporate governance, and his writing tends to have a practical orientation. His books include a coauthored standard reference for *operational auditing, *The Operational Auditing Handbook: Auditing Business Processes* (Chambers and Rand, 1997), and a coauthored overview of modern internal auditing, *Leading Edge Internal Auditing* (Ridley and Chambers, 1998).

A tireless advocate of the importance of internal auditing in modern corporate governance, Andrew Chambers has described auditing as "an old science with well-established principles" (Ridley and Chambers, 1998, xx). He is also a vocal critic of corporate governance initiatives of which he disapproves. On the United Kingdom's *Hampel Report*, for example: "Getting to the heart of the 'final' Hampel report is like groping one's way into a hay stack only to find it largely hollow at its core" (Chambers, A., 1998).

Further reading: Chambers, A. (1997); Chambers, A. (2002); Chambers, A. and Rand (1997); Ridley and Chambers, A. (1998)

Chambers, Raymond John (born 1917) An Australian accounting academic and author. Former foundation Professor of Accounting at the University of Sydney, and visiting professor to a number of universities around the world, R. J. Chambers' achievements include the establishment of the Academic journal *Abacus in 1965 and the founding of the *Pacioli Society in 1968. His written output is vast: *Accounting, Evaluation and Economic Behavior* (1966) is perhaps his most famous work, in which he introduced his controversial theory of continuously contemporary accounting. He has also authored a monumental *Accounting Thesaurus* (1995). An *Accounting Hall of Fame member, Chambers has been a long-standing advocate of the application of scientific rigor to accounting analysis.

Further reading: Chambers, R. J. (1966); Chambers, R. J. (1995); Gaffikin (1994)

chaos theory The proposition that a system, although governed by deterministic laws, displays unpredictability owing to sensitivity to changes in independent variables. Chaos in this sense does not refer to the everyday sense of "utter confusion." Weather patterns are often given as a chaos theory example, in that they combine predictability and unpredictability. A popular image associated with the theory is the notion that the flapping of a butterfly's wings can disturb the atmosphere, contributing to a chain of events that causes an environmental catastrophe elsewhere. Chaos theory is a sophisticated and highly technical branch of physics and mathematics, and some commentators have attempted to apply its implications to investments, and even to auditing.

Further reading: Peters (1994); Vinten (1991)

Chapter 11 A statute of the 1978 *U.S. Bankruptcy Reform Act*. Chapter 11 protection allows an organization or individual to attempt to restructure and reorganize, to minimize the effects of a *bankruptcy. Spectacular Chapter 11 filings in recent years have included *Enron and *WorldCom corporations.

charter See *audit charter.

chartered accountant (CA) The designation of *public accountants in the United Kingdom and many former British colonies. Roughly equivalent to the U.S. term *Certified Public Accountant, the status of chartered accountant is generally awarded following examination success and a period of relevant professional experience. In the British Isles the principal professional organizations for CAs are the *Institute of Chartered Accountants in England and Wales, the *Institute of Chartered Accountants of Scotland, and the *Institute of Chartered Accountants in Ireland.

The term "chartered accountant" is named for the royal charters used in the United Kingdom and the former British Empire to incorporate the professional institutes. As a result, many former British colonies share the same terminology: Chartered accountants are found, for example, in Canada (the *Canadian Institute of Chartered Accountants), India (the *Institute of Chartered Accountants of India), and South Africa (the *South African Institute of Chartered Accountants). Some former British colonies, however, have adopted the U.S. terminology of the Certified Public Accountant. An example is Kenya (the *Institute of Certified Public Accountants of Kenya).

Further reading: Matthews et al. (1998)

Chartered Institute of Management Accountants (CIMA) A British professional *management accounting organization. Headquartered in London, the CIMA was founded in 1919 as the Institute of Cost Accountants, and the organization went through several name changes before adopting its current designation in 1986. Its Web site states that "CIMA members are *Accountants in Business*. We represent financial managers and accountants who work in industry, commerce, *not-for profit and public sector organisations. Our key activity is related to Business Strategy, Information Strategy and Finance Strategy. CIMA members are not trained in audit" (emphasis in original). This clearly indicates CIMA's traditionally low emphasis on auditing, though individual CIMA members may of course move into auditing roles during their careers. In 2003 the institute's international membership was around 135,000, including some 60,000 student members.

Web site: *www.cimaglobal.com*

Chartered Institute of Public Finance and Accountancy (CIPFA) A British professional *public sector accounting organization. Based in London, the CIPFA was incorporated as the Institute of Municipal Treasurers and Accountants in 1901, though it traces its origins to a predecessor organization founded in 1885. It adopted its present name in 1973. The CIPFA Web site states that the "quality of CIPFA's technical output has placed it at the forefront of commentators on public finance, accountancy and audit." CIPFA maintains an active publishing program, mainly on accounting and auditing in the public sector. The institute's membership in 2003 was around 14,000, including students, and members carry the designatory letters CIPFA.

Web site: *www.cipfa.org.uk*

chart of accounts A sequentially numbered list of *general ledger *accounts. In some countries, charts of accounts are set by *legislation, and are intended to facilitate *taxation procedures and the gathering of national economic statistics: The French *plan comptable général* is an example. In most English-speaking countries organizations have discretion in their general ledger numbering systems.

check 1. The verification of the existence or accuracy of something. The performance of checks is central to the obtaining and assessment of *audit evidence. 2. A document that instructs a bank to pay a sum of *money to a named individual or organization on a specific date. Though still an important *disbursement mechanism, the use of checks has been giving way to *wire transfers in recent years.

check digit A numerical digit added to a number to permit verification of its accuracy by a computerized accounting system.

checklist A documented list of *audit steps or other required actions. The completion of checklists is intended to ensure that all steps of a process have been addressed. They are often used in the context of *Control Risk Self Assessment. The use of checklists is frequently criticized on the grounds of their alleged inability to stimulate creative thought. See also *box-ticking approach.

cheque An alternative spelling of *check (definition 2) in the United Kingdom and some other countries influenced by British culture.

Chief Auditing Executive (CAE) The most senior internal auditing post in an organization. There are several other titles typically associated with this executive post, such as Chief Internal Auditor, Director of Audit, General Auditor, Head of Audit, Inspector General, and Principal Auditor. In all cases, CAE or its equivalent term designates the individual responsible for managing an organization's *internal audit function. "[W]hen internal audit services are obtained from outside providers, the CAE is the person responsible for overseeing the service contract" (Anderson, 2003, 127).

Chief Executive Officer (CEO) The most senior individual responsible for the management of an organization. The CEO sits at the top of a *chain of command system.

Chief Financial Officer (CFO) The head of an organization's financial and accounting functions.

Chief Internal Auditor (CIA) An alternative term for *Chief Auditing Executive.

Chinese Institute of Certified Public Accountants (CICPA) China's main professional accounting and external auditing organization. The CICPA was established in 1988, more than a century after its equivalents in most English-speaking countries. Its late foundation reflects China's estrangement from the world economy for much of the twentieth century and, from the 1980s, its gradual liberalization from previously strict *command economy structures. The introduction of capitalist practices to China led to the need for a Western-style accounting and external auditing profession. The CICPA was created to meet this need, adopting the U.S. terminology of the *Certified Public Accountant. Article 3 of its charter (available in English on its Web site) states that it aims to "serve the socialist market economy."

Web site (Chinese only, except for the CICPA charter): *www.cicpa.org.cn*

Chinese walls An information barrier between an organization's departments and divisions to block the dissemination of sensitive information. Chinese walls are intended to prevent *conflicts of interest or the abuse of *price-sensitive information. In multidisciplinary organizations that include external auditors, Chinese walls are an important mechanism to ensure auditor independence. The term derives from the defensive walls erected around ancient China.

circularization **1.** An audit test that consists of written requests to *third parties to confirm the existence and accuracy of items in financial statements. A common example is the circularization by external auditors of a sample of an organization's customers, to obtain documentary evidence of *accounts receivable balances. A positive circularization is one in which the third party is asked to confirm a communicated balance, whether correct or incorrect. A negative circularization is one in which a third party is requested to reply only if a stated balance is incorrect or disputed. Third party evidence is generally considered by auditors to be of high value, and circularization procedures are therefore considered to provide strong *audit evidence. See also *confirmation letter. **2.** The distribution of a leaflet or similar document among a group of individuals or organization. An example is the mailing of the details of sales offers to an organization's customers.

circulating assets An alternative term for *working capital (definition 1).

classification The arrangement or grouping of items into categories on the basis of shared characteristics. An organization's expenses, for example, are classified in appropriate *general ledger accounts.

clean opinion An alternative term for an *unqualified opinion.

clinical auditing The auditing of the activities of hospitals and other medical institutions. Clinical auditing ranges from *qualitative and *quantitative reviews of patient care to assessments of the *Three E's in hospital activities.

Coalition for Environmentally Responsible Economies (CERES) An international organization that promotes corporate environmental best practice. Founded in 1989, CERES is based in Boston, MA. It encourages standardized corporate environmental reporting, and its ten *CERES Principles* aim to enhance corporate environmental conduct. A number of large corporations (e.g., the Ford Motor Company and General Motors Corporation) have adopted the *CERES Principles*, which are available from the CERES Web site. See also the *Global Reporting Initiative.

Web site: *www.ceres.org*

Cohen Commission Report A U.S. report of 1978 that reviewed external auditor responsibilities. The Cohen Commission was established by the *American Institute of Certified Public Accountants, and it was named for its chairperson. The full title of the report was the *Report, Conclusions, and Recommendations of the Commission on Auditors' Responsibilities*. It addressed the role of the external auditor in the context of the *expectations gap.

Further reading: *Cohen Commission Report* (1978)

collateral *Assets pledged to secure or guarantee a *debt. Default on a debt normally leads to surrender of assets provided as collateral. Common items of collateral include *real estate property and *inventory.

collusion A secret arrangement or conspiracy between two or more individuals for *fraudulent or improper purposes. An example is collusion of an organization's employee with a *vendor to overcharge *prices of raw materials.

Combined Code An alternative name for the *Hampel Report*.

comfort **1.** The support given by *audit evidence to address an *audit objective. Auditors generally aim to obtain a high level of comfort to support their *audit opinions. **2.** An alternative term for *assurance.

comfort letter An alternative term for *representation letter.

command and control See *chain of command.

command economy An economy in which the government determines industrial output, the *prices of products and services, and the allocation of economic resources. In a command economy, market forces are subdued or eliminated in favor of national economic planning. Few command economies exist in the early twenty-first century, following the collapse of the Soviet Union (and the subsequent withdrawal of support for its allies and satellites) in the late 1980s and early 1990s. Communist countries ranging from China to Cuba to Vietnam have embraced *free market principles to varying degrees. Further, the existence of *underground economies has tended throughout history to undermine the objectives of government planners.

commission A fee for services performed by an *agent or an intermediary. Commission is often calculated as a percentage of the value of underlying *transactions. Illegal commissions are often termed *kickbacks.

Committee of Sponsoring Organizations of the Treadway Commission (COSO) A U.S.-based organization dedicated to improving *corporate governance and *financial reporting. The COSO Web site describes the organization's aims of "improving the quality of financial reporting through business ethics, effective internal controls, and corporate governance." Founded in 1985 to sponsor the National Commission on Fraudulent Financial Reporting, which produced the *Treadway Commission Report* (1987), COSO comprises five U.S. accounting and auditing organizations: the *American Accounting Association, the *American Institute of Certified Public Accountants, *Financial Executives International, the *Institute of Internal Auditors, and the *Institute of Management Accountants (known as the National Association of Accountants in the 1980s). In 2003 the chair of COSO was John Flaherty.

In addition to the *Treadway Commission Report*, other landmark COSO publications include the 1992 report *Internal Control—Integrated Framework* (often referred to as the *COSO Report*), and the 1999 report *Fraudulent Financial Reporting: 1987–1997* (Beasley et al., 1999), a follow-up to the original *Treadway Commission Report*. At the time of this writing, in 2003, an ongoing COSO project is the development of an *enterprise risk management framework.

Further reading: Beasley et al. (1999); COSO (1992); Treadway Commission (1987)

Web site: *www.coso.org*

commodity **1.** An item of economic value that can be sold, such as a product or a *raw material. **2.** An item obtained from *land, such as foods, fuels, or *raw materials. Commodities are often traded in large quantities through organized *markets.

common law The section of the law in English-speaking countries that is derived from judicial precedent and custom. Unlike *legislation, which is issued by the parliamentary enactment of statutes, common law derives from case law and the accumulated decisions of judges. Common law developed in England and later spread through the British Empire to most parts of the English-speaking world.

common market An international *market created by the reduction or elimination of *customs duties and other trade formalities between nations. Examples of common markets include the Andean Pact, originally founded in

1969, and the European Union, an earlier form of which was created by the 1957 Treaty of Rome.

common stock A share of ownership in a corporation. The owners of common stock normally enjoy voting rights and, ideally, are rewarded for their investment by both *dividends and *appreciation in the market value of the common stock. Common stock is classified as *equity in a balance sheet, and it is normally shown at *par value.

Commonwealth Association for Corporate Governance (CAGC) A London-based international organization that has issued *corporate governance guidance. The CAGC addresses corporate governance in the countries of the British Commonwealth, a group of former members of the British Empire that includes India, Nigeria, and the United Kingdom itself. In association with the Commonwealth Business Council, the CAGC has issued a set of corporate governance principles (*CAGC Guidelines*, 1999). The principles include the importance of adequate communication with *stakeholders (Principle 7) and the importance of corporate *risk assessment (Principle 14).

Further reading: *CAGC Guidelines* (1999)

***Compagnie Nationale des Commissaires aux Comptes* (CNCC)** A French accounting and external auditing organization. Established in 1969 under the authority of the French Ministry of Justice, the CNCC is charged with supervising external auditing in France. All French external auditors must be CNCC members. For this reason, the CNCC's membership of around 16,000 overlaps substantially with that of France's *public accounting organization, the *Ordre des Experts-Comptables*. The CNCC issues French *auditing standards.

Web site (French only): *www.cncc.fr*

compensating balance **1.** An amount a bank can offset between a loan and a deposit. **2.** Two or more accounting *balances that *offset one another.

compensating error A *compensating balance (definition 2) that consists of two errors. A compensating error neutralizes the effects of another error. Items of this nature are frequently undetected in *trial balances.

compensation **1.** Employee *remuneration. Compensation normally covers cash payments in the form of *salaries or *wages, and other perks and *fringe benefits. **2.** Recompense for damage, injury, or wrongdoing.

competition Rivalry in a *market. Competition is often viewed as a positive means of encouraging *efficient markets, and *antitrust laws are among the ways in which countries attempt to promote competitive economic practices.

*Prices in *free markets are established by the interplay of competitive forces among buyers and sellers. Contrast *monopoly and *oligopoly.

compliance An action in conformity with agreed procedures, *regulations, law, or the terms of a *contract. Compliance is central to auditing, in relation to both *external control and *internal control. See also *compliance testing.

compliance audit An *audit of *compliance with external *regulations or *internal control procedures. A compliance audit is not to be confused with *compliance testing—the former has as its *audit objective the verification of compliance with external or internal requirements, while the latter is an auditing procedure used to gather *audit evidence on the reliability of internal controls.

compliance cost The cost of maintaining *compliance procedures. For example, an organization that faces heavy external *regulation may be obliged to keep costly monitoring records, and to employ a team of auditors to perform *compliance audits.

compliance testing Auditing procedures that evaluate the reliability of an entity's *internal controls. In contrast to *substantive testing, which focuses on verifying the accuracy of quantifiable amounts, compliance testing aims to gain *reasonable assurance that underlying procedures (i) reliably reflect an organization's activities and (ii) are suitably controlled. In general terms, auditors tend to reduce the level of substantive testing if compliance testing indicates the satisfactory operation of controls and procedures: "Where a system of accounting and internal control has been well designed and adhered to in operation, and its integrity secured by effective internal check and internal audit, a high degree of reliability may be placed on the data derived from the system" (Flint, 1988, 114). Most audits consist of a mixture of compliance and substantive testing—the balance between the two tends to be determined by factors like the volume of transactions to be tested, and the sophistication and reliability of an entity's computerized accounting systems. Contrast *compliance audit.

compound interest The calculation of *interest on a sum of money by application of an *interest rate to both the original sum of money and previously accumulated interest. Contrast *simple interest.

comprehensive auditing An alternative term for *operational auditing. The term was used widely in the United Kingdom and the British Commonwealth until the 1970s, when it was largely supplanted by the term *value-for-money auditing.

Comptabilité, Contrôle, Audit A French-language, scholarly accounting and auditing journal. Published twice a year by Editions Vuibert on behalf of the Paris-based **Association Francophone de Comptabilité*, the journal is available in print and (partial) online formats. The journal's notes state that it is geared toward all types of accounting research, and its coverage is international.

Web link (French only): *www.afc-cca.com/larevue/presentation.html*

comptroller A rather archaic term for *controller (definition 2). Taken from Anglo-Norman French, the term is still widely used in the modern *public sector.

computer assisted audit techniques (CAATs) Steps taken to gather *audit evidence from and by means of computer software programs. Computer assisted audit techniques (CAATs) can be used for both *compliance and *substantive testing, and they can be applied to existing data and *test data. The latter can be created and evaluated against expected outcomes, in order to test the processing accuracy of computerized systems.

Confederation of Asian and Pacific Accountants (CAPA) A regional accounting organization, based in Kuala Lumpur, Malaysia. Formed in 1976, CAPA's membership comprises national accounting organizations in the Asia and Pacific region. In 2003, CPA had over 30 members. The confederation's Web site describes its mission to be the providing of "leadership in the development, enhancement and coordination of the accountancy profession" in its region. Its activities include publications, conferences, and promoting research and education in accounting and auditing.

Web site: *www.capa.com.my*

confirmation The verification of the existence or accuracy of something.

confirmation letter A written response to an auditor's request to confirm the existence or value of an item. Examples of commonly requested confirmation letters include the *circularization by external auditors of an organization's customers to confirm *accounts receivable balances, and requests to banks for evidence of bank *deposits and *loans. A positive confirmation involves a third party confirming a communicated balance, whether correct or incorrect. A negative confirmation requests a reply only in the case of disagreement with a stated amount. As *third party evidence is generally considered by auditors to be of high value, confirmation letters tend to be viewed as strong *audit evidence. Auditors requesting confirmation letters normally ensure that responses are sent directly to them (rather than via an *auditee) to reduce the potential for the responses being intercepted and amended.

conflict of interest An incompatibility between an individual's rights and responsibilities. *Rewards gained by an individual from a conflict of interest are generally regarded as unethical, and they may also breach *legislation or *regulations. For example, an employee of an organization who negotiates raw material *prices with a family-related *vendor faces a potential conflict of interest between (i) minimizing costs to the employer and (ii) maximizing returns to the family member. External auditors are particularly sensitive to accusations of conflicts of interest that may impair the ability to give an *independent and objective *audit opinion. The supply of lucrative *management advisory services to an *auditee and personal investments in an *auditee's business are aspects of external auditor regulation in most countries.

conglomerate A large, *diversified corporation.

conservatism In accounting, a cautious, prudent, skeptical, or even pessimistic attitude. Conservatism tends to result in the early *recognition of expenses and the later recognition of revenues, as it aims to avoid understating the former and overstating the latter. The *accruals basis of accounting is a manifestation of conservatism in practice.

consideration A legal term for the transfer of *assets or other items of *value in relation to a *contract. Consideration may take the form of (i) *cash payments, (ii) transfers of *tangible assets, (iii) waivers of payments, or (iv) the providing of services.

Consiglio Nazionale dei Dottori Commercialisti Italy's main professional accounting and external auditing organization. The term *dottore commercialista* approximates to the U.S. designation *Certified Public Accountant. Established in 1924 and headquartered in Rome, the *Consiglio* had approximately 50,000 members in 2003. As in other continental European countries, the Italian accounting and external auditing profession is relatively underdeveloped (in both size and scope) in comparison to English-speaking countries. Further, despite the size of Italy's population and the international importance of its economy, the Italian accounting profession has tended to be peripheral to international developments: Italy, for example, was not among the founding members of the *International Accounting Standards Committee in 1973. Perhaps conscious of this, the *Consiglio* has adopted the motto *Insieme per lo sviluppo* (i.e., "developing together"), which reflects its profile-raising activities both domestically and internationally in recent years. The *Consiglio* is one of two large Italian accounting bodies: most of the members of the other organization, the *Consiglio Nazionale dei Ragionieri e Periti Commerciali*, work in industry.
    Web site (Italian only): *www.cndc.it*

consignment 1. A delivery of goods following or pending a sale. 2. An arrangement in which an *agent or intermediary takes physical custody of a vendor's *inventory, pending anticipated sales to *third parties. The agent earns a *commission for storage and sale of the inventory. The *risks and *rewards of the transactions and the inventory normally remain with the vendor.

consistency The regular treatment over time of an accounting item or procedural matter. Consistency is a fundamental concept to both accounting and auditing, and its promotion is one of the main purposes of *Generally Accepted Accounting Principles and *Generally Accepted Auditing Standards.

consolidation accounting The presentation of the *financial statements of two or more organizations as one economic unit. Consolidation accounting techniques require the combining of the financial statements of the individual organizations of a *business combination (i.e. of a *parent organization and its *subsidiaries), subject to *adjustments like the elimination of profits on transactions between the consolidated entities.

Consultative Committee of Accountancy Bodies (CCAB) A British umbrella group of professional accounting organizations. Owing to the institutional fragmentation of the United Kingdom's accounting profession, the CCAB was established in 1974 to allow accountants to take united positions in making representations to the British government on regulatory or technical issues. The CCAB is a corporation and its six members are the *Institute of Chartered Accountants in England and Wales, the *Institute of Chartered Accountants of Scotland, the *Institute of Chartered Accountants in Ireland, the *Association of Chartered Certified Accountants, the *Chartered Institute of Management Accountants, and the *Chartered Institute of Public Finance and Accountancy.

Web link: *www.icaew.co.uk/ccab/intro.html*

consulting The providing of expertise or specialist advice. Consulting performed by auditors tends to focus on improvements to procedures and processes, in contrast to *compliance auditing. The tensions between consulting and compliance for auditors have been described as follows: "The nub of the behavioural challenge of internal auditing is that internal auditors are both inspectors and advisors. They have these two roles which are in conflict with each other...If an auditor were to jettison the inspectorial role, the auditor would become an internal management consultant only and *management would have lost a key element of their *internal auditing function. If the auditor were to jettison the advisory role, the auditor would become merely an authoritarian inspector and much of the practical benefit which would usually result from internal auditing work would be lost... The answer to internal audit role conflict invariably is *not* to drop one of the conflicting roles" (Ridley and Chambers, 1998, 186–187, emphasis in original).

Further reading: McCall (2002); Williams (2003)

consumer An individual or organization that purchases or uses goods and services. See also *consumption.

consumer goods Tangible *merchandise or *products for sale to the general public. See also *consumption and *finished goods.

consumer society A society or country in which individuals place excessive importance on the accumulation and *consumption of material goods. In a consumer society, the conspicuous display of material wealth is deemed to be indicative of high social status.

consumption The use of economic resources. *Consumer consumption refers to the final enjoyment of an item's *worth. In this sense, consumption is the final point in the economic process of production, distribution, and exchange as individuals purchase and use goods. It may be characterized as the underlying purpose of economic activity.

consumption tax An *indirect tax charged on a good or a service. The burden of a consumption tax falls on the individual or organization that enjoys the full *worth of a good or service. It is levied at the final stage of the economic process of production, distribution, and exchange. See also *sales tax and *value added tax.

Contemporary Accounting Research A Canadian scholarly accounting journal. Established in 1984, it is published quarterly by the *Canadian Academic Accounting Association in both print and online formats. The journal frequently covers research into auditing, and its scope is international.

Web link: *www.caaa.ca/publications/index.html*

contingent asset A potential *asset whose existence and quantification are doubtful. Many systems of *Generally Accepted Accounting Principles require the *disclosure of *material contingent assets in financial statements, but do not allow the *recognition of such assets until their *crystallization is very likely. Contingent assets normally depend on the occurrence or outcome of a specific event: an example is a court case whose outcome is uncertain, but which may give rise to financial benefits to an organization. Contrast *contingent liability.

contingent liability A potential *liability whose existence and quantification are doubtful. Most systems of *Generally Accepted Accounting Principles require the *disclosure of *material contingent liabilities in financial statements. Contingent liabilities normally depend on the occurrence or outcome of a specific event. An example of a contingent liability is a court case whose outcome is uncertain, but which may give rise to significant costs against an organization. External auditors use *attorney letters to obtain *audit evidence of this nature. Contrast *contingent asset.

continuing operation An activity or operation within an organization that remains active. Contrast *discontinued operation.

continuous auditing Auditing activity that takes place over an extended time period. A continuous audit is not necessarily an uninterrupted process, as it may involve short breaks in audit activity. A classic example is daily stocktaking to monitor the reliability of a *perpetual inventory system. With potential moves to corporate *real time reporting in the future, the role of continuous *financial auditing is expected by many commentators to grow in importance: "For the listed companies of the world, one can foresee detailed financial information being available by electronic means, possibly on the *Internet. Such information is unlikely to be accompanied by a long form [external] *audit report, nor is it likely to be produced some months afterwards but in real time" (Percy, 1997, 11).
    Further reading: Rezaee et al. (2001)

continuous improvement (CI) A Japanese management philosophy that constantly aims at improvements to all aspects of an organization and its activities. For example, cost reduction targets are often built into CI *budgets and are intended to act as a stimulus to improve (among other things) the *Three E's of *economy, *efficiency, and *effectiveness. CI theories are often known by the Japanese term *kaizen.

contra account A *general ledger *account that *offsets another account. For example, *allowances for bad debts are recorded in contra accounts in relation to *accounts receivable.

contract An agreement between two or more parties that is enforceable in law. Contracts may be written, verbal, or even implied by circumstances, but to be legally binding a contract must normally be accompanied by some form of *consideration.

contract auditing The auditing of *contracts. A specialism of *internal auditing, contract auditing aims to provide *assurance that contractual terms are correctly followed.

contra entry An item booked to a *general ledger account to *offset, cancel, or partially reduce another item. A contra entry is not restricted to the same general ledger account as the item to which it relates—the related item may be made in any general ledger account. The Latin word *contra* means "against" or "opposite."

contribution The element of *income (definition 2) that is attributable to sales income less *variable costs. *Fixed costs are excluded from contribution calculations.

control The exercising of influence, regulation, or restriction over an activity, process, or individual. In an auditing context, control is often understood to be an action or practice that assists an organization to achieve its objectives, though this definition is probably cast too widely—it would include making a sale or securing the employment of a promising candidate. A narrower definition of control is a procedural or physical mechanism to address a *risk or to enhance the *economy, *efficiency, or *effectiveness of operations. A control may or may not be *embedded in an organization's day-to-day operations. Organizational control is often analyzed into separate *external and *internal control components: *External control is exercised by *stakeholders, and *internal control is effected by *boards of directors, managers, and employees.

Control & Governance Series *Corporate governance guidelines issued by the *Criteria for Control (CoCo) Board (renamed the Risk Management and Governance Board in 2001) of the Canadian Institute of Chartered Accountants. The first report in the series was *Guidance on Control*, issued in 1995.
   Web link: *www.cica.ca*

control account A *general ledger account used to record and monitor the accuracy of amounts transferred from *subsidiary ledgers.

control framework A conceptual basis for understanding and analyzing *internal controls and *external controls. Well-known control frameworks include the *Internal Control—Integrated Framework* of the *Committee of Sponsoring Organizations of the Treadway Commission (COSO), and the *Canadian Institute of Chartered Accountants' *Guidance on Control*.

controllable cost An expense that is incurred at the discretion of an organization's managers. The performance of individuals is often appraised, in part, in relation to efficient use of controllable costs. Most costs in this category are *variable, but some *fixed costs may also be discretionary. See also *avoidable cost and *unavoidable cost.

controller **1.** The individual with major "hands-on" responsibility for an organization's financial and accounting functions. In large organizations the financial controller reports to the *Chief Financial Officer, while in smaller organizations the two roles may be combined. **2.** Alternative term for *Chief Financial Officer in some *public sector organizations.

controlling account An alternative term for *control account.

control risk **1.** The *risk that items in financial statements are *misstated as a result of problems in an organization's *internal control systems. Control risk is considered alongside *inherent risk and *detection risk as one of three components of external *audit risk (definition 1), and it is usually assessed through *compliance testing. A system of weak internal controls implies a high control risk. **2.** The *risk of a breakdown in *internal controls.

Control Risk Self Assessment (CRSA) A *risk assessment methodology in which an organization's employees identify and assess areas of *risk and *control for which they are responsible. Control Risk Self Assessment (CRSA) mechanisms include the use of *questionnaires or the gathering of information through interviews, workshops, and *brainstorming exercises. CRSA can take many forms, though it tends to concentrate on the identification and assessment of risks and related *internal controls. Although CRSA processes involve risk assessments made by an organization's employees, the concept is often promoted by an organization's *internal audit function: "It is likely that internal audit will need to facilitate and monitor CRSA if it is to survive and prosper" (Chambers, 2002, 311). The term is sometimes abbreviated to Control Self Assessment (CSA).

Further reading: Hubbard (2000); Hubbard (2003)

Control Self Assessment (CSA) An alternative term for *Control Risk Self Assessment.

conversion cost Production costs incurred in converting *raw materials into *finished products. Raw materials costs are usually excluded from conversion cost calculations.

convertible security A *bond or *security that can be converted into *common stock during a specified time period. The exercise of rights over convertible securities can *dilute a corporation's common stock, and the effects of this dilution are normally factored into *earnings per share calculations.

cookie jar reserves A semi-humorous term for *reserves or accrued expenses created with the intention of manipulating *financial statements. The term derives from the image of dipping at one's convenience into a jar of cookies. By analogy, reserves of this type are released at the convenience of the managers of an organization to inflate *earnings at times of weak financial performance. Selective use of reserves in this manner is a subversion of the *accruals basis of accounting, and is forbidden by most systems of *Generally Accepted Accounting Principles. The term "cookie jar reserves" was used in a speech in 1998 by Arthur Levitt, then chair of the *Securities and Exchange Commission. See also *big bath reserves.

cooking the books A semi-humorous term for *false accounting or other *fraudulent manipulation of accounting data.
Further reading: Schilit (2002)

Cooper, Cynthia (born c.1964) A U.S. internal auditor who played a major role in uncovering accounting malpractice at *WorldCom, the *multinational telecommunications corporation that filed for *Chapter 11 bankruptcy in 2002. Cooper was WorldCom's *Chief Internal Auditor, and for her role in uncovering the accounting *fraud she was nominated by *Time* magazine as one of its "Persons of the Year 2002." This publicity helped to bring the importance of internal auditing to public attention. Cooper's tenacity when faced with senior management resistance to her auditing reviews prompted her to work through the night to uncover and analyze accounting entries that had *capitalized billions of dollars of *operating expenses. Media reports have often described Cooper's activities at WorldCom as *whistle-blowing, but her actions can perhaps be categorized as tenacious internal auditing.
Further reading: Barrier (2003); Jeter (2003); Ripley (2002)

copyright An exclusive legal right to benefit from the authorship of a text or artistic creation. In most jurisdictions, copyright typically covers periods ranging from 50 to 75 years.

corporate audit Depending on the context, an alternative term for either *external audit or *internal audit.

corporate governance The ways in which an organization is controlled and regulated, and the manner in which an organization conducts its activities. It has been suggested that the "basic [corporate] governance issues are those of power and *accountability. They involve where power lies in the corporate system, and what degree of accountability there is for its exercise" (Cadbury, 2002, 3). Corporate governance frameworks are molded by many influences, including *legislation, custom, *ethics, *stakeholder pressure, public opinion, and professional and academic literature. In classical economic theory, *profit-seeking firms seek to maximize revenues above all other considerations (Friedman, 1982). While corporate governance theory does not necessarily seek to contradict or undermine this objective, it attempts to establish socially accepted rules for the pursuit of profit. In addition, corporate governance is applicable to *public sector and *not-for-profit organizations, for which the alternative term *organizational governance is frequently used.

Governance tends to be differentiated from the management of an organization: Governance is concerned with strategy and overall oversight, while management is concerned with the day-to-day implementation of governance strategies. The *Organization for Economic Co-operation and Development has described corporate governance as "a set of relationships between a company's *management, its *board, its *shareholders, and other *stakeholders. Corporate governance also provides the structure through which the objectives of the company are set, and the means of attaining those objectives and monitoring performance are determined. Good corporate governance should provide proper incentives for the board and management to pursue objectives that are in the interests of the company and shareholders and should facilitate effective monitoring" (OECD, 1999, 1). A former chairperson of the SEC has referred to corporate governance as "the link between a company's management, directors, and its financial reporting system" and has described it as "indispensable to effective *market discipline" (Arthur Levitt, quoted in Hermanson and Rittenberg, 2003, 26).

Some commentators identify two main aspects of corporate governance: (i) an external side with accountability of *stewardship to stakeholders and *external controls; and (ii) an internal side of procedures, *internal controls, and internal auditing. See also *corporate social responsibility and *risk management.

Further reading: Cadbury (2002); Cohen et al. (2002); Gugler (2001); Hermanson and Rittenberg (2003); Keasey and Wright (1999); Lipton and Lorsch (1992); OECD (1999); Roussey (2000)

Corporate Governance Site, the A U.S. online resource center for *corporate governance. Established in 1995, the Corporate Governance Site contains news, Internet links, and discussions of corporate governance issues.

Web site: *www.corpgov.net*

Corporate Library, the A U.S. online resource center for *corporate governance. Established in 1999, the Corporate Library is an independent investment firm. Its Web site has many free resources as well as subscriber-only services, and it has valuable links to other corporate governance Web sites.

Web site: *www.thecorporatelibrary.com*

Corporate Report, The A British *corporate governance report of 1975. *The Corporate Report* was published as a discussion paper by the British Accounting Standards Committee. It aimed to establish a consensus of opinion on the theory and practice of corporate *financial reporting.

Further reading: Accounting Standards Committee (1975)

corporate social reporting (CSR) See *corporate social responsibility and *social and environmental reporting.

corporate social responsibility (CSR) The encouragement of correct social and environmental practice by organizations. The term corporate social responsibility (CSR) is used widely, in contexts as varied as the following: (i) environmental considerations (as elaborated by organizations like the *Coalition for Environmentally Responsible Economies); (ii) ethical and transparent conduct in relation to investors, employees, customers, vendors, and the other *stakeholders of an organization; (iii) *ethical investing; (iv) the encouragement of volunteer work by an organization's employees to improve local communities; and (v) contributions to nation-building in recently independent countries.

Corporate social responsibility is a controversial and disputed area, both in its principles and its advocacy of *social and environmental reporting. For example, the concept of the "triple bottom line reporting" of financial, environmental, and social matters to underpin sustainable economic activity is not universally accepted. The economist Milton Friedman has argued that "Few trends could so thoroughly undermine the very foundations of our free society as the acceptance by corporate officials of a social responsibility other than to make as much *money for their *stockholders as possible. This is a fundamentally subversive doctrine" (Friedman, 1982, 133). See also *sustainability.

Further reading: *Bruntland Report* (1997); Davis (1975); Deegan (2002); Henderson (2001); Lehman (2001); Woodward et al. (2001)

corporation An organization recognized as a legal entity separate from its owners. Corporations are characterized by the *limited liability of their *investors. Large, modern corporations are typically run by professional managers who act as *agents on behalf of *stockholding *principals. The separation of ownership from management gives rise to questions of *accountability, *agency costs, and a vast range of *corporate governance considerations. Compare *partnership.

corrective action Steps taken to resolve a problem or to minimize the likelihood of occurrence of a problem. *Audit recommendations often include suggested corrective actions to address weaknesses in procedures and *internal controls.

corrective control An *internal control designed to remedy or minimize the damage caused by a breakdown in other internal controls. Compare *detective control and *preventative control.

correlation The degree of correspondence between variations in the behavior of two or more items. For example, an ice cream retailer's sales may be highly correlated with hot weather conditions. Correlation relationships can be calculated statistically, and analysis of this nature is often used to support *pricing decisions. See also *scatter graph.

corruption Dishonest or unethical behavior. Corruption is normally associated with personal gain, and its pernicious influence on organizations is of great concern to auditors. Corruption covers both *bribes and the *fraudulent manipulation of financial statements (or *cooking the books). See also the *Foreign Corrupt Practices Act and *Transparency International.
Further reading: Balkaran (2002)

COSO Report An alternative name for the *Internal Control—Integrated Framework* report of 1992.

cost 1. A *quantifiable item of expenditure. Costs can refer to expenditure on (i) *long-term *assets, (ii) *overheads and *operating costs, (iii) *short-term *expenses, and (iii) *manufacturing activities. 2. The nonquantifiable (see *quantifiable), harmful effects of an activity or action. Cost in this sense includes reference to a benefit foregone.

cost accounting The recording and analysis of *costs for management information purposes. Cost accounting often focuses on the costing of *units of *inventory, for which there are several methodologies, including *absorption costing, *activity based costing, and *backflush costing. Cost accounting is sometimes used to establish a product's selling price through *cost-plus pricing.

cost-benefit analysis An appraisal of the costs of an undertaking (or potential undertaking) in comparison with its *rewards. Cost-benefit analysis is often used to determine the economic viability of *capital expenditure and *investments. See also *zero-base budgeting.

cost center An activity, unit, or individual within an organization with which costs can be identified. In contrast to a *profit center, a cost center usually incurs costs only, and does not generate income. Cost centers are often used for cost control and decision-making purposes. They are also used to allocate *overhead costs to manufactured products in *absorption costing methodologies.

cost driver An activity or factor with a *quantifiable relation to costs incurred in the achievement of an organization's objectives. For example, the number of hours for which a production machine operates may be related to production costs in a manufacturing process. In *absorption costing methodologies, production volumes tend to be used as a cost driver to allocate costs to products, while *activity based costing (ABC) uses activities (like machine hours) as cost drivers.

cost of capital The rate of *return a corporation must pay for the *capital used to finance its activities. As capital in its widest sense is drawn from various forms of *debt and *equity (*common stock, *preferred stock, and *retained earnings), the cost of capital is usually a *weighted average of the costs of the individual sources of capital. A corporation's cost of capital is normally expressed as a percentage, and it is often used as a *hurdle rate in *discounted cash flow analysis and other investment appraisal techniques: A proposed investment's anticipated *return must exceed a corporation's cost of capital if it is to be accepted. See also *internal rate of return.

cost of goods sold (COGS) An alternative term for *cost of sales. Use of the term is particularly common in the United Kingdom and in other countries with a history of British influence.

cost of sales (COS) The *direct costs of a product sold. Cost of sales includes *raw material costs, and costs directly attributable to production, but it excludes nonproduction *overheads. The *gross income of an item is calculated as its revenue less cost of sales.

cost-plus pricing The establishment of a product's selling price by adding a predetermined *markup to the product's costs.

coupon A document or voucher entitling the holder to a benefit or right. For example, an organization may issue gift coupons entitling customers to purchase items for the value stated on the coupons. See also *token (definition 3).

coupon rate The interest rate stated on a *bond or other debt instrument.

CPA Australia™ An Australian professional accounting organization. CPA Australia differs from the country's other large accounting organization, the *Institute of Chartered Accountants in Australia, by having a smaller proportion of its members in public practice and external auditing. Many members of CPA Australia work in the public sector. However, there is much overlap between the two organizations, and a merger between the two has often been discussed. The name CPA Australia was adopted in 2000, but the organization traces itself back through preceding organizations to the nineteenth century.

The acronym CPA stands for Certified Practicing Accountant, rather than *Certified Public Accountant. The organization's membership in 2003 was approximately 100,000, and in recent years it has expanded its membership into a number of Asian countries.

Web site: *www.cpaaustralia.com.au*

CPA Ireland A commonly used name for the *Institute of Certified Public Accountants in Ireland.

CPA Journal® A U.S. accounting and external auditing magazine. Published monthly by the New York State Society of *Certified Public Accountants (CPA), the magazine is available in both print and online formats. It focuses on professional developments and news in accounting and external auditing, with particular emphasis on the United States. The magazine was established in 1930 as the *Bulletin of the New York State Society of Certified Public Accountants*, and it adopted its present name in 1970. Online archives are available from 1989.

Web site: *www.cpajournal.com*

CPA Letter A U.S. accounting and external auditing newsletter. Published ten times a year by the *American Institute of Certified Public Accountants, the *CPA Letter* is available online. It focuses on professional developments and news in accounting and external auditing, and it is aimed at AICPA members. Its coverage is concentrated mainly in the United States.

Web link: *www.aicpa.org/pubs/cpaltr/index.htm*

creative accounting The manipulation of *financial statements through the use of imaginative or unusual accounting techniques. Creative accounting techniques include, among other things, the following: (i) extension of the *amortization periods of *long-term assets to reduce amortization expenses in the initial years of an asset's life; (ii) manipulation of *reserves through * cookie jar accounting; (iii) the use of *off-balance sheet items; and (iv) *window dressing techniques. Creative accounting techniques may or may not contravene *Generally Accepted Accounting Principles (GAAP), as creative accountants tend to dance around the outer boundaries of GAAP. However, by "operating in the gray area between legitimacy and outright fraud" (Beattie et al., 2001, 5), creative accountants are generally viewed as motivated by attempts to mislead *investors and others.

In recent years, systems of GAAP and Generally Accepted Auditing Standards (GAAS) around the world have aimed to narrow the scope for auditor acquiescence to creative accounting transactions. As has been memorably stated, creative accountants have tended to become more bold in pushing the boundaries of accounting acceptability: "[Auditors giving] the green light to risky transactions was the accounting equivalent of providing Viagra to a sex addict; it fuelled the desire to push harder" (Toffler and Reingold, 2003, 245).

Further reading: McBarnet and Whelan (1999); Schilit (2002); Smith, T. (1996)

creative auditing Auditor acquiescence to an *auditee's *creative accounting practices. The term is nearly always used pejoratively, to express a sense of insufficiently *independent auditing.

credit **1.** The facility to purchase a good or service or to take a *loan on the promise of payment at a future date. **2.** An abbreviated term for *credit entry. **3.** An abbreviated term for *credit limit. **4.** Public praise or recognition.

credit control A function in an organization that monitors the granting of *credit to customers, and which oversees the collection of *accounts receivable.

credit entry An accounting transaction under *double entry bookkeeping which increases *liabilities, *revenues, and *equity, or reduces *assets and *expenses. A credit entry has a corresponding *debit entry (or debit entries) of equal value.

credit limit The maximum amount of *credit offered to a customer. The use of credit limits is a common *internal control over *accounts receivable.

credit line An amount of *money offered by a bank to its customer for potential borrowing. Once offered, the credit line is a facility that may be used at the customer's discretion.

credit note A document showing that an amount is owed to a customer. Credit notes are issued to refund or reimburse customers for matters such as the following: (i) *discounts, (ii) *price adjustments, (iii) goods returned, and (iv) the correction of invoicing errors.

creditor **1.** An individual or organization owed *money for transactions made on *credit. Compare *debtor. **2.** [plural] A British term for *accounts payable.

credit risk The *risk that a borrower may default on amounts owed on a *loan or other *credit arrangement.

Criteria for Control (CoCo) Board A body established in the early 1990s by the *Canadian Institute of Chartered Accountants to provide guidance on *corporate governance and *internal control. Its *Control & Governance Series included the well-known *Guidance on Control. In 2001 the CoCo Board changed its name to the *Risk Management and Governance Board.

critical accounting A reformist movement that challenges current accounting and auditing practices. Largely university based, the critical accounting
movement is a broad school of thought that seeks emancipation from current
social, economic, and power structures. Its aim is to "unfreeze and challenge
conventional discourses and practices" (Sikka and Willmott, 1997, 161). The
practices and institutional structures of external auditing are frequent targets
for the movement's critiques. The movement owes its intellectual origins to
various strands of critical social theory—it contains Marxists, environmentalists,
and admirers of Theodor Adorno, Michel Foucault, and Jürgen Habermas,
among others. In broad terms, it is left-leaning and radical in tone.

Depending on how far one wishes to cast the definition of "critical accounting,"
major figures in the movement may be said to include *Austin Mitchell,
*Michael Power, and *Prem Nath Sikka, though many individuals commonly
identified as critical accountants might deny their adherence to the movement.
(In addition, there is much squabbling among critical accountants who adhere
to competing ideologies.) Important critical accounting journals include
Accountancy, Business, and the Public Interest and *Critical Perspectives on
Accounting*. The *Association for Accountancy and Business Affairs is a promi-
nent critical accounting forum.

The quotations that follow indicate the tone and concerns of some of the
movement's complex and varied philosophies. The large external auditing
firms have been described as "pre-occupied with fees and client appeasement"
(Cousins et al., 1998, 9), as "accessories to casino capitalism" (Mitchell et al.,
1991, 3), and even as "emperors of darkness" (Dunn and Sikka, 1999, 4). On
auditing: "The social practice of 'audit' does not have a single unambiguous
meaning but rather, numerous competing meanings that exist side by side...
This is not to say that 'audit' is meaningless, but rather that its meaning is contingent and negotiable: its fixing within relations of power is precarious and
subject to redefinition" (Sikka et al., 1998, 303–304); the *audit society "can be
understood as a label for a loss of confidence in the central steering institutions
of society, particularly politics... it may be that a loss of faith in intellectual,
political and economic leadership has led to the creation of industries of checking
which satisfy a demand for signals of order" (Power, 2000, 188). On accounting:
"Class warfare is institutionalised and perpetuated by accounting practices"
(Sikka et al. (1999).

Further reading: Cousins et al. (1998); Dunn and Sikka (1999); Mitchell and
Sikka (2002); O'Regan (2003b); Power (1997); Sikka and Willmott (1997)

Critical Infrastructure Assurance Office (CIAO) The agency that coor-
dinates the U.S. Federal Government's initiatives on information security and
*assurance. The CIAO has worked to raise awareness of the *risks associated

with information and cyberspace security in the *private and *public sectors. Founded in 1998, the CIAO Web site states its primary focus to be as follows: To "raise issues that cut across industry sectors and ensure a cohesive approach to achieving continuity in delivering critical infrastructure services." In 2003 CIAO was integrated into the Department of Homeland Security (DHS) under the Information Analysis and Infrastructure Protection (IAIP) Directorate.

Web site: *www.ciao.gov*

critical path analysis (CPA) A decision-making philosophy that seeks to minimize the time required to complete an activity by reference to the longest (or "critical") path of activity. The aim of critical path analysis is to improve efficiencies along the critical path in order to speed up the entire process. It was developed by U.S. military project planners following World War II, and its use has spread to the business world. Critical path analysis is normally prepared as a diagram that shows the various routes and events that occur in a pattern of sequential activities.

Critical Perspectives on Accounting An international scholarly accounting journal. Established in 1990, the journal is published in eight issues a year by Elsevier Science in print and online formats. The journal's notes describe its aim as follows: To "provide a forum for the growing number of accounting researchers and practitioners who realize that conventional theory and practice is [sic] ill-suited to the challenges of the modern environment, and that accounting practices and corporate behavior are inextricably connected with many allocative, distributive, social, and ecological problems of our era." Its approach places it within the framework of the *critical accounting movement, in its challenging of mainstream notions of accounting and auditing. The journal's auditing focus is mainly on external auditing, and its coverage is international.

Web link: *www.elsevier.com/locate/issn/1045-2354*

crore The term used in India for 10 million. See also *lakh.

crystallization Becoming definite, clear, or unambiguous. The term "crystallization" is often used to refer to the triggering of an *asset or *liability by the occurrence of an event.

CSA Sentinel A U.S. newsletter of the CSA (*Control Self Assessment) Group of the *Institute of Internal Auditors. Established in 1997 and published three times a year, the newsletter is available online. Its Web page describes its coverage of "all aspects of control self-assessment, particularly as they relate to successful implementation by internal auditors." In particular, it aims to "support the development of knowledge surrounding the implementation of self-assessment workshops and techniques."

Web link: *www.theiia.org/ecm/newsletters.cfm?doc_id=744*

currency A system of *money that is widely accepted as a medium of exchange in a specific country or region. Gold is often considered to be an international currency, owing to its acceptability throughout the world. See also *hard currency, *soft currency, *functional currency, and *managed currency.

current asset A *short-term *asset with an anticipated economic life of less than one year. Examples of current assets include *accounts receivable, *cash, and *inventory.

current cost The *cost of replacing an *asset with an identical one of the same condition. Current cost can refer to either the purchase *price or the manufacturing cost of an asset. Contrast *historical cost.

current liability A *short-term *liability with an anticipated settlement date of less than one year. Examples include *accounts payable and short-term bank *loans.

current ratio A *liquidity measure calculated by dividing *current assets by *current liabilities. Compare the *acid test ratio, which is generally considered to be a sharper test of liquidity.

customer The buyer of goods or services. Organizations manage their *credit transactions with customers through *accounts receivable records.

customer return *Goods and *products returned from a customer to a supplier in line with *contractual terms or industry practice. Common purposes for returns include (i) defective or damaged products, (ii) unsold items, and (iii) product *obsolescence.

customs duty A form of *taxation levied on the *importation or *exportation of goods or services.

cutoff The point of time at which a *financial reporting period ends. Cutoff dates are important in determining the allocation of transactions to time periods in accordance with the *accruals basis of accounting. For example, an auditor may verify that sales are reported in correct periods by reference to the timing of underlying sales transactions around a cutoff date. The deliberate manipulation of transactions around cutoff dates is known as *window dressing.

cycle counts The regular undertaking of *physical inventory checks. Cycle counts are often performed in the context of a *perpetual inventory system, and the term normally refers to the cyclical checking of *inventory that covers all categories of products in all locations of a warehouse.

data Information, facts, and statistics. In its general use, the term refers to both numeric and alphabetic information.

database A structured bank of *data held in a computerized information system. The information stored in a database is normally maintained by a *database management system and is made available for analysis or processing by one or more computer programs.

database management system (DBMS) A software program used to manage information in a *database.

data privacy Restricted access to information in a *database. Data privacy is required by legislation in many parts of the world: In particular, the countries of the European Union have stringent privacy requirements, and penalties for infractions can be severe.

data processing The operations undertaken in a computerized information system to record, sort, process, analyze, and report data.

daybook A rather archaic term for an accounting *ledger used to record primary transactions (principally sale and purchase transactions) before the daily transfer of its total balances to a *general ledger account. Compare *subsidiary ledger.

debenture A *bond issued by a corporation. There are many types of debentures, but typically (unlike *common stock) they carry no voting rights. The issuer of a debenture agrees to pay the holder the debenture's *face value at a specific *maturity date, along with periodic *interest payments.

debit entry An accounting transaction under *double entry bookkeeping that increases *assets and *expenses, or reduces *liabilities, *revenues, and *equity. A debit entry has a corresponding *credit entry (or credit entries) of equal value.

debt *Money or *assets owed to an individual or organization. Debts include *short-term trading debts with customers as well as *long-term items like bank *loans and corporate *bonds—in all these cases, the debts arise from enforceable *contracts.

debt-equity ratio The ratio of a corporation's *long-term *debt to its *equity. The elements of equity used in the ratio include *common stock, *preferred stock, and *retained earnings. The debt-equity ratio measures a corporation's *leverage.

debtor 1. An individual or organization with a legally enforceable obligation to settle money due on *credit transactions. Compare *creditor. 2. [plural] A British term for *accounts receivable.

debug, to 1. To detect and remove errors or flaws (i.e., *bugs) from a computer software program. 2. To correct an error in the operation of computer hardware.

decentralization Within an organization, the granting of autonomy in activities, powers, and decision-making authority. The delegation of responsibility can occur both geographically and across layers of management. Contrast *centralization.

decision theory The systematic analysis of strategies for the optimal selection of alternative courses of action. Decision-making in conditions of uncertainty is fundamental to the management of organizations, and decision theory has developed a sophisticated range of methodologies—see, for example, *critical path analysis, *decision trees, and *discounted cash flow analysis. Compare *game theory.

decision tree A pictorial decision-making tool that portrays possible actions and choices in order to complete an activity. Decision trees normally include estimated outcomes for individual decisions, and the *probability of success of each decision. This permits the calculation of *quantifiable *expected values for various decisions.

deconsolidation The exclusion of the *financial statements of an organization from the *consolidated accounts of a *business combination. Deconsolidation may occur if a *parent organization reduces its investment in a *subsidiary to levels that no longer require consolidation into *group financial statements.

deep discounted bonds *Bonds issued at very large *discounts to their *face value. Deep discounted bonds typically offer very low *interest payments, and holders tend to anticipate income from *appreciations in the bonds' *market value.

defalcation An alternative term for *embezzlement.

default, to 1. To fail to honor the terms of a *contract. 2. To fail to pay amounts of *money at specified *due dates. 3. In a computerized accounting system, to revert to a predetermined position when no alternative action has been specified.

deferred charge An alternative term for *prepaid expense.

deferred income An alternative term for *unearned revenue.

deferred (income) tax An asset or liability that arises on timing differences between *income (definition 2) calculated under *Generally Accepted Accounting Principles and income calculated according to *taxation rules. See also *temporary differences and *permanent differences.

deferred revenue An alternative term for *unearned revenue.

deficit 1. An alternative term for *loss. 2. A debit balance in accumulated *retained earnings in a *balance sheet. 3. A shortfall in expected *cash balances.

defined benefit pension plan A *pension plan that arranges its funding on the basis of predetermined amounts payable to members. The amounts payable to members on retirement are usually a function of a combination of some or all of the following (items ii and iii refer to occupational pension plans): (i) age, (ii) length of service, and (iii) salary on retirement. Contrast *defined contribution pension plan.

defined contribution pension plan A *pension plan that arranges its payments and benefits to members on the basis of the amounts contributed by active members. Unlike in a *defined benefit pension plan, members are not guaranteed specific levels of payments or other benefits on retirement.

deflation A sustained reduction in the general sales *prices of consumer goods. Contrast *inflation and *disinflation.

Deloitte Touche Tohmatsu A global accounting, auditing, and professional services firm. One of the *Big Four firms, Deloitte Touche Tohmatsu operates some of its individual country firms under the name Deloitte. The firm's origins can be traced to the United Kingdom in the nineteenth century, while the Tohmatsu element of the name reflects the inclusion of a Japanese organization into the firm's structures.
    Further reading: Matthews et al. (1998)
    Web site: *www.deloitte.com*

demand 1. The desire or need of participants in a *market to purchase a good or service. In unregulated markets, *prices are (in theory) established by the "invisible hand" of buyers' and sellers' demand and *supply decisions. 2. A request for payment.

denationalization An alternative term for *privatization.

department A separately identifiable part of an organization that undertakes a discrete, specialized activity. See also *cost center and *profit center.

deposit 1. *Money invested at a bank. 2. The first payment installment for the purchase of a good or service.

depreciation 1. A reduction in the value of an asset. Contrast *appreciation. 2. A cost allocation method used to record the reduction in the value of an asset over time. See *amortization.

depression A severe or prolonged economic *recession in a *market or territory. Depressions often result in high *unemployment levels. The Great Depression in the United States, Germany, and other countries started in the late 1920s and stretched through to the late 1930s, and the experience of massive unemployment contributed to the conditions that led to World War II.

deregulation The reduction or elimination of *regulations, government controls, and other restrictions over a *market. The aims of deregulation include the following: (i) the stimulation of *competition, (ii) the encouragement of *price reductions, and (iii) the removal of *barriers to entry to a market.

derivative A *security whose value derives from uncertain or variable underlying conditions. Examples of derivatives include *futures contracts and *options. The underlying conditions that give rise to uncertainty include fluctuations in the *prices of *commodities, *currencies, and *securities. Derivatives are often customized to the requirements of individual investors. The complexity and high *risk of some forms of derivatives require extreme caution from an auditing perspective. Specialist expertise in understanding and assessing the impact of derivatives is often necessary to reach a reliable *audit opinion.

detailed audit An audit characterized by extensive *substantive testing of a large number of *transactions. In a detailed audit there is only a limited reliance on *compliance testing.

detection risk The *risk that the *misstatement of items in *financial statements may not be found through an auditor's *substantive and *compliance tests. Detection risk is considered alongside *inherent risk and *control risk as one of three components of external *audit risk. Unlike inherent risk and control risk, detection risk can be considered as directly controllable by the auditor, who can perform *audit tests devised expressly to minimize it.

detective control An *internal control designed to identify the occurrence of an unwanted event. Compare *corrective control and *preventative control.

devaluation A reduction in the value of a *currency in relation to other currencies. Contrast *revaluation (definition 2).

developed country A country of advanced economic standing. A collective term for developed nations is the *North. Contrast *developing country, the *South, and the *Third World.

developing country A country of modest economic standing. The economies of developing countries tend to be dominated by agricultural sectors and the supply of *raw materials, and are therefore vulnerable to fluctuations in *commodity *prices. Alternative terms for developing country include less developed country (LDC), *Third World country, and (collectively) the *South. There are many international institutions that work to assist the economic progress of developing countries. Examples include the *African Development Bank Group, *Asian Development Bank, the International Development Association of the *World Bank, and several other agencies of the *United Nations. Contrast *developed country.

Dicksee, Lawrence Robert (1864–1932) A British *external auditing pioneer. Dicksee was a prolific writer on the practice and theory of external auditing and, almost self-handed, he produced most of the important English-language auditing literature of his generation. A *chartered accountant who qualified at the *Institute of Chartered Accountants in England and Wales in 1886, Dicksee spent several years in public practice. His first book, *Auditing: A Practical Manual for Auditors*, was published in 1893. The book was aimed at auditing practitioners and students, and it placed heavy emphasis on the role of the auditor in *fraud detection. The book was not the first on external auditing (e.g., Pixley, 1888), but it is now regarded as an early auditing classic. The book was a huge success and ran to 15 editions over the following decades. The success of *Auditing* also spread across the Atlantic, and its U.S. edition edited by *Robert Hiester Montgomery also went through several editions. With the passage of time, Dicksee's *Auditing* has understandably lost most of its relevance to current auditing issues: It stands today as a text of historical interest only. However, it is a significant milestone in the development of auditing theory. Dicksee is also remembered for his pioneering academic teaching on auditing and accounting, and for a number of other important books, including a study of *window dressing.

Further reading: Brief (1980); Dicksee (1893); Dicksee (1927); Kitchen and Parker (1994)

dilution A reduction in *value. In the case of *common stock, dilution refers to a reduction in the value of a *stockholder's share of *equity, or a reduction in the proportion of shares held by a stockholder. This can occur when a corporation issues additional common stock, or *investors exercise their rights to *convertible securities, without a corresponding increase in the corporation's underlying assets.

diminishing returns **1.** The notion that the incremental satisfaction derived from the consumption of a good or the use of a service decreases with each additional unit. For example, a smoker may derive a great deal of satisfaction, or *utility, from the first cigarette of the day. The amount of satisfaction obtained from subsequent cigarettes decreases progressively. **2.** The theory that the use of an incremental unit of one *factor of production, with all the other factors held constant, will result in a reduced level of incremental output.

direct cost **1.** An alternative term for *variable cost. **2.** Costs directly attributable to the manufacture of a specific product.

director An individual with formal responsibility for the *stewardship of an organization. Directors usually exercise their responsibilities through the structure of a *board of directors. Directors employed by organizations are known as *inside directors, while those who are based externally are referred to as *outside directors.

directors' report An annual report from a *board of directors to an organization's *stockholders and other *stakeholders. Directors' reports normally accompany annual *financial statements, which they are intended to amplify and interpret. Under most systems of *Generally Accepted Auditing Standards, external auditors are required to report any *material discrepancies between a directors' report and related financial statements.

direct taxation A tax deducted from the income or wealth of an individual or organization. Contrast *indirect taxation.

disaster recovery planning An alternative term for *business continuity planning.

disbursement A payment of *money. Disbursements can be made in the form of (i) *cash payments, (ii) *checks, and (iii) *wire transfers.

disclaimer An external auditor's judgment that it is impossible to give an *audit opinion on an entity's *financial statements. Disclaimers are issued when an auditor is faced with the following types of problems: (i) insufficient *audit evidence, (ii) *scope limitations, or (iii) *material uncertainties surrounding an organization's financial health. Under most systems of *Generally

Accepted Auditing Standards, external auditors are obliged to explain the reasons for a disclaimer. Compare *adverse opinion, *qualified opinion, and *unqualified opinion.

disclosure Information given in the narrative notes to *financial statements. Disclosure of items is either (i) required by *Generally Accepted Accounting Principles or (ii) offered as a means of amplifying and explaining financial statement items. The legal writer L. C. B. Gower stated in 1969 that "as the fundamental principle of investor protection, [disclosure] only works if the information disclosed can be safely taken as accurate. Unless checked by some independent authority this cannot be relied on; so as far as the accounts are concerned the auditors are this *independent (and usually reliable) authority" (quoted in Chambers, R. J., 1995, 73).

discontinued operation The sale or closure of an activity or operation within an organization. Most systems of *Generally Accepted Accounting Principles require separate analysis of *continuing and discontinued operations in published *financial statements.

discount, to 1. To deduct an amount from the standard sales *price or *cost of a good, service, or *security. In a trading context, discounts can be offered to customers for several reasons: (i) as an inducement to purchase an item, (ii) to encourage prompt payment, and (iii) to generate customer *goodwill (definition 3). **2.** To recalculate future cash flows in *present value terms. See *discounted cash flow analysis.

discounted cash flow (DCF) analysis An investment appraisal method that assesses the *net present value of future incremental *cash flows that would arise from the implementation of a decision. In acknowledgment of the *time value of money, future cash flows are *discounted to *present values by the use of an appropriate *cost of capital rate. Discounted cash flow (DCF) analysis is frequently used to assess *capital expenditure proposals. See also the *internal rate of return.

discretionary cost An alternative term for *controllable cost.

diseconomies of scale Increases in the *unit costs of manufactured items in line with increases in *production levels. Contrast *economies of scale.

disinflation A reduction in the rate of *inflation. Compare *deflation.

distress price A low sales price offered by a seller in financial or operational difficulty. A distress price is often established in relation to a seller's *fixed costs, which must be covered if a seller is to continue as a *going concern.

distribution **1.** The mechanisms of *supplying goods and services to consumers. Distribution covers the storage, delivery, and also (under some definitions) the *wholesaling and *retailing of items for sale. **2.** Payments of a corporation's *income to *stockholders in the form of *dividends. **3.** The pattern of items in a population of data. See *normal distribution.

diversification **1.** The holding of a *portfolio of varied *investments to spread and thereby reduce *risk. See *portfolio theory. **2.** An increase in the range and variety of operations undertaken by an organization or an individual. *Multinational corporations tend to reduce their *risks by geographical diversification, as well as by entering different sectors of activity—these moves are typically intended to reduce overreliance on a small number of markets. However, although diversification generally leads to a spreading of (and therefore reduction of) risk, overdiversification can be counterproductive. A corporation that takes on an excessively wide range of operations may find that it loses strategic focus, and the range and variety of extensive activities may absorb an excessive amount of management time. In such cases, the negative effects of overdiversification can be mitigated by the *divestment of some operations.

divestment **1.** The sale or liquidation of assets or investments. Contrast *investment. **2.** The sale or liquidation of a subsidiary organization. Contrast *acquisition and *merger.

dividend The distribution of a corporation's *net income to its *stockholders. Dividends are normally paid in cash, in proportion to the sizes of stockholdings. Dividend payments to holders of *preferred stock take priority over those to holders of *common stock. For investors in a corporation's *common stock, dividends are a major form of investment return. The other major source of investment income is *appreciation of the common stock's market value.

division A unit of an organization that is responsible for two or more *branches. Divisions may be organized by (i) type of activity, (ii) geographical distribution, or (iii) a combination of the two. Divisions are used to control activities in large organizations and *multinationals, as the direct control of dispersed operations may be beyond the capability of a *board of directors or *head office management.

division of duties An alternative term for *segregation of duties.

division of responsibilities An alternative term for *segregation of duties.

dottore commercialista An Italian term that approximates to *Certified Public Accountant. In Italy the *Consiglio Nazionale dei Dottori Commercialisti is the professional association for *public accountants.

double entry bookkeeping A system of recording accounting *transactions with corresponding *debit entries and *credit entries of equal value. The mathematical integrity of the dualistic aspects of double entry bookkeeping can be established, through preparation of a *trail balance, by reference to the accuracy of the *accounting equation. The efficiency of the mechanics of double entry bookkeeping has long been recognized: It has been described as "simple, symmetrical, logical and beautiful" (Sawyer and Vinten, 1996, 204). The origins of double entry bookkeeping are widely attributed to the Italian mathematician and monk *Luca Pacioli, though Pacioli only summarized and synthesized pre-existing practices.

doubtful debt See *bad debt.

downloading The transmission of a file from a central location in a computerized information system to an individual or remote user.

downsizing **1.** A reduction in the scale of an organization's operations, through the sale or closure of activities, assets, or *subsidiary organizations. **2.** A reduction in the numbers of employees in an organization.

down time A period of time in a manufacturing environment when a machine is not working as a result of mechanical failure.

draft **1.** An interim version of a document. **2.** An alternative term for *bill of exchange.

due date A specific date at which there is a promise of *payment, delivery of a good, or performance of a service. See also *cut-off date.

due diligence The appraisal and assessment of an investment. The term is normally used in the context of corporate *acquisitions and *flotations, and it covers financial, legal, and operational considerations. In many organizations, internal and external auditors (the latter in their capacity as *consultants) perform financial due diligence procedures.

dumping The offloading in an overseas *market of *commodities or goods that arc difficult to sell in a domestic market. The effects of dumping can be devastating on a local market, and many countries have antidumping *legislation.

duty **1.** Money collected through tax and *tariff mechanisms. **2.** The existence of a responsibility, need, or obligation.

earnings 1. An alternative term for *net income. 2. *Sales revenues accruing to an organization or individual. 3. Employee *remuneration.

earnings per share (EPS) *Net income accruing to a corporation's stockholders, expressed in terms of individual shares of ownership. The earnings per share (EPS) is calculated by dividing net income by *common stock. In practice, this basic calculation can require adjustments to the net income figure for the *dividends of *preferred stock, which have preference over *common stock in the distribution of *earnings. The basic calculation may also require adjustments to the common stock figure, to take account of the potential dilution of stockholdings from *convertible securities and *stock options. The EPS is a highly sensitive figure for corporations, and investment analysts place great emphasis on the evolution of EPS over time. Pressures to meet market expectations of EPS were a prominent factor in the earnings manipulation scandals at *Enron and *WorldCom: One commentator mused that the acronym stood for the "eventual prison sentence" of individuals tempted to manipulate EPS (quoted in Jeter, 2003, 179).

Eastern, Central and Southern African Federation of Accountants (ECSAFA) A regional accounting organization, based in Kenya. Formed in 1989, ECSAFA's membership consists of national accounting organizations in the African regions of its title. In addition, it has a number of "observer" members, including the *Institute of Chartered Accountants in England and Wales and the *World Bank. The ECSAFA Web site describes its mission as follows: To "build and promote the accountancy profession in the Eastern, Central and Southern regions of Africa in order that it is, and is perceived by accountants, businesses, financiers and governments, to be an important factor in the economic development of the region." Its activities include publications and conferences.

Web site: *www.ecsafa.org*

e-commerce The conducting of business *transactions through the *Internet. It is an abbreviation of the term electronic commerce.

Further reading: Debreceny et al. (2003); Marcella (1998); Murphy and Bruce (2003)

economic life See *useful economic life.

economic order quantity (EOQ) A volume of *inventory intended to minimize *inventory-related administrative, holding, and transport costs. An optimal EOQ can be calculated through either differential calculus or subjective estimation.

economies of scale Reductions in the *unit costs of manufactured items with increases in *production levels. Contrast *diseconomies of scale.

economy **1.** As one of the *Three E's of *operational auditing, economy refers to the obtaining of resources at the lowest possible cost. Chambers and Rand (1997, 12) define economy in this context as "the ratio between planned inputs and actual inputs in terms of unit costs." **2.** The administration and management of a nation's resources, and of the production and distribution of a nation's wealth.

effectiveness The degree of success in undertaking activities in order to fulfill objectives. As one of the *Three E's of *operational auditing, Flint (1988, 175, n.6) defines effectiveness as "[s]uccess in achieving the objective of a policy or course of action as a consequence of the input of resources." Chambers and Rand (1997, 12) define effectiveness in this context as "the ratio of actual outputs to planned outputs."

efficiency The performance of an activity with an optimal use of resources and minimal waste. As one of the *Three E's of *operational auditing, Flint (1988, 175, n.5) defines efficiency as "[o]btaining maximum useful output from the resources devoted to an activity; utilising minimum resources necessary to achieve a required output or objective; or adopting the policy or course of action to achieve a required objective which requires least input of resources." Chambers and Rand (1997, 12) define efficiency in this context as "the ratio of actual inputs to actual outputs."
Further reading: Radcliffe (1999)

efficient markets hypothesis (EMH) The theory that abnormal profit cannot be made by investing in *securities in a *market in which information is shared by all participants. There are three forms of efficient markets: (i) a strong form, in which the prices of *securities fully reflect all available information (as all information is known publicly); (ii) a semi-strong form, in which the value of a security reflects all publicly held information, but there may be some privately held information which is withheld and which can lead to investors making abnormal profits; and (iii) a weak form, in which the use of secret information makes movements in the prices of securities difficult to estimate. The existence of profits through *arbitrage and *speculation suggests that the strong form of market exists only rarely—if at all—in practice.

elasticity The sensitivity or responsiveness of *demand for a good or service to changes in its sales *price.

Electronic Accountant, The The former title of *WebCPA.

electronic data interchange (EDI) The transfer of *transactions and other information between the computers of a buyer and seller. Electronic data interchange (EDI) practices are common in large commercial corporations, and in banks.

electronic mail The full term for *e-mail.

electronic office An alternative term for *paperless office.

e-mail An abbreviated term for electronic mail, which consists of documents transferred between geographically dispersed computers. Files can be attached to e-mail documents, which are normally channeled through individually identifiable e-mail accounts. See also *spam.

embargo The prohibition of economic activity between one country and another. Embargoes tend to be introduced for political reasons: A classic example is the United States' trade embargo on Fidel Castro's Cuba, declared in 1961. See also *boycott and *sanction.

embedded Incorporated within (or intrinsic to) an activity or procedure. *Internal controls are often embedded in organizations by means of integration into standard operating procedures. Some forms of *audit test are embedded in an organization's computer programs (see *computer assisted auditing techniques).

embezzlement The criminal misappropriation of *money placed under one's custody and control.

Emerging Issues Task Force (EITF) A committee of the *Financial Accounting Standards Board (FASB). The EITF was established in 1984 and was charged with reviewing the implications of urgent accounting issues: The FASB's processes for setting and interpreting accounting standards is considered too slow to deal with urgent issues on a timely basis. The EITF's members include both accountants and nonaccountants, and its model has been imitated elsewhere—for example, in the United Kingdom's *Urgent Issues Task Force.
Web link: *www.fasb.org/eitf*

empowerment The delegation of decision-making authority to individuals at lower levels of an organization. Management theory frequently advocates empowerment of employees as a way of mitigating some of the dysfunctional effects of traditional *chain of command structures.

encryption The protection of *data transferred between computers through the use of codes or combinations of characters that can only be understood by authorized individuals. Data transferred, stored, or processed in this way is usually decrypted (decoded) before it can be interpreted.

  Further reading: Friedlob et al. (1997)

endorsement **1.** An authorizing signature on a *check or other payment order. **2.** A public declaration of approval. For example, the manufacturers of clothes washing machines and of washing powders may endorse one anothers' products to mutual advantage. **3.** A clause in an *insurance policy that excludes an item from the terms of the policy.

engagement See *audit engagement.

engagement letter A *contractual document that confirms the terms, conditions, and costs of an *audit engagement. An engagement letter usually summarizes the rights and responsibilities of both the auditor and the *auditee.

Enron® A U.S. *multinational corporation that filed for Chapter 11 bankruptcy reorganization in December 2001. At the time, it was the largest bankruptcy in U.S. corporate history. The uncovering of false accounting and fraud forced Enron to make a write-down of stockholder *equity of more than $1 billion in its *financial statements in 2001. One of the contentious accounting mechanisms used by Enron was a web of *Special Purpose Entities. Some of these semi-independent, off-balance sheet investment partnerships were used to mask debts and losses. These investment mechanisms skirted some of the looser acceptability frontiers of *Generally Accepted Accounting Principles and many were essentially elaborate accounting hoaxes. Enron's problems exploded in late 2001 and last-minute attempts to arrange for the corporation to be acquired by a rival failed. Following its collapse, Enron has been described as representing "greed and hubris, deceitful accounting, and Wall Street favors" (Fox, 2003, v).

  The importance of Enron in the history of auditing was the effect of its fall from grace. First, it was a major contributory factor in the demise of the *Big Five external auditing firm *Arthur Andersen (AA). A perception of collusion between the senior management of Enron and AA led to a hemorrhage of AA's audit clients, the secession of some of AA's international practices, and the firm's criminal indictment. Most notoriously, AA's shredding of literally tons of

Enron-related auditing documents left its reputation in tatters. Even worse was to follow, as the Enron accounting scandal was followed by an even larger one at *WorldCom, another AA auditing client. Arthur Andersen itself collapsed in 2002.

The second way in which Enron is important to auditing is the effect of its accounting scandal on public opinion. The Enron affair changed the entire climate of auditing, and it led to shifts in the parameters of business legislation and *corporate governance. Words like *Enronitis entered the English language. The most tangible post-Enron changes to corporate governance crystallized in the *Sarbanes-Oxley Act* of 2002.

Further reading: Baker (2003); Bryce (2002); Fox (2003); Hala (2003); Schwartz and Watkins (2003); Toffler and Reingold (2003)

Web site: *www.enron.com*

Enronitis An ironic adjective referring to a loss of investor faith in corporate financial reporting and corporate governance. The term was coined by the media following the *Enron corporation's accounting scandals. For example, "Wall Street began talking regularly about Enronitis infecting stocks, as pundits ascribed various declines in the broad market to worries about corporations' accounting" (Fox, 2003, 294).

Further reading: Vinten (2003)

enterprise **1.** A *profit-seeking undertaking or activity. See also *entrepreneur. **2.** A display of initiative and *risk-seeking attitudes.

enterprise risk management (ERM) The identification, analysis, and management of the entire range of an organization's *risks. Enterprise risk management (ERM) is essentially the holistic and integrated application of *risk management principles, and it has been described as "a systematic and disciplined approach to managing risk throughout [an] organization" (Funston, 2003, 60). At the time of this writing, in 2003, an ongoing project of the *Committee of Sponsoring Organizations of the Treadway Commission is the development of an *enterprise risk management framework.

Further reading: Chapman (2001); Funston (2003)

entity A separately identifiable economic unit that can be subjected to auditing. An entity in this sense does not necessarily have a separate legal identity: it can refer to a *corporation, *partnership, or *public sector body, or to an activity or department within an organization.

entrepreneur An individual who uses the *factors of production to create *wealth. In classical economic theory, a *profit-seeking entrepreneur operates in the *private sector, taking *risks to achieve *income. The term is taken from the French, and it literally means "an individual who undertakes an *enterprise."

entry The recording of an accounting *transaction in a *general ledger or *subsidiary ledger. Under the conventions of *double entry bookkeeping, entries take the form of *debit entries and *credit entries.

environmental auditing The auditing of an organization's adherence to environmental laws, regulations, and best practices. This branch of auditing assesses the impact of an organization's activities on the environment, in areas such as the following: (i) pollution levels, (ii) the handling of waste, and (iii) health and safety considerations for employees and the wider community. Environmental auditing increased in importance in the late twentieth century, alongside a general increase in environmental awareness. A leading professional organization in the field is the *Board of Environmental, Health & Safety Auditor Certifications.
Further reading: Hillary (1998)

equilibrium A condition in a *market at which *supply and *demand are in harmony. An equilibrium point establishes a *price for a product or service, and it can be achieved in both the *short and *long terms.

equity 1. The ownership interest of *stockholders in a corporation. Under the conventions of *double entry bookkeeping and the *accounting equation, stockholders' equity is calculated as total *assets less total *liabilities. It is recorded in the *balance sheet. 2. An alternative term for *common stock. 3. An alternative term for the combined value of *common stock, *preferred stock, and *retained earnings. 4. In a general sense, justice and fairness. 5. A legal right over an asset. 6. A body of English law distinct from (and which generally prevails over) *common law. Equitable law derives in part from principles of natural justice, and equitable doctrines have entered legal systems throughout the English-speaking world.

equity method A means of accounting for *business combinations in contexts where an investment in an organization is too small to effect control. The equity method operates through (i) the inclusion of an appropriate proportion of the organization's *income in the *income statement of the investor and (ii) the inclusion of the original amount invested (plus a share of *retained earnings) in the investor's *balance sheet. See also *consolidation accounting techniques.

Ernst & Young® A global accounting, auditing, and professional services firm. One of the *Big Four firms, Ernst & Young was established in its current form

in 1989 with the merger of Ernst & Whinney and Arthur Young & Co. The firm traces its roots to the United States in the early twentieth century.
Web site: *www.ey.com/global*

error An inaccuracy, mistake, miscalculation, or misrepresentation. In general, the term error is used to refer to nonintentional inaccuracies or deviations from control, in contrast to deliberately *fraudulent actions. Systems of *internal control are intended to reduce the likelihood of errors.

escapable cost An alternative term for *avoidable cost.

ethical investment The restriction of investments to organizations that avoid unethical, immoral, or questionable activities. The concept of ethical investing is hotly disputed, owing to the subjective nature of the ethical judgments that underpin it. Criteria used to underpin ethical investing include (i) the nature of an organization's activities (tobacco and armaments tend to be among disapproved activities), (ii) a record of good environmental practices, and (iii) equitable treatment of employees. See also *Corporate Social Responsibility.

ethics Systematic moral judgments and principles of intrinsic value. High ethical standards are central to the credibility of *professions, and to the *corporate governance standards of organizations, and they are often formalized in written codes of practice.
Further reading: Blank (2003); Dittenhofer (1983); Dittenhofer and Sennetti (1983); Preuss (1998); Shafer et al. (2001)

European Accounting Association (EAA) A European scholarly accounting organization. Established in 1977 and headquartered in Brussels, Belgium, the EAA's Web site states that it aims "to link together the Europewide community of accounting scholars and researchers, to provide a platform for the wider dissemination of European accounting research and to foster and improve research." Its activities include an annual congress, workshops, and publication of the academic journal *European Accounting Review.
Web site: *www.eaa-online.org*

European Accounting Review A European scholarly accounting journal. Established in 1992, the journal is published quarterly in English by Routledge on behalf of the *European Accounting Association, in both print and online formats. It focuses on academic research, and its notes emphasize "its European origins and the distinctive variety of the European accounting research community." The notes also draw attention to the journal's "openness and flexibility, not only regarding the substantive issues of accounting research, but also with respect to paradigms, methodologies and styles of conducting that research." The journal frequently covers auditing topics.

Web link: *www.tandf.co.uk/journals/routledge/09638180.html*

European Corporate Governance Institute (ECGI) A European *corporate governance body. The ECGI is based in Brussels, Belgium, and was launched in 2002 as successor to the European Corporate Governance Network. Its primary objective, as stated on its Web site, is "to undertake and disseminate impartial and objective research on corporate governance and undertake any other activity that will improve understanding and exercise of the highest standards in corporate governance." The ECGI cooperates with other institutions in the field, like the *Global Corporate Governance Forum and the *International Corporate Governance Network.

Web site: *www.ecgi.org*

European Federation of Accountants The English name of the *Fédération des Experts Comptables Européens.

Web site: *www.fee.be*

evaluation **1.** The assessment of evidence. Evaluation skills are central to auditing, in both the assessment of *audit evidence and the reasoning used to arrived at *audit opinions. See also *assurance. **2.** A *quantitative or *qualitative measurement. For example, qualitative evaluations of staff performance are common in most large corporations.

event **1.** A *transaction or significant happening in an organization that can influence an *audit opinion. **2.** In *critical path analysis, a point that represents the start or end of an activity or series of sequential activities. **3.** In *probability analysis, an outcome of an activity to which a probability estimate can be applied.

event after the balance sheet date A *material *event that can potentially affect *financial statements despite its occurrence after a *balance sheet date. An event of this type may lead to *disclosure in the notes that accompany financial statements, or to adjustments to financial statements. See also *contingent assets and *contingent liabilities.

evidence See *audit evidence.

examination **1.** The inspection or investigation of a matter. The examination of records and procedures is central to the gathering and *evaluation of *audit evidence. An 1888 editorial of the *Accountant magazine described an audit as "an intelligent examination of the *books" (quoted in Chambers, R. J., 1995,

73). **2.** A formal test of competence or knowledge. Along with supervised work experience, examinations are central to the certification of auditors by *professional associations. **3.** An archaic term for *audit.

exception An item that does not follow a general pattern. For example, an organization's *internal controls may specify that all *disbursements over a given threshold should be *authorized by a senior employee. If this procedure is not followed in only rare cases, the nonadherence to the internal control may be deemed to be exceptions. Auditors are required to apply judgment to *errors to decide whether (i) they are merely isolated exceptions or (ii) they indicate a systematic breakdown in procedures and internal controls.

exceptional item A *transaction separately reported or disclosed in an *income statement on account of its *materiality, unusual nature, or infrequency. Exceptional items arise from normal operating activities, and examples may include the write-off of a significant *accounts receivable balance, or unusually large *reorganization costs. A material, unusual transaction arising from events beyond the scope of normal operating activities is usually referred to as an *extraordinary item.

exception report A report of errors or other *exceptions arising from an activity or procedure. Exception reports are convenient mechanisms for focusing on potential breakdowns in *internal controls, and they are a common management tool. Auditors also frequently use the contents of exception reports as *audit evidence. Exception reports may be either manually prepared or generated by a computer program.

exchange The buying and selling of items in a *market. Simple exchange is effected through *barter transactions, but in modern economies *money is used as the main medium of exchange.

exchange rate **1.** The rate at which one unit of a *currency can be exchanged for one unit of another currency. **2.** The *value of a commodity, good, or service measured in terms of its ability to be exchanged for other items, without the intermediary of *money. See also *barter.

executive director The British term for *inside director.

executive remuneration *Compensation paid to an organization's *directors and senior *management. Levels of executive remuneration are a sensitive topic, and they are subject to *disclosure in financial statements under most systems of *Generally Accepted Accounting Principles. Other *corporate governance measures in this area can include (i) the existence of *remuneration committees to determine executive remuneration, (ii) the linking of remuneration levels to individual and organizational performance (including changes in the *value of a corporation's *common stock), (iii) internal audits of executive pay, and (iv) the releasing of executive remuneration details to the media in the interests of openness.

Further reading: Keasey and Wright (1999)

exemption 1. The releasing of an individual from an obligation or responsibility. **2.** A permitted deduction or exclusion from computations of taxable income.

ex gratia The giving of an item, such as a gift* or a payment of *money, without any obligation intended to be placed on the recipient. The term derives from Latin, and it usually refers to an action that originates from a moral decision rather than from a legal requirement.

existence Objective, verifiable reality. The *verification of the existence of both *tangible and *intangible items is a fundamental *audit objective.

expectations gap Discrepancies between the expectations of auditors and the expectations of *auditees, other parties interested in an audit, and public opinion. The term is normally used in the context of external auditing, and it tends to be painfully apparent when external auditors are perceived to have failed to detect a corporate *fraud or other *material *irregularity in a corporation's financial statements. The expectations gap has been described as "the difference between how financial auditors are perceived (responsible for the detection of *fraud) and how they see themselves (primarily responsible for forming a professional opinion on the financial statements)" (Power, 1994a, 24) and "a representation of the feeling that auditors are performing in a manner at variance with the beliefs and desires of those for whose benefit the audit is being carried out" (Humphrey, 1991, 7).

Further reading: Sikka et al. (1998); Wolf et al. (1999)

expected value (EV) The quantifiable, expected result of a course of action whose outcome is uncertain. Expected values are often used in *decision theory, and are calculated by multiplying the expected outcomes of decisions by the *probabilities of their occurrence. See also *decision tree.

expediting payment An alternative term for *facilitating payment.

expenditure *Money spent to cover *costs and *expenses. See *capital expenditure and *revenue expenditure.

expense 1. A *cost incurred in a specific time period. Expenses are deducted from revenues in an *income statement to calculate *net income for a defined time period. The cost of *long-term assets is expensed to individual time periods through the mechanism of *amortization. The terms cost and expense are often used synonymously. **2.** [plural] Travel expenses incurred for a business journey.

expert-comptable A French term that approximates to *Certified Public Accountant. It is used in France and in a number of other francophone countries. In France the *Ordre des Experts-Comptables* is the professional association for *public accountants, while the Paris-based *Fédération Internationale des Experts Comptables Francophones* is a forum for French-speaking public accountants around the world.

exponential increase A quantifiable increase that becomes increasingly rapid.

exportation The selling of goods and services to customers based in a foreign country. Contrast *importation.

exposure draft A draft *accounting standard or *auditing standard that is disseminated for public comment and discussion prior to being finalized and issued.

extended trial balance A mechanism for the preparation of financial statements from a *trial balance. The listing of *general ledger accounts in a trial balance is "extended" by the recording of adjustments (like *accrued expenses) and reclassifications, and by the identification of each account with the *balance sheet and *income statement.

external audit An *audit of *financial statements by *independent individuals or organizations. *Robert Khun Mautz has suggested that "the role of [external] auditing in an advanced economic society can be and has been stated in very simple terms—to add credibility to financial statements" (quoted in Flint, 1988, 6), while *Tom A. Lee has described external auditing as a "technical process to independently ᴬverify and attest the quality of externally reported... financial statements" (1993, 115). Another definition has been offered by the American Accounting Association: "Auditing is a systematic process of objectively obtaining and *evaluating evidence regarding assertions about economic actions and events to ascertain the degree of correspondence between those assertions and established criteria and communicating the results to interested parties" (American Accounting Association, 1973).

Modern external auditing is the result of almost two centuries of continuous evolution. It emerged as a *professional discipline in the United Kingdom in the nineteenth century, when the creation of limited liability *corporations resulted in separation of the providers of *capital from the managers who administered it. To monitor that investments were appropriately managed and controlled, the external auditing profession offered providers of capital an independent and objective opinion on published financial statements, traditionally the primary record of corporate accountability. As has been suggested, "capitalism is a complicated enterprise, and the system won't work without referees" (Fox, 2003, 313).

The early emphasis of external auditing was on the detection of *errors and *fraud, but it gradually developed into an assessment of the *fair presentation of financial statements. With the establishment of the *American Institute of Certified Public Accountants in 1887, external auditing's center of gravity shifted from the United Kingdom to the United States, where it has since remained.

A notable feature of the external auditing profession is the existence of powerful auditing firms of astonishing longevity. The auditing firms of nineteenth century London included the forerunners of today's global auditing and accounting firms. Among the names of London auditing firms in 1886 were several that have survived, in various combinations, to the modern era: Price, Waterhouse, and Cooper Brothers (now *PricewaterhouseCoopers) and Deloitte, Dever, Griffiths (now *Deloitte Touche Tohmatsu). See also *agency theory and *internal auditing.

Further reading: Flint (1988); Lee (1993); Porter et al. (2003); Power (1997); Schandl (1978); Wolnizer (1987)

external auditing The process or action of undertaking an *external audit. Although the gerund auditing places greater emphasis on action than the simple noun audit, the two terms are largely interchangeable.

external auditor An individual who performs an *external audit. In most countries, external auditors are drawn from the ranks of *Certified Public Accountants, or are individuals of equivalent *professional standing.

external audit risk See *audit risk (definition 1).

external control **1.** Aspects of *corporate governance related to the controls exercised by *stakeholders over their interests in an organization. Elements of external control include (i) the preparation of published *financial statements, (ii) the *external auditing of financial statements, and (iii) other mechanisms of *accountability for *boards of directors. **2.** The monitoring of *internal controls in a *vendor or other outside organization. For example, some retail corporations seek to ensure the achievement of their objectives by monitoring the activities and internal controls of their major vendors.

extraordinary item A *transaction separately reported or disclosed in an *income statement on account of its *materiality, unusual nature, or infrequency. Extraordinary items arise from events outside normal operating activities, and examples may include large-scale, one-off costs arising from natural disasters, fire damage, or government appropriation of *assets. An unusual event arising from normal operating activities is often referred to as an *exceptional item.

extrapolation The extension of trends indicated by a *sample of data to an entire *population of data. For example, if 10 percent of a representative sample of *accounts receivable balances exceeds agreed *credit limits, an auditor may assume that 10 percent of the entire accounts receivable balances exceed their credit limits. Caution must be exercised in extrapolating the results of any sample, however, owing to *sampling risk. Compare *interpolation.

face value 1. The *nominal value of a *bond or other debt instrument. The purchase price of a bond when issued may differ from its face value, owing to a *discount or *premium on issuance, and the *market values of traded bonds also tend to differ from face values. However, a bond's value at *maturity and its *interest payments tend to be calculated in relation to face value. The term face value is sometimes used synonymously with *par value, though careful users restrict the former to debt instruments and the latter to *common stock. **2.** The monetary value stated on a coin or bank note.

facilitating payment A minor payment made to an individual or organization in order to encourage the correct and timely performance of duties. The term facilitating payment (or expediting payment) is associated with the *Foreign Corrupt Practices Act, which distinguishes it from a *bribe. In essence, a facilitating payment is made to ensure the performance of an individual's routine duties, and no more, while the intention of a bribe is to gain influence and procure preferential treatment. Compare *questionable payment.

factoring The sale of *accounts receivable to a *third party, known as a factor. A factor purchases accounts receivable at a discount to their total value, and assumes responsibility for collection and *credit risks. The advantages of factoring for the seller include (i) the saving of accounts receivable administrative costs and (ii) improved *cash flow and *working capital. The main advantage for the factor is the *income (definition 2) arising from the difference between the purchase price and collectible value of the acquired accounts receivable.

factors of production The resources and inputs required for the *production of goods of economic *value. Famously defined by the economist Alfred Marshall (1842–1924) as the "things necessary for making a commodity," the factors of production have traditionally been grouped into three categories: (i) land (including *raw materials), (ii) *labor, and (iii) *capital (definition 4). Some economists add *entrepreneurship as a fourth factor of production.

Fair Labor Association (FLA) An international *not-for-profit organization dedicated to the promotion of ethical *labor practices. The FLA is based in Washington, DC, and its mission (as stated on its Web site) is founded on "combining the efforts of industry, *non-governmental organizations (NGOs), colleges and universities to promote adherence to international labor standards and improve working conditions worldwide." The FLA's activities include the issuing of a code of conduct for labor practices, and the monitoring of adherence to the code by its participating corporations, which include a number of large clothing *brands.

Web site: *www.fairlabor.org*

fair market value The *price of an asset in the context of an *arm's length transaction in a *free market. Compare *book value and *market value.

fair presentation A term used in external auditing in the United States to refer to *financial statements that portray underlying economic conditions in an accurate, reliable, honest, and *understandable manner. External auditors are required to give an *audit opinion on the extent to which financial statements fairly present underlying economic circumstances. See also *Generally Accepted Accounting Principles.

fair value *A British alternative term for *fair market value.

false accounting The *fraudulent manipulation of accounting data. A more informal term is *cooking the books.

fast moving consumer goods (FMCG) A term used to describe tangible *consumer goods of portable size that are characterized by high volume activity.

favorable variance In *budgeting, the incurring of smaller than anticipated costs or the earning of larger than anticipated revenues. A favorable variance indicates that actual performance is better than expected. The term is also used in *standard costing. Contrast *unfavorable variance.

feasibility study An evaluation of the impact of undertaking an activity or making an investment. Quantifiable evaluation techniques like *discounted cash flow analysis and *payback period analysis are commonly used in feasibility studies.

***Fédération des Experts Comptables Européens* (FEE)** A European accounting organization. Based in Brussels, Belgium, and known in English as the European Federation of Accountants, the FEE was founded in 1987. Its members consist of European national accounting organizations, and in 2003 they numbered more than 40. The FEE Web site describes its mission to be "the leading representative body of the European accountancy profession to the institutions of the European Union." The FEE's activities include publications, technical research, and policy initiatives.

Web site: *www.fee.be*

fee A payment to an individual or organization for the providing of a service. The term is often used for the remuneration of external auditors and other *professionals. Compare *compensation.

feedback The providing of information on the performance of an activity or project. In *budgeting, timely feedback on *variances is generally considered to be essential in order to take appropriate corrective action.

fiduciary An individual or organization responsible for administering another party's assets. *Agents, for example, are fiduciaries to *principals, and trustees are fiduciaries to the beneficiaries of *trusts.

field auditor An auditor who undertakes assignments geographically distant from an organization's head office. The *internal audit functions of *multinational corporations typically use field auditors to cover a range of international operations.

fieldwork Detailed *audit testing performed at an *auditee's premises or away from an organization's head office.

finance **1.** The management of the *monetary resources and *funding of an individual, organization, or government. *Financial auditing is concerned principally with the auditing of *financial statements. **2.** An alternative term for *capital (definitions 1 and 4). **3.** An alternative term for *money. **4.** An alternative term for *funding.

finance lease A British alternative term for *capital lease.

Financial Accountability and Management A British scholarly accounting journal. It is published quarterly by Blackwell Publishing in print and online formats. The journal's notes describe its aim as follows: To publish "new thinking and research in the financial accountability, accounting, and financial and resource management of all types of governmental and other non-profit organizations and services." The notes also point toward an interdisciplinary approach: The "journal includes contributions from economics, political science, social and public administration, and management sciences, as well as accounting and finance." The journal's coverage is international, and it occasionally addresses auditing topics.
    Web link: *www.blackwellpublishing.com/journals/FAM*

financial accounting The maintenance of *accounting records and the preparation of *financial statements and related documents. Financial accounting, in contrast to *management accounting, tends to focus on accounting records for use outside an organization—by *investors, *creditors, *debtors, and *tax authorities, for example.

Financial Accounting Foundation (FAF) The U.S. organization responsible for overseeing *financial reporting standards. Founded in 1972, the FAF has overseen both the *Financial Accounting Standards Board (FASB) and its *public sector equivalent, the *Governmental Accounting Standards Board (GASB). The FAF appoints the members and advisory councils of both standard-setting bodies. The FAF's own board of trustees are nominated by a number of organizations, including the *American Accounting Association and the *American Institute of Certified Public Accountants.

Prior to 2003, the FAF was also responsible for the funding of both the FASB and the GASB. However, following the mandatory funding model requirements of listed corporations introduced by the *Sarbanes-Oxley Act of 2002, the FAF has stopped offering membership in support of the FASB. It will allow existing memberships to expire. The FAF has, however, retained funding responsibilities for the GASB.

Web site: *www.fasb.org/faf*

Financial Accounting Standards Advisory Council (FASAC) An advisory committee of the *Financial Accounting Standards Board (FASB). Set up in 1973 at the time of the FASB's creation, the council advises the FASB on its activities relating to U.S. *Generally Accepted Accounting Principles. The composition of FASAC reflects several constituencies with an interest in financial reporting: It includes accountants, corporate executives, and academics. The FASAC does not have the authority to overrule the FASB's decisions, but its views are an important part of the FASB's decision-making processes.

Web site: *www.fasb.org/fasac*

Financial Accounting Standards Board (FASB) The U.S. accounting standards-setting organization. Based in Norwalk, CT, the FASB was established in 1973 as successor to the *Accounting Principles Board. The FASB's Web site states that its mission is "to establish and improve standards of financial accounting and reporting for the guidance and education of the public, including issuers, auditors, and users of financial information." The FASB is, therefore, the custodian of *Generally Accepted Accounting Principles in the United States, and it issues accounting standards in the form of *Statements of Financial Accounting Standards (SFAS), often referred to as *FASB Statements. The SFAS are recognized by the *Securities and Exchange Commission and other important financial reporting and accounting organizations. Unlike its predecessor, the *Accounting Principles

Board, the FASB is formally independent of the *American Institute of Certified Public Accountants.

The FASB also issues *FASB Staff Positions* that offer guidance on the application of the SFAS, and *Statements on Financial Accounting Concepts* that set out a fundamental theoretical framework to underpin accounting practice. The FASB also has an *Emerging Issues Task Force that looks at the implications of urgent accounting issues, and an advisory committee known as the *Financial Accounting Standards Advisory Council.

Web site: *www.fasb.org*

financial auditing The auditing of *financial statements and related information. Financial auditing has been described as "an inferential practice which seeks to draw conclusions from a limited inspection of documents, such as budgets and written representations, in addition to reliance on oral testimony and direct observation" (Power, 2000, 111). The term is often used interchangeably with *external auditing.

financial controller An alternative term for *controller.

***Financial Executive Magazine*®** A U.S. professional finance magazine. Published in ten issues a year by *Financial Executives International, *Financial Executive* is available in print and online formats. It focuses on business and management issues in an international context, in addition to finance and accounting topics. Auditing issues are frequently covered.

Web link: *www.fei.org/mag*

Financial Executives Internationalˢᴹ **(FEI**ˢᴹ**)** A U.S. professional association for corporate financial executives. Established in 1931 as the Controllers Institute of America, the FEI adopted its current name in 1962. It had approximately 15,000 members in 2003. Despite its relatively small size, the FEI is an influential organization. Its Web site states that the association "speaks vigorously on behalf of the profession to legislative and regulatory bodies in Washington, DC, and other corridors of power. FEI provides a corporate perspective to Congress and policymaking bodies such as the SEC, the FASB and the IASB." The association is one of the five sponsoring organizations of the *Committee of Sponsoring Organizations of the Treadway Commission. The FEI's activities include conferences and publications: The latter includes e-newsletters, research publications, and the *Financial Executive* magazine. The FEI has been active in analyzing and contributing to the debates surrounding the *Sarbanes-Oxley Act* of 2002. In May 2002, for example, the FEI's Research Foundation issued *Internal Control Reports Required by Sarbanes-Oxley*, an online report.

Web site: *www.fei.org*

financial instrument A paper *investment that confers a claim or a potential claim to income. In the widest sense of the term, there are many types of financial instruments, including *common stock and *bonds. They can be issued by corporations and governments, and they may or may not be traded. However, some users of the term reserve it only for traded bonds.

financial reporting The preparation and dissemination of *financial statements. "Corporate financial reporting is essentially an information system designed to construct and represent abstractions of the state and effects of specific empirical events which comprise the business activity of a corporate organziation" (Lee, 1993, 138). Financial reporting in most countries is guided by a combination of *legislation and *Generally Accepted Accounting Principles, and it is normally subject to *external auditing.

Financial Reporting Council (FRC) A British accounting regulatory authority. The FRC has five operating boards, including the Accounting Standards Board (ASB) and the Financial Reporting Review Panel (FRRP), to which it provides policy guidance. The FRC's main objective, as stated at its Web site, is to "promote and secure good financial reporting" in the United Kingdom. The ASB is responsible for issuing British *accounting standards, while the FRRP examines alleged contraventions of British *Generally Accepted Accounting Principles.
    Web site: *www.frc.org.uk*

financial reporting period A period of time covered by *financial statements. An *income statement reports revenues and costs for a financial reporting period, normally 12 months under most systems of *Generally Accepted Accounting Principles, and a *balance sheet reports *assets, *liabilities, and *equity on the final date of the reporting period. See also *fiscal year.

financial reporting standard Rules and guidance on accounting practice and *disclosure in *financial statements. Along with *legislation and custom, financial reporting standards (sometimes referred to as *accounting standards) are the foundation of *Generally Accepted Accounting Principles (GAAP). In the United States, the *Financial Accounting Standards Board issues *Statements of Financial Accounting Standards*, which form the basis of U.S. GAAP. Moves toward the *harmonization of international GAAP are based on the *International Financial Reporting Standards* of the *International Accounting Standards Board.

financial statements Summaries of the accounting transactions and financial position of an organization or individual at a specific date. The main elements of financial statements are the *balance sheet, which offers a snapshot of *assets, *liabilities, and *equity at a given date, and the *income statement, which sets out operating results and *net income for a defined time period leading to the balance sheet date. Under most systems of *Generally Accepted Accounting Principles, other components of financial statements typically include a *cash flow statement, explanatory notes, and a *directors' report. The quality of financial statements is often judged in terms of relevance, reliability, and usefulness in decision-making. See also *fair presentation.

financial year (FY) An alternative term for *fiscal year, used in the United Kingdom and some other countries with a history of British influence.

finished goods The final products of a *manufacturing process that are held as *inventory, pending their sale. Compare *raw materials and *work-in-process.

firm 1. [noun] An organization established to undertake business or professional activity. A firm is not necessarily a *corporation, as the term covers *partnerships and other legal forms of economic unit. **2.** [adjective] Not subjected to uncertainty or negotiation. Examples of the use of the term are in the expressions "firm order" and "firm sale."

first-in first-out (FIFO) An *inventory valuation method that assumes inventory is consumed or sold in the order in which it is purchased or manufactured. The FIFO methodology, which allocates older inventory costs to *cost of sales, is acceptable under most forms of *Generally Accepted Accounting Principles. Compare *last-in first-out (LIFO) and *next-in first-out (NIFO).

fiscal Relating to government finances, especially *taxation.

fiscal year (FY) A *financial reporting period of 12 months' duration used for *taxation assessments. As corporate financial reporting periods tend to be used as the basis for tax computations, the term fiscal year also refers to standard corporate financial reporting periods.

Five E's See the *Six E's.

fixed asset 1. A *long-term, *tangible or *intangible asset. **2.** A British term for *property, plant, and equipment.

fixed budget An alternative term for *static budget.

fixed charge 1. An alternative term for *fixed cost. **2.** Costs related to the setting up of production batches. All things being equal, large production batches minimize the impact of fixed charges like the setting up and calibration of machines. **3.** The right of a lender to take possession of a specific asset should a borrower *default on the repayment of a *loan, or should another specified event (such as *bankruptcy) take place. A fixed charge establishes an asset as *collateral for a debt: An example is a *mortgage on a property. Compare *floating charge.

fixed cost An item of expenditure that is not directly sensitive to changes in activity levels. Rental, insurance, and salary costs are typical fixed costs for many manufacturing organizations. Contrast *variable cost and *semi-variable cost.

fixtures *Fixed assets that take the form of attachments to larger assets. For example, depending on their *materiality, security devices attached to motor vehicles could be classified as fixtures.

fixtures and fittings An alternative term for *fixtures.

flag of convenience In international maritime practice, the registering of a ship in a country other than the ship's country of origin. A flag of convenience tends to be used to simplify administrative requirements, or to avoid or minimize taxation and regulatory responsibilities.

flash report **1.** An internal report in an organization that summarizes important or sensitive information in advance of detailed *management accounts. Sales data is a typical component of flash reports. **2.** An alternative term for *exception report.

Flesher, Dale L. (born 1945) A U.S. academic, author, and accounting and auditing specialist. A professor at the University of Mississippi's Patterson School of Accounting, Flesher has written extensively on auditing and accounting, with (by 2003) at least 300 articles and 35 books. A noted historian of accounting and auditing, he is the author of *50 Years of Progress Through Sharing* (1991), which covers the history of the *Institute of Internal Auditors from its foundation in 1941 through 1991. He has also co-authored a ten-year supplement to this title (Flesher and McIntosh, 2002). Flesher is a former president of the *Academy of Accounting Historians, and former editor of the * *Accounting Historians Journal*. His other areas of interest include *operational auditing (Flesher, 1982) and auditing in the hospitals sector (Flesher, 1976).

Further reading: Flesher (1976); Flesher (1982); Flesher (1991); Flesher and McIntosh (2002); Flesher et al. (2003)

Web link: *www.olemiss.edu/depts/accountancy/dflesher.html*

flexible budget A *budget that provides information on various levels of activity. In contrast to a *static budget, a flexible budget is a dynamic management tool that caters for changes in operational circumstances. Its flexibility can simplify *variance analysis.

float **1.** An amount of *money held as *petty cash. **2.** The time difference between the deposit of checks at a bank and their processing by the bank. During this time, the *money is available to neither payer nor payee.

flotation The launching of a new *corporation via the issuing of *securities in a *market.

floating charge The right of a *lender to take possession of unspecified assets should a borrower *default on the repayment of a *loan, or should another specified event (such as *bankruptcy) take place. Compare *fixed charge (definition 3).

flowchart A diagram that depicts the sequential flow of an activity's inputs, processes, and outputs. Flowcharts portray flows of transactions, data, and documents, and its conventional symbols include (i) rectangles for descriptions of activities, (ii) diamonds for decision points, and (iii) circles for links.

footing The totaling of individual items in a list or in an *account.

forecast A quantifiable estimate of future activities. The term forecast is used in several ways: (i) as a synonym for *budget, (ii) for a period of time shorter than that of a budget, and (iii) for a period of time longer than that of a budget. See also *cash flow forecast.

Foreign Corrupt Practices Act (FCPA) *Anticorruption *legislation passed by the U.S. Congress in 1977. The *FCPA* requires U.S. corporations to maintain adequate *internal control systems throughout their international operations. The *FCPA* also forbids the payment of *bribes to foreign officials. In some countries, small *gifts are an essential means of doing business: The *FCPA* acknowledges this by permitting *facilitating payments, which are intended merely to encourage the correct and timely performance of routine duties. However, the difference between a bribe and a facilitating payment is often a thin one, and is sometimes decided in court. Owing to the increase in auditing and monitoring that it stimulated, the *FCPA* has been described humorously as the "internal auditor full-employment act" (Izzard, 1988). (Similar comments were heard following the passing of the *Sarbanes-Oxley Act* in 2002.) Contravention of the *FCPA* can result in severe fines and custodial sentences, and it has had an enormous impact on the manner in which U.S. *multinational corporations manage their affairs. Although many countries have anticorruption legislation, the United States is unique in having laws of the *FCPA*'s reach and severity.

Further reading: Vanasco (1999)

Web link: *www.usdoj.gov/criminal/fraud/fcpa.html*

foreign currency A *currency other than one used as a *functional currency by an individual or organization.

forensic auditing Investigative auditing undertaken specifically to support actions in a court of law. Forensic auditing is associated with practices like the investigation of *money laundering transactions, and it is often aimed at uncovering *fraudulent and illegal activity.

forfeiture The loss or deprival of an *asset or legal right. Forfeiture can be a punishment for wrongdoing, or it can arise from the nonoccurrence of an event in a commercial contract. An example of the latter is the loss of a deposit required for the submission of bids to win a contract, when the deposit is refundable only to the winner of the contract.

forgery The *fraudulent copying or imitation of an asset or document. Items typically subject to forgery include (i) signatures, (ii) money, and (iii) works of art.

format 1. The manner in which an item is structured and presented. The format of an *audit report, for example, is often central to its success as a communication medium for *audit recommendations. **2.** The initial preparation of a medium of computer data storage (like a diskette or CD-ROM) to permit the future recording of data.

forward rate An *exchange rate specified in a foreign exchange *contract. The contract involves either a commitment or an *option to buy or sell a specified amount of a foreign currency at a specified date.

franchising 1. A *contractual authorization given by one party (a franchisor) to another (a franchisee) to undertake economic activity using the franchisor's *brand name. The franchisee usually pays a *royalty for the use of the brand name. Fast-food outlets are a classic example of a franchise arrangement. **2.** The granting by a government of *monopoly rights to an organization. In this context, franchising is often used for the providing of public *utilities.

fraud Illegal, dishonest, or improper activity. Fraud appears in many guises, including (i) the manipulation of accounting data (or *cooking the books), (ii) the theft of *assets, and (iii) the sale to *competitors of confidential or sensitive information about an organization. Fraud can be committed by an individual working alone, in contrast to *collusion, which requires the cooperation of two or more individuals. Fraud involving deceit by an organization's *directors or senior *management can be difficult to detect, yet it can have potentially disastrous consequences. The difference between fraud and *error originates in the intentions behind the actions.

Fraud has always been of concern to auditors, particularly during the development of modern auditing in the nineteenth and twentieth centuries. In 1843 the accounting writer B. F. Foster remarked that "no system of accounts is secure from the designs of the fraudulent" (quoted in Chambers, R. J., 1995, 72). The legacy of the importance of fraud in external auditing is evident in the *expectations gap—the continuing discrepancy between public and professional opinion on the extent to which external auditors are responsible for fraud detection.

Further reading: Apostolou et al. (2001); Genaldi (2002); Graham and Bedard (2003); Hillison et al. (1999); Makkhawi and Schick (2003); Shelton et al. (2001); Vanasco (1998)

Fraudulent Financial Reporting: 1987–1997 A report issued in 1999 by the *Committee of Sponsoring Organizations of the Treadway Commission (COSO). The full title of the report was *Fraudulent Financial Reporting: 1987–1997: An Analysis of U.S. Public Companies.* Thematically and chronologically, the report updated the *Treadway Commission Report* of 1987, and its executive summary stated its objectives as follows: "To identify instances of alleged fraudulent financial reporting... To examine certain key company and *management characteristics for a sample of these companies involved in instances of *financial statement fraud... [and to] provide a basis for recommendations to improve the corporate financial reporting environment." Among the report's findings was that *audit committees in corporations that had suffered fraud tended to be weaker than average in terms of independence and expertise.

Further reading: Beasley et al. (1999)

Web site: *www.coso.org*

free-market economy An economy dominated by private enterprise. In a free-market economy industrial output, the *prices of products and services, and the allocation of economic resources are determined by the unhindered interplay of the forces of supply and demand. In practice, a pure free-market economy is unlikely to exist today, as most nations have significant *public sector activity and *regulations over commerce and trade. A *mixed economy is currently the norm.

free port 1. A sea or air port that does not charge *customs duties on transactions conducted through it. 2. A sea or air port that is open to traders of all nationalities.

frequency A measure of the occurrence of an event or item. Frequency is normally expressed as the number of occurrences within a defined time period.

frequency distribution An analysis of the number of times an item appears in a *population of data. See *normal distribution.

fringe benefit An item of *compensation, other than *money, paid to an employee of an organization. Sometimes referred to simply as benefits, common fringe benefits include (i) the use of a motor vehicle, (ii) health care insurance, and (iii) travel insurance.

front office The trading (as opposed to administrative) functions of a *brokerage operation that buys and sells *securities, *commodities, and *currencies. Compare *back office.

functional currency A *currency used in the primary location of an individual or organization, which is normally adopted for *financial reporting purposes. For example, a *multinational corporation based in the United States would usually adopt the U.S. dollar as its functional currency.

fund An amount of *money set aside for specific operational or *investment purposes. Examples of funds include *pension funds, *sinking funds, and *petty cash funds.

funding The providing of *capital to invest in economic activity. In this sense, funding is synonymous with *finance (definitions 2 and 3).

fungibles Items that can be interchanged without any loss in *value. Examples of fungibles include bank notes and identical units of a *commodity.

furniture and fittings A category of *property, plant, and equipment that consists of *fixed assets found typically in administrative offices.

futures contract A *contract to buy or sell a defined quantity of a *commodity, *currency, or *security at a specified date at a specified *price. Unlike an *option, a futures contract involves a firm commitment to buy or sell in accordance with the terms of the contract.

future value (FV) The quantifiable amount to which a sum of *money will grow if invested at a defined *interest rate.

G

gain **1.** An increase in *value. Gains arising on the *appreciation of the value of an *asset may be *realized or *unrealized. **2.** An alternative term for *income (definition 2).

galloping inflation An archaic term for *hyperinflation.

game theory The systematic analysis in competitive conditions of strategies for the optimal selection of alternative courses of action. In game theory, unlike *decision theory, the outcomes of an individual's decisions depend on the actions of other participants. An important assumption underpinning game theory is that participants act rationally in self-interest. Very often, as in *zero-sum games, the participants have conflicting interests: in other cases (so-called "cooperation games"), collusion and cooperation between partici-pants is possible. See also *prisoner's dilemma.
  Further reading: Chau (1996a, 1996b)

Gaming Auditorium The newsletter of the Gaming Audit Group of the *Institute of Internal Auditors. Published quarterly, the newsletter is available online. Its Web page describes its coverage of internal auditing and related issues in the context of "casinos, lotteries, racetracks, other gaming enterpris-es, and government regulatory commissions or agencies."
  Web link: *www.theiia.org/ecm/newsletters.cfm?doc_id=743*

Gantt chart A graphical portrayal of a project or activity that shows the com-parative distribution of operations and responsibilities over time. Gantt charts typically display activities through the plotting of horizontal bands across a time scale.

gearing A British term for *leverage.

General Accounting Office (GAO) The auditing, evaluation, and inves-tigative arm of the U.S. Congress. The GAO was founded in 1921, and its Web site states that it "exists to support the Congress in meeting its Constitutional responsibilities and to help improve the performance and ensure the account-ability of the federal government for the American people." It also states that the GAO "examines the use of public funds, evaluates federal programs and activities, and provides analyses, options, recommendations, and other assistance to help the Congress make effective oversight, policy, and funding decisions." Headquartered in Washington, DC, the GAO issues *Government Auditing Standards*—popularly known as the *Yellow Book*. Many of the GAO's audit reports are available online from its Web site.

Web site: *www.gao.gov*

General Agreement on Tariffs and Trade (GATT) The forerunner to the *World Trade Organization. Established in 1948, GATT's objectives included support for free trade, with emphasis on the reduction or abolition of *tariffs and other *protectionist mechanisms. In 1995 GATT was replaced by the *World Trade Organization.

general fund **1.** A *fund characterized by the setting aside of *assets and * liabilities without a specific or dedicated purpose. The term is frequently used in the context of *public sector and *not-for-profit organizations. Contrast *sinking fund. **2.** An investment *fund with holdings in a range of corporate sectors.

general ledger (GL) A series of *accounts used as the foundation for preparation of *financial statements. The general ledger contains accounts for *assets, *liabilities, *equity, *revenue, and *expenditure, and the accounts are traditionally analyzed into a *trial balance en route to the preparation of financial statements. Some accounting transactions may be recorded in *subsidiary ledgers prior to their transfer to a general ledger account.

Generally Accepted Accounting Principles (GAAP) Rules, guidance, and concepts for accounting practices and the content of *financial statements. GAAP covers the *recognition, *measurement, *reporting, and *disclosure of accounting items, and it is derived from several sources: *financial reporting standards (or *accounting standards), *legislation, custom, industry-specific conventions, and the pronouncements of authoritative professional and academic bodies. The importance of each of these elements varies from country to country. For example, in continental Europe legislation has tended to be the main source of GAAP. In the United States, in contrast, legislation has tended to play a less important role: U.S. GAAP derives from the *Statements of Financial Accounting Standards* of the *Financial Accounting Standards Board, and the pronouncements and interpretations of professional bodies like the *American Institute of Certified Public Accountants, as well as from law, industry practice, and academic literature. The *harmonization of international GAAP started to gather significant momentum around the turn of the twenty-first century. The countries of the European Union, for example, agreed to adopt the *International Financial Reporting Standards* of the *International Accounting Standards Board for listed corporation GAAP by 2005.

Generally Accepted Auditing Standards (GAAS) Rules and guidance for the conduct of external auditing. GAAS is derived from several sources, including *legislation, custom, industry-specific conventions, and academic and professional literature. However, the announcements of professional auditing organizations are by far the most important source of GAAS. In the United States the *Auditing Standards Board of the *American Institute of Certified Public Accountants issues *Statements on Auditing Standards*. On a global scale, the *International Auditing and Assurance Standards Board of the *International Federation of Accountants aims at international *harmonization of GAAS through its *International Standards on Auditing*.

Generally Accepted Government Auditing Standards (GAGAS) An alternative term for *Government Auditing Standards.

geometric progression A sequential pattern of numbers in which the ratio of each number to its predecessor is constant. An example is 2, 4, 8, 16, and so on. Contrast *arithmetic progression.

gift An item presented free of charge to an individual or organization. Gifts are generally intended to express gratitude or friendship, and are common in business circles in some cultures. However, a gift may become a *bribe if it is intended (or is perceived as intended) to gain undue influence over an individual or organization. Typical *internal controls over the giving of gifts in an organization include the following: (i) their recording on a timely basis, (ii) a statement of their purpose, (iii) prior authorization by a senior official, (iv) value thresholds to discourage the giving of expensive or extravagant gifts, and (v) the forbidding of certain types of gift.

Global Auditing Information Network (GAIN) A *benchmarking service for internal auditors. Established by the *Institute of Internal Auditors in 1993, GAIN offers its participants comparative data for topics like the costs and working practices of *internal audit functions. GAIN has dozens of industry-specific specialty groups, and it also offers networking services.
   Web link: *www.theiia.org/ecm/gain.cfm?doc_id=319*

global corporation An alternative term for *multinational corporation.

Global Corporate Governance Forum (GCGF) An international *corporate governance body. The GCGF was founded in 1999 by the *Organization for Economic Co-operation and Development and the *World Bank. Its sponsors include a number of countries, among which are India, the United Kingdom, and the United States, and it is based at the World Bank headquarters at Washington, DC. The GCGF's aims, as stated on its Web site, are to help countries "improve the standards of governance for their corporations, by fostering the spirit of enterprise and accountability, promoting fairness, transparency and responsibility." Its emphasis is on developing countries and nations in transition from *command economies to liberal democracies. The GCGF's activities range from technical assistance to institution building.

Web site: *www.gcgf.org*

globalization **1.** The increasing internationalization of economic, political, and cultural activity. Globalization is both characterized by and stimulated by improvements in telecommunications and travel infrastructures that facilitate the movement of people, capital, ideas, and consumer goods across geographical and political borders. Deregulation has also stimulated globalization, notably in the liberalization of China, India, and the former Soviet bloc. **2.** The emergence of transnational organizations: "Globalization does not mean merely the expansion of communications, contacts, and *trade around the globe. It means the transfer of social, economic, political, and juridical power to global organizations... in the form of *multinational corporations, international courts, or transnational legislatures" (Scruton, 2002, 127).

Further reading: Micklethwait and Wooldridge (2003); Norberg (2003); Scruton (2002)

Global Reporting Initiative (GRI)™ An international body dedicated to the promotion of *corporate social responsibility. The GRI is headquartered in Amsterdam, in the Netherlands, and its Web site describes it as a "multi-stakeholder process and independent institution whose mission is to develop and disseminate globally applicable *Sustainability Reporting Guidelines." The GRI was established in 1997 by the *Coalition for Environmentally Responsible Economies (CERES), but it became an independent organization in 2002. Its activities include the development of environmental and social performance indicators and reporting methodologies, and it works in collaboration with the environmental programs of the United Nations.

Web site: *www.globalreporting.org*

going concern The assumption used in accounting and auditing that an organization will continue to operate for the foreseeable future. The consequences of an organization under audit not being a going concern (e.g., mounting debts raise the prospect of *bankruptcy or the significant curtailment of activities) are normally reflected in changes to a range of assumptions concerning the *valuation of *assets and the *matching of revenues and costs across accounting periods.

golden handcuffs *Contractually agreed monetary *remuneration or other benefits designed to encourage an employee to continue to work at an organization. The term is an informal one, and it is normally used to refer to generous *compensation packages designed to discourage employees from being poached by rival organizations.

golden parachute A *contractually agreed element of *executive remuneration that guarantees an individual significant amounts of *money or other benefits in the event of a forced departure from an organization. Golden parachutes tend to be devised with the potential effects of corporate *acquisitions in mind.

golden share An investment held by a government in a *privatized organization that confers special rights. Governments choose to retain golden shares in denationalized corporations in order to keep a degree of strategic control over key decisions. For example, a golden share may give a government the right to block a *takeover bid or to regulate the *prices of services supplied by public utilities.

goods See *consumer goods.

goodwill **1.** In an *acquisition, the excess of the *consideration paid by an acquiring company over the *fair value of acquired *net assets. Contrast *negative goodwill. **2.** The value of an organization's reputation and *brands that allow it to generate *income. **3.** A favorable or friendly disposition toward an individual or organization.

Governance A British *corporate governance newsletter. Founded in 1992, the newsletter is published monthly in both hard copy and online formats. Its coverage is international.

Web site: *www.governance.co.uk*

Governmental Accounting Standards Advisory Council (GASAC) An advisory committee of the *Governmental Accounting Standards Board (GASB). The members of GASAC comprise a variety of constituencies with an interest in public sector accounting, and GASAC's responsibilities include the provision of technical advice, opinions on GASB projects, and aiding the *Financial Accounting Foundation to raise funds for GASB.

Web site: *www.gasb.org/gasac*

Governmental Accounting Standards Board (GASB) The U.S. *public sector accounting standards-setting organization. Based in Norwalk, CT, and established in 1984, the GASB's Web site states that its mission is "to establish and improve standards of state and local governmental accounting and financial reporting that will result in useful information for users of financial reports and guide and educate the public, including issuers, auditors, and users of those financial reports." The GASB is the public sector equivalent of the *Financial Accounting Standards Board (FASB), and it is overseen by the *Financial Accounting Foundation. It issues *accounting standards and also guidance on the standards, thereby acting as the custodian of public sector *Generally Accepted Accounting Principles in the United States. The GASB is advised by *Governmental Accounting Standards Advisory Council (GASAC), which has a larger set of responsibilities than the FASB's *Financial Accounting Standards Advisory Council.

Web site: *www.gasb.org*

Government Auditing Standards The U.S. *public sector auditing standards. Issued by the *General Accounting Office, and often referred to as either the *Yellow Book* or as Generally Accepted Government Auditing Standards, GAS address the audit of government and government-assisted operations and organizations. The Advisory Council on Government Auditing Standards keeps the standards under review, and invites public comment on any changes.

Web site: *www.gao.gov*

graduated tax An alternative term for *progressive tax.

graft **1.** Dishonest, *fraudulent, or improper behavior. See also *bribe and *corruption. **2.** Work, or hard work.

grand livre (GL) The French term for *general ledger. The expression *grand livre* literally means "large book," and by coincidence its abbreviation is identical to its equivalent English term.

grant Assistance given by a government to an individual or organization for a particular purpose. Grants can take several forms: (i) sums of *money, (ii) the giving or use of *assets, or (iii) the provision of training and technical assistance.

gratis Free of charge. The term derives from the Latin expression "out of kindness."

gray economy Economic activity that combines legitimate behavior with elements of the *underground economy.

great salad oil swindle, the The popular name of a landmark 1963 U.S. court case that featured the Allied Crude Vegetable Oil Refining Corporation. The corporation's sales were over $100 million annually, an enormous sum for the time, and the founder of the corporation was indicted (along with other individuals) on criminal charges of *fraud and deception. The indictment arose from the discovery that the corporation regularly inflated its *inventory records of vegetable oil. To deceive a representative from a bank, who visited the corporation weekly to perform inventory checks, Allied Crude undertook a series of tragi-comic irregularities. For example, it pumped oil from one oil tank to another as the visitor walked from tank to tank to undertake measurement tests, and in some cases it simply filled oil tanks with sea water. The case had indirect repercussions for external auditors: The swindle prompted external auditors to enhance their inventory verification tests, including the use of independent technical experts where appropriate.

Further reading: Miller (1965)

green audit An alternative term for *environmental audit.

Greenbury Report A British *corporate governance report of 1995. The report was prepared by a study group under Sir Richard Greenbury, and it addressed *executive remuneration. It was later revised as part of the *Hampel Report (or Combined Code) of 1998.

Further reading: *Greenbury Report* (1995)

gross **1.** An amount or *price stated before the deduction of *allowances, *discounts, *taxation, or other items. Contrast *net. **2.** An archaic term for twelve dozen (144).

Gross Domestic Product (GDP) The total *value of a country's economic output over a specified time period. Gross Domestic Product comprises the output of both goods and services, and *per capita GDP is often used as a ready measure of a country's economic prosperity.

gross income Total sales revenues less *costs of goods (or services) sold. Nonproduction *overheads (such as administration and distribution costs) are excluded from the calculation of gross income. Contrast *net income.

gross margin An alternative term for *gross income.

gross profit An alternative term for *gross income.

gross risk A *risk before the application of *risk management procedures. See also *inherent risk and *net risk.

gross sales Total sales before the deduction of *discounts, *allowances for bad debts, and *customer returns.

group financial statements The *consolidated accounts of a *business combination.

guarantee **1.** A *contractual undertaking to provide financial security for an *asset or *transaction.

    2. A *contractual assurance or promise that specified conditions will be fulfilled. For example, the manufacturer of a product can offer a guarantee that the product will be replaced within a specified time period should it be faulty. See also *warranty.

Guidance on Control *Corporate governance and *internal control guidelines issued in 1995 by the *Criteria for Control (CoCo) Board of the *Canadian Institute of Chartered Accountants. The report was the first of CoCo's *Control & Governance Series*.

    Further reading: CoCo (1995)

Guidelines for Internal Control Standards Guidance for *public sector auditing issued by the *International Organization of Supreme Audit Institutions. The guidelines were first published in 1992, and cover the role of *internal controls in government operations.

    Web link: *www.intosai.org/3_INTCOe.html*

hacker An individual who attempts to gain unauthorized access to computer networks or files. Hackers may be motivated by a desire to corrupt files or to commit another criminal act, or even by the enjoyment of a sense of danger in testing the security of a computerized system.

Hampel Report A British *corporate governance report of 1998. The full title of the report was *Final Report: the Committee of Corporate Governance*, and it was named for Sir Ronald Hampel, the chairperson of the committee that prepared it. The *Hampel Report* is popularly known as the *Combined Code*, as it combined and revised guidance given in two earlier British corporate governance initiatives: the *Cadbury Report* of 1992 and the *Greenbury Report* of 1995. The *Hampel Report* stressed that corporate prosperity may be hindered by excessive bureaucratic corporate governance procedures, and it did not impress all commentators. *Andrew Chambers, for example, commented that "getting to the heart of the... Hampel report is like groping one's way into a hay stack only to find it largely hollow at its core" (Chambers, 1998, 1). The *Combined Code* was revised in 2003 to incorporate aspects of the *Higgs Report* and the *Smith Report*.
Further reading: *Hampel Report* (1998)

hard asset An alternative term for *tangible asset.

hard copy A document printed from a computer system that records data or information.

hard currency A *currency that is widely accepted throughout the world and freely convertible in currency *markets. Contrast *soft currency.

harmonization The reduction or elimination of differences between things. In an auditing context, the term is frequently used to refer to the elimination of inconsistencies between different national systems of *Generally Accepted Auditing Standards and *Generally Accepted Accounting Principles.

hash total An addition of numbers for *internal control purposes in computer applications. Hash totals are typically used to identify potentially missing items in a data *population.

Head 2 Head A British newsletter aimed at *Chief Audit Executives. Published quarterly by the *Institute of Internal Auditors UK and Ireland, the newsletter is available in both print and online formats. It focuses mainly on developments in British internal auditing and *corporate governance.
Web link: *www.iia.org.uk/knowledgecentre/heads/head2headnewsletter.cfm*

Head of Audit An alternative term for *Chief Auditing Executive.

hedge An arrangement or transaction intended to protect against fluctuations in the *price of an asset. Hedges are typically used as *risk management measures against price movements of *currencies, *securities, and *commodities.

Higgs Report A British *corporate governance report of 2003. The report's formal title was *Review of the Role and Effectiveness of *Non-executive Directors* and it was named for Derek Higgs, the chairperson of the committee that prepared it. The *Higgs Report* appeared at the same time as the *Smith Report* on *audit committees. The *Higgs Report* added to guidance provided in the 1998 *Hampel Report*.
Further reading: *Higgs Report* (2003)

hire purchase (HP) A British term for *installment credit.

historical cost The unadjusted, original *cost of purchasing an *asset or an item of *inventory.

holding company A corporation that controls one or more *subsidiary organizations. Control can be effected through either a majority of *common stock voting rights or through dominance influence on a subsidiary's management or operating policies. Holding companies can be distinguished from *parent organizations on two grounds: (i) the term holding company is frequently used to designate the ultimate parent entity in an organization, rather than an intermediary company that both controls other entities and is itself controlled by another organziation; and (ii) the term holding company is often used for a parent organization that exists principally to hold shares (and also perhaps to employ senior management and to perform head office services), rather than to carry on regular trading or other operations. However, the terms holding company and parent organization are often used interchangeably.

holding cost The *cost of storing items of *inventory. Holding costs typically include (i) *warehouse expenses, (ii) *insurance costs, (iii) *shrinkage, and (iv) obsolescence.

holding gain An *appreciation in the *value of an asset over a period of time. The *gain may be *realized or *unrealized.

holding loss A *depreciation in the *value of an asset over a period of time. The *loss may be *realized or *unrealized.

holy cow See *sacred cow.

horizontal analysis The analysis of *financial statements over time. The technique typically looks at percentage changes in the amounts of specific items between *financial reporting periods. The reasonableness of changes over time is a common aspect of auditors' *analytical review procedures. Also known as trend analysis, horizontal analysis can be used to forecast future activity through the analysis of past trends. Compare *vertical analysis.

hostile takeover An *acquisition (definition 2) that is unwelcomed by an acquired organization.

housekeeping controls *Internal controls that relate to relatively minor, day-to-day activities in an organization. Although the areas addressed by housekeeping controls may not be of major significance (e.g., the formal *authorization of individual *petty cash vouchers), the quality of such controls is often considered to be indicative of the quality of an organization's wider internal control environment.

hurdle rate A *rate of return used as a threshold for accepting or rejecting proposed *investments. It represents a required rate of return. See *cost of capital.

hyperinflation An excessively high rate of *inflation. A common yardstick for defining hyperinflation is a rate of 100 percent or more. Hyperinflationary conditions can lead to a collapse of a country's monetary system, with recourse to systems of *barter or the use of foreign *currencies to undertake transactions. Contrast *deflation and *disinflation.

IASC Foundation® (IASCF®) The U.S. registered parent organization of the London-based *International Accounting Standards Board (IASB). Formed in 2001, the IASC foundation is an independent organization whose trustees oversee the IASB by appointing its members and raising funds for its activities. The acronym IASC reflects the foundation's origins in the IASB's predecessor, the *International Accounting Standards Committee.

Web site: *www.iasb.org.uk*

illiquid 1. Not readily convertible into *cash. Examples of illiquid items include *fixed assets and some types of *current asset, such as *inventory (which by convention is excluded from the *acid test ratio, a key liquidity measure). Contrast *liquid. **2.** Without sufficient cash resources to meet *current liabilities.

impairment 1. A *long-term *depreciation in the *value of an asset. **2.** *Long-term physical damage to an asset.

importation The purchase of goods and services from a seller based in a foreign country. Contrast *exportation.

imprest fund An alternative term for *petty cash.

income 1. An alternative term for *sale. **2.** The excess of *sales revenues over related costs in a specified time period. Also known as profit. See also *gross income, *net income, and *loss. **3.** An increase in the *net assets of an individual or organization. In this sense, income can be described as a *return to a *factor of production. **4.** A flow of *money, a promise of money, goods, or services arising from *investments, employee *compensation, or *dividends.

income statement An accounting summary of the results of operations of an organization or individual for a defined time period. An income statement establishes *net income from *revenues and *expenses, in line with the conventions of *double entry bookkeeping and *Generally Accepted Accounting Principles. Financial analysts place great emphasis on *net income and *earnings per share information included in income statements. The income statement and *balance sheet are the primary elements of *financial statements.

independence The absence of a relationship, obligation, or *conflict of interest that could comprise an auditor's *judgment. In external auditing, independence can be subverted (or can be perceived to be subverted) by many factors, including the following: (i) a financial interest in an *auditee's business or in an audited transaction; (ii) family or personal relationships with *auditees; (iii) excessive entertaining or hospitality by or with auditees; (iv) lavish *gifts to and from auditees; (v) restrictions on the scope of audit work; (vi) an auditor's overde-pendence on fees from one customer; and (possibly) (vii) the provision of lucra-tive *management advisory services. In addition to these aspects of independ-ence, most of which are manifestations of potential conflicts of interest, the concept is often discussed in terms of a state of mind, involving personal char-acter, ethics, and honesty. Therefore, while it has been suggested that auditing "requires a high level of technical knowledge, *integrity*, and interpersonal skills" (Beattie et al., 2001, 285, emphasis added), it has also been argued that independence "is an attitude of mind which goes deeper than any formal rules or standards" (Newman, 1964, 148). It is little wonder that Lee (1993, 100) refers to auditor independence as a "multi-dimensional concept."

Independence is considered to be essential for an objective, unbiased external *audit opinion: "It is primarily on the basis of its independence that the [external] audit derives its authority and its acceptance" (Flint, 1988, 29). Or, expressed more evocatively, "the auditor, like Caesar's wife, must be above suspicion" (Toffler and Reingold, 2003, 251).

Further reading: AICPA (1997); Caswell (1999); Mutchler et al. (2001); Stevenson (2002); Windsor and Ashkenasy (1995); Youkins (1983)

indirect cost **1.** Costs that are difficult to attribute to specific units of production. **2.** An alternative term for *fixed cost.

indirect taxation A tax that is not deducted from the income of an individual or organization. *Consumption and *sales taxes are examples of indirect taxation, and they are charged on goods and services. Indirect taxes bear a less obvious relation to an individual's ability to pay than is the case with *direct taxation. See also *regressive tax.

inflation A sustained increase in the general sales *prices of consumer goods. Inflation can be interpreted as a decrease in the value of *money. See also *deflation, *disinflation, and *hyperinflation.

informal economy An alternative term for the *underground economy.

information age A term denoting the importance of rapid telecommunications in the modern era. The information age derives from technological advances in broadcasting, communications, and computer software, and it is one of the driving forces of *globalization. The effects on society of advances in telecommunications has often been described as revolutionary. One example of the ramifications of the information age can be seen in the educational sector: Many universities now offer online degrees, whose entire delivery is handled via the *Internet and *e-mail. In such cases, it is possible for students scattered throughout the world to undertake a university's entire online degree course, without a need for a physical visit to the university.

information risk *Risks arising from incorrect, incomplete, or outdated information. Information risk can distort decision-making, subvert an organization's objectives, or result in misleading *audit evidence.

Information Systems Audit and Control Association® (ISACA) A U.S.-based international organization dedicated to information systems auditing and security. Established in 1969, ISACA is headquartered at Rolling Meadows, IL. Its activities include conferences, education, and publication of the *Information Systems Control Journal*. The association also administers the *Certified Information Systems Auditor and the Certified Information Security Manager qualifications. Another ISACA initiative is the *I.T. Governance Institute. In 2003 the ISACA had over 25,000 international members.

    Web site: *www.isaca.org*

Information Systems Control Journal A U.S. magazine, published bimonthly by the *Information Systems Audit and Control Association. Available in print and hard copy formats, the journal's Web site states that it aims to provide "professional development information to those spearheading IT governance and those involved with information systems audit, control and security."

    Web site: *www.isaca.org/jrnlhome.htm*

inherent risk The *risk that items in financial statements are *misstated. Inherent risk is considered alongside *control risk and *detection risk to be one of three components of external *audit risk (definition 1). The term is sometimes also used in the sense of *gross risk.

In Our Opinion A U.S. external auditing newsletter. Published quarterly by the Auditing Standards Team of the *American Institute of Certified Public Accountants (AICPA), the newsletter is available in hard copy format only. The AICPA Web site describes the newsletter as "designed to keep interested parties up-to-date on recent pronouncements, current projects, and new publications of the *Auditing Standards Board and the Accounting and Review Services Committee." The views expressed in the newsletter are not designed to be definitive in status, and do not necessarily reflect official AICPA policy.

    Web link: *www.aicpa.org/members/div/auditstd/opinion/pub.htm*

inside director A member of an organization's *board of directors who is also an employee of the organization.

insider dealing The illegal or improper use of secret or *price sensitive information to benefit from sales and purchases of a corporation's *securities.

insider trading An alternative term for *insider dealing.

insolvent Unable to settle liabilities and debts. See also *bankruptcy.

inspection A careful *examination. Inspection is central to the gathering and *evaluation of *audit evidence. See also *physical inspection.

installment One of a series of payments of sums of *money. Installment payments are frequently, but not necessarily, of equal amounts.

installment credit A *lease agreement in which a *lessee takes ownership of a leased *asset after a specified number of payments. Installment credit is a common means of financing the sale of *consumer goods.

Institut der Wirtschaftprüfer in Deutschland e.V. Germany's main professional accounting and external auditing organization. The *Wirtschaftprüfer is the German equivalent of the *Certified Public Accountant, but the *public accounting profession is less extensive in Germany than in the English-speaking world. The Institut was established in 1931, and it had approximately 10,000 members in 2003. This is a very small number in relation to the size of the German population and the power of the German economy. While membership of the Institut is voluntary, all external auditors must by law register with the country's Wirtschaftprüferkammer. The latter may be translated as "accountants' chambers."
Web site (German only): *www.idw.de*

Institute of Certified Public Accountants in Ireland An Irish professional accounting organization, often referred to under the shorter name of CPA Ireland. The institute had around 2,500 members in 2003; therefore, it is considerably smaller than the main Irish accounting and external auditing organization, the *Institute of Chartered Accountants in Ireland. CPA Ireland is headquartered in Dublin, and it publishes a quarterly magazine, the *CPA Journal of Accountancy*, available in print and (partially) online formats.
Web site: *www.cpaireland.ie*

Institute of Certified Public Accountants in Israel Israel's main professional accounting and external auditing organization. Established in 1948, soon after the creation of the modern Israeli state, the institute had approximately 9,000 members in 2003. The institute is headquartered in Tel Aviv, and it sets Israeli *auditing standards. The institute was also responsible until 1997 for setting Israeli *accounting standards, but in that year it relinquished those responsibilities to the newly established, independent Israeli Accounting Standards Board.

Web site (partially in English): *www.icpas.org.il*

Institute of Certified Public Accountants of Kenya (ICPAK) Kenya's main professional accounting and external auditing organization. Established in 1977 from pre-existing professional bodies dating back to the British colonial period, the ICPAK adopted the U.S. terminology of *Certified Public Accountant rather than the United Kingdom's *chartered accountant designation. The ICPAK is headquartered in Nairobi, and it had approximately 2,300 members in 2003. It is Kenya's leading professional organization for both accounting and external auditing.

Web site: *www.icpak.com*

Institute of Chartered Accountants in Australia (ICAA) An Australian professional accounting and external auditing organization. The ICAA differs from the other large accounting organization in Australia, *CPA Australia, by having a larger proportion of its members in public practice and external auditing. However, there is much overlap between the two organizations, and a merger between the two has often been discussed. The ICAA was established in 1928 by royal charter, from the merger of pre-existing accounting bodies. It is based on the British models of *chartered accountants' institutes, and its membership in 2003 was approximately 38,000.

Web site: *www.icaa.org.au*

Institute of Chartered Accountants in England and Wales (ICAEW) Britain's main professional accounting and external auditing organization. The ICAEW was incorporated by royal charter in 1880 by combining pre-existing regional English accounting institutes. Headquartered in London, it is the United Kingdom's most important *Recognised Qualifying Body for external auditors. Its publications include a number of journals, magazines, and newsletters, such as *Accountancy*, *Accounting and Business Research*, *Audit News*, *Internal Control*, and *True and Fair*. Its Web site describes its main activities as the "education and training of students, continuing professional development for members, maintenance of professional and ethical standards, cutting-edge work on technical accounting issues, and provision of advice and services to members."

ICAEW members are known as *chartered accountants and are allowed the designatory letters ACA or FCA. The latter represents fellowship and is determined by seniority. ICAEW membership in 2003 was approximately

135,000, including 9,000 students and 15,000 members based outside the United Kingdom.

Further reading: Habgood (1994); Matthews et al. (1998)

Web site: *www.icaew.co.uk*

Institute of Chartered Accountants in Ireland (ICAI) Ireland's main professional accounting and external auditing organization. Established by royal charter in 1888 during the British colonial period, the ICAI is Ireland's main professional body for accounting and external auditing. It is headquartered in Dublin, and its Web site describes its mission as follows: To "serve the public and promote chartered accountancy through achieving and maintaining the highest standards in the professional and technical competence of its members, in their education and training, and in their professional conduct." The ICAI publishes the magazine *Accountancy Ireland*, and in 2003 it had approximately 13,000 members.

Web site: *www.icai.ie*

Institute of Chartered Accountants of Bangladesh (ICAB) Bangladesh's main professional accounting and external auditing organization. Established in 1973, the ICAB (as in other South Asian countries) has roots in predecessor organizations that date from the British colonial period. The ICAB is headquartered in Dhaka, and although it has a modest membership of around 700, it is Bangladesh's leading professional organization for accounting and external auditing. (The members of another Bangladeshi accounting organization—the Institute of Cost and Works Accountants of Bangladesh—work mostly as management accountants in industry.)

Web site: *www.icab-bd.com*

Institute of Chartered Accountants of India (ICAI) India's leading professional organization for accounting and external auditing. Headquartered in New Delhi, and established in 1949 from predecessor bodies founded during the British colonial period, the Indian *chartered accountants' institute is large, sophisticated, and influential. Through its committee structures, the ICAI issues English-language Indian *accounting standards and *auditing standards, details of which are available from the ICAI Web site. Also available from the ICAI Web site are interpretations and clarifications of Indian accounting standards.

The ICAI had approximately 100,000 members in 2003, including many members based outside India (e.g., among Indian expatriate communities in Africa and the Mid East). The ICAI is one of two large Indian accounting organizations—the other is the Calcutta-based Institute of Cost and Works

Accountants of India, whose members work mostly as management accountants in industry.

Web site: *www.icai.org*

Institute of Chartered Accountants of New Zealand (ICANZ) New
Zealand's main professional accounting and external auditing organization.
The ICANZ adopted its current name in 1996, before which it was known as
the New Zealand Society of Accountants. Although New Zealand is a small
country, the ICANZ's membership in 2003 was relatively large (at approximately 27,000) with many of its members working outside New Zealand. The
ICANZ is based in Wellington, and it is internationally renowned for the
sophistication of its activities, that range from issuing *accounting standards
and *auditing standards to publication of the monthly *Chartered Accountants
Journal.*

Web site: *www.icanz.co.nz*

Institute of Chartered Accountants of Nigeria (ICAN) Nigeria's main
professional accounting and external auditing organization. Established in
1965 from predecessor bodies of the British colonial period, the ICAN is headquartered in Lagos. It has 12,000 members, and is Nigeria's leading professional organization for accounting and external auditing.

Web site: *www.ican.org.ng*

Institute of Chartered Accountants of Pakistan (ICAP) Pakistan's
main professional accounting and external auditing organization. Established
in 1961 from predecessor bodies founded during the British colonial period, the
ICAP is headquartered in Karachi. Although it has a relatively modest membership of around 3,000, the ICAP is Pakistan's leading professional organization for accounting and external auditing. (The members of another Pakistani
accounting organization, the Institute of Cost and Works Accountants of
Pakistan, work mostly as management accountants in industry.)

Web site: *www.icap.org.pk*

Institute of Chartered Accountants of Scotland™ **(ICAS**™**)** A British
professional accounting and external auditing organization. The ICAS was
established by royal charter in 1854. Although much smaller than the *Institute
of Chartered Accountants in England and Wales (ICAEW), its English counterpart, the Scottish ICAS benefits from significant prestige and authority as the
world's oldest organization of its type. The ICAS, headquartered in Edinburgh,
is a tenacious preserver of its independent status within the United Kingdom's
community of *chartered accountants. Unlike the ICAEW's designation of
ACA, Scottish chartered accountants bear the designatory letters CA. The

ICAS is one of the United Kingdom's five *Recognised Qualifying Bodies for external auditors, and it publishes the *CA Magazine and well-respected research monographs. It had a membership of around 15,000 in 2003.

Web site: *www.icas.org.uk*

Institute of Chartered Accountants of Sri Lanka (ICASL) Sri Lanka's main professional accounting and external auditing organization. Established in 1959 from predecessor bodies of the British colonial period, the ICASL is headquartered in Colombo. The ICASL has only around 2,000 members, but its influence is larger than this modest number would suggest. It is Sri Lanka's leading professional organization for accounting and external auditing, and it is the country's sole standards-setting authority for both *accounting standards and *auditing standards.

Web site: *www.icasrilanka.com*

Institute of Internal Auditors (IIA)® The world's leading organization for *internal auditing. Established in 1941 and headquartered in Altamonte Springs, FL, the IIA grew impressively in the twentieth century as it simultaneously encouraged and benefited from the growth of internal auditing. Its early years in the 1940s saw a stimulus for internal auditing in the form of the pressures of a war economy: Increasing government regulations and shortages of labor and *raw materials led to corporations' efforts to control their operations more efficiently. The IIA's activities include certification programs (including the *Certified Internal Auditor qualification), research activities, and conferences. It also has a vigorous publications program, covering practice guides, research monographs, and magazines and newsletters. The latter include *Auditwire, *CAE Bulletin, *CSA Sentinel, *Gaming Auditorium, and *Internal Auditor.

Although its certification program is well-respected, the IIA does not have monopolistic control over internal auditing, and many internal auditors operate outside its framework. However, the IIA has done much to professionalize the discipline, and many internal auditors who are not formal IIA members follow the spirit of the IIA's professional standards (O'Regan, 2001). The organization's motto is "Progress Through Sharing," and in 2003 its international membership stood at approximately 80,000.

The growing complexity of organizations, the implications of *globalization, and the ever-increasing profile of internal auditing in *corporate governance prompted the IIA to establish a new Professional Practices Framework (PPF) in 1999. The PPF consists of Standards and Ethics; Practice Advisories; and Development & Practice Aids. Standards and Ethics are mandatory for IIA members, and they include the IIA's *Code of Ethics* and its *Standards for the Professional Practice of Internal Auditing*. Practice Advisories are strongly recommended to IIA members, but are not mandatory, while Development & Practice Aids offer practical guidance and research findings.

Further reading: Brink (1977); Flesher (1991); Flesher and McIntosh (2002); IIA (1999); O'Regan (2001)

Web site: *www.theiia.org*

Institute of Internal Auditors UK and Ireland The United Kingdom's national institute of the *Institute of Internal Auditors (IIA). Established in 1948 as the first IIA chapter outside of North America, the IIA UK became a national institute in 1979. The IIA UK is now an influential body for internal auditing and *corporate governance in the United Kingdom and the Republic of Ireland. It publishes briefing notes on internal auditing topics, and the monthly magazine *Internal Auditing & Business Risk*. It also maintains a UK-specific certification program, separately from the IIA's main *Certified Internal Auditor program.

Web site: *www.iia.org.uk*

Institute of Management Accountants™ (IMA) A U.S. professional accounting organization. Established in 1919 (and originally called the National Association of Cost Accountants), the IMA focuses on *management accounting and financial management. It has little overlap with the external auditing and *public accounting focus of the *American Institute of Certified Public Accountants. The IMA is headquartered in Montvale, NJ, and its activities include certification programs, educational events, research programs, and publications, such as the monthly magazine *Strategic Finance* and the academically-oriented *Management Accounting Quarterly*. The IMA also issues *Statements on Management Accounting*, ethical standards for members, and "comment letters" that set out the official IMA positions on accounting developments. In 2003 the IMA had approximately 75,000 members.

Web site: *www.imanet.org*

Institute of Social and Ethical Accountability See *AccountAbility.

institutional investor An organization that invests on a large scale in *securities, *bonds, and other assets. Institutional investors are often *pension funds or *insurance companies and (owing to the size of their investments and the volume of transactions they can generate) they tend to enjoy significant clout in the corporate investment environment. In recent years institutional investors have altered the nature of *corporate governance by an increasing willingness to assert their power over the *boards of directors of corporations. This has reversed the trend of the dispersion of stockholder power following the end of World War II—as stockholding became more diffuse, it became increasingly difficult for investors to combine forces to challenge the directors of corporations. The large institutional investors have reversed this trend to a degree, with proactive involvement in the governance of the organizations in which they have invested. Major institutional investors in the United States include the *California Public Employees' Retirement System (CalPERS) and the *Teachers Insurance and Annuity Association College Retirement Equities Fund (TIAA-CREF), both of which have addressed corporate governance policies in recent years.

***Instituto dos Auditores Independentes do Brasil* (IBRACON)** Brazil's main accounting and external auditing organization. The acronym IBRACON is based on the organization's previous name *Instituto Brasiliero do Contadores*—the name of the organization changed in 2001, but the well-known acronym was retained. IBRACON was established in 1971 from pre-existing accounting and external auditing organizations. It issues Brazil's *accounting standards and *auditing standards. The former are based on IAS but with some modifications.

Web site (Portuguese only): *www.ibracon.com.br*

insurance policy A *contractual arrangement to compensate for potential future illness or loss of life, or for the loss or *impairment of *assets. Insurance is a means of *risk management, and insurance cover is normally arranged through the regular payment of a *premium.

intangible asset A *long-term *asset that does not possess physical substance. Examples include *brands, *goodwill, and *intellectual capital. The recognition of some intangible assets is carefully controlled by most systems of *Generally Accepted Accounting Principles.

intellectual capital Technical knowledge and expertise held by individuals or an organization. Intellectual capital can be a source of competitive advantage for a business *enterprise. See also *know-how.

Further reading: Mouritsan (2003); Usoff et al. (2002)

inter alia A Latin expression meaning "among other things." An example of its use is as follows: "The framework for corporate governance includes, *inter alia*, legislation, custom, stakeholder pressure, and public opinion." The term inter alia refers to inanimate things. When referring to people, the phrase *inter alios* ("among other people") should be used. Use of the expression *inter alia* is surprisingly common in accounting and auditing literature, especially in the United Kingdom, for reasons which are unclear. However, it is a cliché with an antiquated and even rather pompous tone, and it is best avoided in favor of its English equivalent.

intercompany transaction A *transaction made between two members of a *business combination. Intercompany transactions like *sales and *loans are normally eliminated under *consolidation accounting.

interest **1.** The cost of borrowing *money, or the *reward for lending money. Interest is calculated by applying an *interest rate to a sum of money. See also *compound interest, *simple interest, *Islamic finance, and *usury. **2.** A legal right or a share in an asset or corporation. See, for example, *minority interest. **3.** Curiosity, concern, or fascination (with something).

interest cover The extent to which an organization's *interest expenses are covered by its income before interest and taxation. The ratio is a measurement of an organization's *leverage, and it can indicate the vulnerability of an organization in meeting interest payment commitments when faced by changes in either *interest rates or income levels.

interest coverage ratio An alternative term for *interest cover.

interest rate A percentage rate applied to a sum of *money to calculate *interest charges.

interest rate risk The potential adverse consequences of unexpected changes in *interest rates.

interim audit A *preliminary or intermediate audit performed in advance of a main audit. In external auditing, interim audits often focus on *audit planning and *compliance testing, and are intended to reduce the burden of work during the subsequent, final audit.

internal audit A branch of auditing developed in the twentieth century as a means of monitoring an organization's *risks, *internal controls, procedures, and *management accounting. As *corporations and *public sector organizations became increasingly complex in the twentieth century, and "as direct, personal contacts of managers with the respective operational areas for which they were responsible became more restricted, a greater need developed for the kind of managerial service provided by internal auditors" (Brink, 1977, 9).

The remit of internal auditing extends beyond the audit of financial statements traditionally associated with external auditing. In 1945, *Robert B Milne, one of the founding fathers of the IIA, wrote that although internal auditing's "roots are in accountancy, its key purpose lies in the area of management control" (quoted in Flescher, 1991, ix). Among other things, internal auditing encompasses (i) *fraud detection, (ii) the safeguarding of assets,

(iii) legal and regulatory compliance, (iv) reviews of management accounting, (v) *internal control assessment, and (vi) *risk assessment. It covers both *compliance and *consulting reviews.

The *Institute of Internal Auditors is the main internal auditing institution, and it defines the discipline as follows: an "*independent, objective *assurance and *consulting activity designed to add value and improve an organization's operations. It helps an organization accomplish its objectives by bringing a systematic, disciplined approach to evaluate and improve the effectiveness of risk management, control, and governance processes" (*www.theiia.org*).

The evolution of internal auditing has been described in the following terms: "Internal auditing as practised in the *developed countries has passed through two dominant paradigms and is poised on the edge of a third. The first internal auditing paradigm focused on *observing and counting... [later] a new concept of the system of internal control... changed the internal audit paradigm from a focus on *reperformance* to a focus on *controls... a third paradigm for internal auditing is emerging, based on auditing the business process through a focus on *risk" (McNamee and Selim, 1998, 6, emphasis in original). Traditionally, internal auditors were described as the eyes and ears of an organization's management: They have recently been called the eyes and ears of the *audit committee (Hermanson and Rittenberg, 2001, 54). Compare *external audit.

Further reading: Bailey et al. (2003); Brink (1977); Flescher (1991); IIA (1999); Pickett (2003); Ramamoorti (2003); Ridley and Chambers (1998); Sawyer and Vinten (1996); Ziegenfuss (1994)

internal audit charter A document that sets out the purpose, authority, responsibilities, and scope of work of an *internal audit function (IAF). The charter is often considered to be an audit function's constitution, and its subject matter typically includes some or all of the following: (i) The IAF's reporting lines within an organization, (ii) the scope of the IAF's work, (iii) the IAF's rights of access to information, (iv) IAF budgetary information, and (v) a formal statement of the IAF's adherence to professional standards (principally the Professional Practices Framework of the *Institute of Internal Auditors).

internal audit function (IAF) The department within an organization responsible for internal auditing. The IAF is headed by a *Chief Auditing Executive.

internal auditing The process or action of undertaking an *internal audit. Although the gerund auditing places greater emphasis on action than the simple noun audit, the two terms are largely interchangeable.

Internal Auditing & Business Risk A British internal auditing magazine. Published monthly by the *Institute of Internal Auditors UK and Ireland, the magazine is available in print and online formats. It focuses on professional developments and news in internal auditing and *corporate governance, with particular focus on the United Kingdom and the European Union.

Web link: *www.iia.org.uk/knowledgecentre/iiamagazine*

Internal Auditing Standards Board (IASB) The standards-setting committee of the *Institute of Internal Auditors (IIA). Established under its current name in 1990, it replaced the IIA's Professional Standards Committee. The IASB issues *Standards for the Professional Practice of Internal Auditing*, which are mandatory for IIA members. Before revising or issuing standards, the IASB invites discussion of exposure drafts. The standards and exposure drafts are available from the IIA Web site.

Web link: *www.theiia.org/ecm/guidance.cfm?doc_id=1499*

internal auditor An individual who performs an *internal audit. The primary professional organization for this auditing specialism is the *Institute of Internal Auditors.

Internal Auditor A U.S. internal auditing magazine. Founded in 1944, the magazine is published bimonthly by the *Institute of Internal Auditors. Available in both print and online formats, it concentrates on news and developments in internal auditing, *corporate governance, and *risk management. The magazine's notes state that its emphasis is on "sharing timely, helpful information... for professionals who want to keep pace with the diverse, dynamic field of internal auditing." Its coverage is international.

Web link: *www.theiia.org/ecm/magazine.cfm?doc_id=540*

Internal Auditors World Wide Web (IAWWW) An online resource center for internal auditing. The Web site of the IAWWW contains links to publications, Internet-based resources, and careers information.

Web site: *www.bitwise.net/iawww*

internal audit shop An alternative term for *internal audit function.

internal control A physical or procedural mechanism that monitors and reduces *risk in an organization's financial and operational activities. In its 1992 report **Internal Control—Integrated Framework,** the *Committee of Sponsoring Organizations of the Treadway Commission (COSO) offered an influential definition of internal control as "a process, effected by an entity's board of directors, management and other personnel, designed to provide reasonable assurance regarding the achievement of an organization's objectives." The objectives of internal control were analyzed by COSO into three categories: (i) the *effectiveness and *efficiency of operations, (ii) the reliability of *financial reporting, and

(iii) *compliance with applicable laws and regulations. The safeguarding of *assets is often identified in corporate governance literature as a separate internal control objective, but it is included in category (i) under the COSO framework.

The existence of a satisfactory system of internal control is one of the *postulates of auditing elaborated by *Robert Khun Mautz and Hussein A. Sharaf. Although many of the concepts of internal control appear to be relatively recent ones, the underlying philosophies of internal control (like the safeguarding of assets and the effectiveness of operations) have a long history. The concept of internal control has even been analyzed in the context of the ancient Jerusalem Temple from the ninth century BCE to the first century CE (Fonfeder et al., 2003).

See also *control risk, *detective control, and *preventative control.

Further reading: Chambers, A. (2002); COSO (1992)

Internal Control—Integrated Framework A landmark report issued in 1992 by the *Committee of Sponsoring Organizations of the Treadway Commission (COSO). Commonly known as the *COSO Report*, it sets out (in its own words) "a standard against which businesses and other entities... can assess their control systems and determine how to improve them." The COSO model portrays *internal control as a process effected by an entity's senior management to provide reasonable *assurance on the achievement of objectives in three areas: (i) the *effectiveness and *efficiency of operations, (ii) the reliability of *financial reporting, and (iii) *compliance with applicable laws and regulations. The report also states that effective internal control consists of five interrelated components: (i) the control environment, (ii) *risk assessment, (iii) control activities, (iv) information and communication, and (v) *monitoring. The COSO control model continues to exert immense influence on internal auditing and *corporate governance around the world. An executive summary of the report is available from the COSO Web site.

Further reading: Applegate and Wills (1999); COSO (1992); Root (1998)

Web link: *www.coso.org*

Internal Control Newsletter A British auditing and *corporate governance newsletter. Edited by *Andrew Chambers for the *Institute of Chartered Accountants in England and Wales, the newsletter is published in ten issues a year by Croner.CCH Group in London. It is available in print format only, and its coverage relates mainly to the United Kingdom.

Web link: *www.management-audit.com/internal-control-newsletter*

internal rate of return (IRR) The *rate of return on an investment derived by comparing the *net present value of future, incremental cash flows with the initial investment. Under IIR analysis, the IIR is used as a *hurdle rate, and

an investment is normally accepted only when its IRR exceeds an organization's *cost of capital.

Internal Revenue Service (IRS)   In the United States, a federal government agency responsible for administering and collecting most forms of *taxation.

International Accountant   A British professional accounting magazine.
Published quarterly by the *Association of International Accountants (AIA),
the magazine is available in printed format, with a limited amount of online
material. Its Web page states that it is "designed to convey news of accountancy innovations and developments," and it has strong international coverage
that reflects the AIA's international character.
   Web link: *www.aia.org.uk*

International Accounting Bulletin   A British accounting newsletter.
Published 20 times annually by Lafferty Publications, it is available in both
print and online formats. The newsletter's Web page claims that it is "the only
industry newsletter to focus exclusively on the activities, performance and
strategies of the world's largest accounting firms." The newsletter's focus,
therefore, is on international accounting and external auditing, and each issue
has a country survey that analyzes the activities of the major accounting firms.
   Web link: *www.lafferty.com/newsletter/newsletter_02_publication.asp?PubID
=IAB*

International Accounting Standards **(IAS™)**   *Accounting standards
issued by the now defunct *International Accounting Standards Committee
(IASC). The intention behind IAS has been to promote global harmonization of
accounting and financial reporting. The adoption of IAS around the world has
to date been mixed, although some developing nations without preexisting
accounting standards (such as Malaysia and Nigeria) have adopted IAS with
little modification. A major coup for IAS was their endorsement in 2000 by the
*International Organization of Securities Commissions. The *International
Accounting Standards Board, the IASC's successor, adopted IAS at the time of
its creation in 2001 as part of its *International Financial Reporting Standards
framework. The IASB is gradually withdrawing IAS as they are superseded by
its new and revised standards.
   Web site: *www.iasb.org.uk*
   Further reading: Nobes and Parker (2002)

International Accounting Standards Board (IASB®)   The international
accounting standards-setting organization. In 2001, the IASB replaced its

predecessor, the *International Accounting Standards Committee. The IASB is based in London, and its Web site states that its main aim is to develop "a single set of high quality, understandable and enforceable global accounting standards." In its promotion of international accounting and financial reporting convergence, the IASB adopted the existing *International Accounting Standards* of its predecessor into its own framework of *International Financial Reporting Standards*. A major coup in the global accounting harmonization process has been the European Union's decision to adopt the IASB standards for listed corporations by 2005. The parent body of the IASB is the *IASC Foundation.

Web site: *www.iasb.org.uk*

International Accounting Standards Committee (IASC) The predecessor of the *International Accounting Standards Board (IASB). Established in 1973, the IASC's founder members were representatives of the accounting professions of Australia, Canada, France, Germany, Japan, Mexico, the Netherlands, the United Kingdom (and Ireland), and the United States. The IASC issued *International Accounting Standards* (IAS) to encourage standardization and *harmonization of financial reporting throughout the world, but its success was limited. The preponderance of English-speaking members at the higher echelons of the organization made some countries' accounting standards-setters reluctant to embrace the IASC's harmonization drives. To many, IAS were too close to U.S. or British practices. As one commentator put it: "[I]t is in continental Europe and Japan that there has been the greatest ambivalence towards the IASC. To some extent the IASC [has been] seen as a Trojan horse which conceals the Anglo-Saxon accounting enemy inside a more respectable international façade. The horse is wheeled into the heart of Europe and then its contents subtly contribute to the undermining of traditional continental accounting" (Nobes and Parker, 2002, 82). Reform of the IASC led to its dissolution, and its replacement by the more geographically representative *IASC Foundation and its standards-setting body, the IASB.

Further reading: Carsberg (1996); Nobes and Parker (2002)

International Association for Accounting Education and Research (IAAER) An international, scholarly accounting organization. The IAAER was founded in 1984, and its Web site states its mission as follows: To "promote excellence in accounting education and research on a worldwide basis and to maximize the contribution of accounting academics to the development and maintenance of high quality, globally recognized standards of accounting practice." Institutional members of the IAAER include the *American Accounting Association, the *British Accounting Association, and the *Canadian Academic

Accounting Association. Its activities focus on the promotion of accounting research and teaching, and its publications include the **Journal of International Financial Management and Accounting* and a newsletter, the *Cosmos Accounting Chronicle*.

Web site: *www.iaaer.org*

International Association of Airline Internal Auditors (IAAIA) An internal auditing specialty organization. The IAAIA is a *not-for-profit association for internal auditors in the airline industry, and its Web site describes the following as among its objectives: To "help develop and maintain standards of the practice of internal audit in the airline industry...to promote the study of and research into the internal audit management and practice in the airline industry and to organize conferences, seminars and other activities conducive to these aims." As its name suggests, the IAAIA is international in scope, and it held its first conference in London in 1991.

Web site: *www.iaaia.com*

International Auditing and Assurance Standards Board (IAASB) A committee of the *International Federation of Accountants. Founded in 2002 as the successor to the *International Auditing Practices Committee, the IAASB issues *International Auditing* and *International Auditing Practice Statements*, the latter offering practical guidance on the former.

Web site: *www.ifac.org/IAASB*

International Auditing Practices Committee (IAPC) The predecessor of the *International Auditing and Assurance Standards Board of the *International Federation of Accountants.

***International Auditing Practice Statements* (IAPS)** External auditing guidance issued by the *International Auditing and Assurance Standards Board of the *International Federation of Accountants (IFAC). The IAPS provide practical guidance on the implementation of *International Standards on Auditing* (ISA), and cover specific industry and audit issues, like auditing in the context of banks and small enterprises. The IAPS are available online from the IFAC Web site.

Web link: *www.ifac.org/Guidance/index*

International Corporate Governance Network (ICGN) An organization dedicated to the global promotion of *corporate governance. Founded in 1995, and with its administrative base in London, the ICGN is a forum for auditors, bankers, corporate governance experts, *institutional investors, and others to exchange views and to reach common positions on corporate governance issues.

The ICGN publishes reports and public statements on matters ranging from *financial reporting standards to *executive remuneration to the responsibilities of institutional investors.

Web site: *www.icgn.org*

International Federation of Accountants (IFAC) An international accounting and external auditing organization. The IFAC was established in 1977 and is headquartered in New York. The IFAC Web site states that its objective is to "develop the [accounting] profession and *harmonize its standards worldwide to enable accountants to provide services of consistently high quality in the public interest." It also states that membership "is open to accountancy organizations recognized by law or general consensus within their countries as substantial national organizations in good standing." In 2003 the IFAC had over 150 member bodies. The organization's activities include the issuing of international guidance on auditing, education, *ethics, *financial accounting, *management accounting, information technology, and public sector accounting. It is a key member of the *International Forum on Accountancy Development.

The IFAC's auditing guidance includes *International Standards on Auditing* and *International Auditing Practice Statements*, issued by the IFAC's *International Auditing and Assurance Standards Board. The organization has a news subscription service, details of which are available from its Web site. The IFAC itself does not issue *International Financial Reporting Standards*, which are the responsibility of the *International Accounting Standards Board (IASB), but it supports the IASB's role in the *harmonization of international financial reporting. The IFAC's predecessor body was the International Coordination Committee for the Accountancy Profession (ICCAP), founded in 1972.

Web site: *www.ifac.org*

International Financial Reporting Standards (IFRS™) *Financial reporting standards issued by the *International Accounting Standards Board (IASB). The IFRS are intended to encourage global convergence of financial reporting practices. The IASB accepted the *International Accounting Standards* of its predecessor body, and is gradually revising and superseding them within its IFRS framework. The first IFRS, titled *First-time Adoption of International Financial Reporting Standards*, was issued in 2003. It covered ways of making a transition from local GAAP to IFRS. The name change from *International Accounting Standards* to *International Financial Reporting Standards* reflects the fact that the latter explicitly cover more than merely accounting matters— they touch on all aspects of financial reporting, including directors' reports.

Web site: *www.iasb.org.uk*

International Forum on Accountancy Development (IFAD) An international accounting group. Established following the devastating effects of the financial crises in Southeast Asia and the Pacific Rim in the late 1990s, the IFAD is a forum for a range of organizations that include the *Big Four accounting firms, the *International Federation of Accountants, the *International Organization of Securities Commissions, the *Organization for Economic Co-operation and Development, and the *World Bank. It first met in 1999. Among the IFAD's objectives listed on its Web site are the promotion of "understanding by national governments of the value of transparent financial reporting, in accordance with sound corporate governance" and assistance to "harness funds and expertise to build accounting and auditing capacity in developing countries." Global *harmonization of financial reporting practices are of major interest to the IFAD, and its Web site gives country by country surveys of *Generally Accepted Accounting Principles.

Web site: *www.ifad.net*

International Journal of Auditing A British scholarly auditing journal. Established in 1997 and edited by *Andrew Chambers, the journal is currently published in three issues a year by Blackwell Publishing. (Previous volumes were published by John Wiley & Sons, Inc. and *Management Audit Ltd.) The journal is available in print and (from 2003) in online formats. Academic in tone, the journal covers a range of auditing topics. The journal's notes describe its primary aim as follows: To "communicate clearly to an international readership the results of original auditing research conducted in practice and in research institutions. Articles have an international appeal either due to the research topic transcending national frontiers, or due to the clear potential for readers to apply the results, perhaps with adaptation, to their local environments." As its title suggests, the journal's coverage is global.

Web site: *www.blackwellpublishing.com*

International Journal of Government Auditing An international journal for *public sector auditing. Published quarterly by the *International Organization of Supreme Audit Institutions (INTOSAI), the journal is available in online format. It focuses on *government accounting news and articles.

Web link: *www.intosai.org/2_IJGA_.html*

International Monetary Fund (IMF) A specialized agency of the United Nations. Headquartered at Washington, DC and founded at the 1944 Bretton Woods Conference, the IMF operates under the co-ordinating machinery of the United Nation's Economic and Social Council. Its activities are linked to those of the *World Bank. At its Web site, the IMF lists the following as among its objectives: To "promote international monetary cooperation, exchange stability, and orderly exchange arrangements; to foster economic growth and high levels of employment; and to provide temporary financial assistance to countries to help ease balance of payments [problems]." The IMF exercises surveillance over the exchange rate policies of its members (more than 180 nations) to encourage the effective operation of the international monetary system, and it also provides technical assistance in areas like fiscal and monetary policy. Its financial resources are obtained from member countries' subscriptions (known as "quotas"), which are based on a formula that reflects the economic strength of individual countries.

The IMF promotes improvements in *corporate governance and *financial reporting practices around the world. Its activities in this field include research, publications, hands-on advice, and participation in initiatives such as the *International Forum on Accountancy Development. The IMF Web site has a full listing of its extensive range of publications, many of which address issues in developing nations.

Web site: *www.imf.org*

International Organization for Standardization (ISO) The global body for international voluntary standardization. Headquartered in Geneva, Switzerland, ISO was founded in 1947. The short name ISO is the same for all languages, and is based on the Greek word isos, meaning equal. On its Web site, ISO states that it acts "as a bridging organization in which a consensus can be reached on solutions that meet both the requirements of business and the broader needs of society, such as the needs of stakeholder groups like consumers and users." Its activities focus on the issuing of international standards (ISO Standards) that encourage global conformity and the consistent treatment of matters ranging from technological aspects of manufacturing processes to information technology developments. ISO has issued in excess of 14,000 international standards. Two of the most well-known "families" of ISO standards are ISO 9000 and ISO 14000, which refer to *quality management and environmental management systems respectively.

Web site: *www.iso.org*

International Organization of Securities Commissions (IOSCO) The organization that represents the world's securities commissions and similar governmental regulatory bodies. Headquartered in Madrid, Spain, and founded in 1987, the IOSCO Web site states that the organization's objectives include the promotion of "high standards of regulation in order to maintain just, efficient and sound markets" and "effective surveillance of international securities transactions." The organization advocates the removal of barriers for international capital markets, and it supports the *harmonization of international accounting and external auditing practices. The IOSCO is a member of the Standards Advisory Council of the *International Accounting Standards Board, and in 2000 it officially endorsed *International Accounting Standards. It has also undertaken a review of the *International Federation of Accountants' *International Standards on Auditing, an endorsement of which it is also considering at the time of this writing. The organization also participates in the *International Forum on Accountancy Development.

Web site: *www.iosco.org*

International Organization of Supreme Audit Institutions (INTOSAI)

The international body for national *public sector auditing organizations. Based in Vienna, Austria, INTOSAI was founded in 1953. Its members numbered in excess of 170 in 2003. The INTOSAI Web site states that *Supreme Audit Organizations (SAI) "play a major role in auditing government accounts and operations and in promoting sound financial management and accountability in their governments." It also states that "governments depend on SAIs to help ensure public accountability... [and] INTOSAI supports its members in this task by providing opportunities to share information and experiences about the auditing and evaluation challenges facing them." The organization's activities include training, the international exchange of information, and the preparation of auditing guidelines. The latter cover *Guidelines for Internal Control Standards* (1992), *Guidelines on Best Practice for the Audit of Privatizations* (1998), and *Guidance for Planning and Conducting an Audit of Internal Controls on Public Debt* (2002). It also publishes the *International Journal of Government Auditing*. All these texts are available from the INTOSAI Web site. INTOSAI also organizes triennial congresses in which international bodies like the *World Bank participate.

Web site: *www.intosai.org*

International Standards on Auditing (ISA)

External auditing guidelines issued by the *International Auditing and Assurance Standards Board of the *International Federation of Accountants (IFAC). The IFAC Web site states that ISA are "intended for international acceptance" as part of the IFAC's mission to encourage international *harmonization of accounting practices. It also states that ISA "contain basic principles and essential procedures together with guidance in the form of explanatory and other material." Some countries have adopted ISA, while other countries have agreed to reconcile national auditing standards with ISA. The ISA are available online from the IFAC Web site. The IFAC also issues *International Auditing Practice Statements*, which are intended to assist in the practical implementation of ISA.

Web link: *www.ifac.org/Guidance/index*

Internet An series of interlinked international information networks that are available, via computer access, to the general public. The Internet permits *e-mail communication and the transfer of computer files. Compare *Intranet.

interperiod income tax allocation An alternative term for *temporary difference.

interpolation The estimation of an unknown, intermediate value by comparing mathematical relationships between surrounding known values. Interpolation is commonly used in *internal rate of return calculations. Compare *extrapolation.

Intranet An organization-specific information network created by using *Internet technology. Unlike the *Internet, an Intranet is made available only to members of a specific organization.

inventory 1. Supplies used and goods manufactured in *production processes. Inventory is normally categorized into (i) *raw materials, (ii) *work-in-process, and (iii) *finished goods. Under most systems of *Generally Accepted Accounting Principles, inventory is usually valued at the lower of *cost and either *market value or *net realizable value. **2.** An alternative term for *physical inventory.

investigation A formal enquiry, or the undertaking of research. Investigation is central to the gathering of *audit evidence, especially in the context of *fraud or other *irregularities. See also *forensic auditing.

investment The allocation of economic resources to activities, *assets, or *securities in the hope of obtaining a satisfactory *rate of return. See also *capital (definition 4) and *factors of production.

invisible asset An alternative term for *intangible asset.

invoice A document that formally records, *quantifies, and requests payment for the *sale of goods or services.

irregularity An inaccuracy, mistake, or occurrence outside normal patterns. An irregularity can be either intentional (as in a *fraud) or unintentional (as in an *error), but the term is perhaps loaded toward matters arising from intent. Two of the *postulates of auditing elaborated by *Robert Khun Mautz and Hussein A. Sharaf Mautz concern accounting irregularities: (i) *Financial statements and other information submitted for *verification are free from *collusive and other unusual irregularities and (ii) the existence of a satisfactory system of *internal control eliminates the *probability of irregularities.

Islamic banking A slightly archaic term for *Islamic finance. The term Islamic banking suggests that *Shari'a* finance concepts apply exclusively to banking institutions, while Islamic finance more accurately places the concept in a wider economic and social context.

Islamic finance Financial practices in accordance with Islamic *Shari'a* law. Among other things, the *Shari'a* forbids usury and the charging of *interest. *Shari'a* law is considered by Muslims to be divine and its principles therefore immutable, and its financial practices operate in their purest form in countries like Iran and Saudi Arabia. In some other Muslim-majority nations (like Malaysia and Pakistan) *Shari'a* law coexists with Western financial practices. For example, some Malaysian and Pakistani financial institutions charge interest, while others do not. The *Accounting and Auditing Organization for Islamic Financial Institutions has established auditing principles for Islamic finance.

itemization The preparation of a detailed list of specific items in a *data population.

IT Governance Institute® A U.S.-based resource center for information technology and *corporate governance. Established in 1998 by the *Information Systems Audit and Control Association, the Institute's Web site states that its main objective is "to assist enterprise leadership in ensuring long-term, sustainable enterprise success and increased stakeholder value by expanding awareness of the need for and benefits of effective IT governance." It also aims to offer "best practice guidance on the management of IT-related risks," and its activities include publications, conferences, and Web-based resources.
Web site: *www.itgovernance.org*

Iwata, Iwao (1905–1955) A Japanese accounting and auditing theorist. Known for his reformist agenda, Iwata (along with *Kiyoshi Kurosawa) was a major figure in Japan's establishment of U.S.-style corporate external auditing requirements following World War II. He played an important role in the establishment of the Japanese *Certified Public Accountant profession, which played a vital part in Japanese economic life in the period of post-war reconstruction when the country was setting down the roots of its economic "miracle." In his academic writings, Iwata drew attention to the importance of (indeed, the indispensability of) external auditing in encouraging reliable corporate *financial statements. Illness and his early death, in the view of some commentators, left some of his theories only partially elaborated.
Further reading: Morita (1994)

J

Japanese Institute of Certified Public Accountants (JICPA) Japan's main professional accounting and external auditing organization. Headquartered in Tokyo, the JICPA was established in 1949 during the period of U.S. occupation following World War II. JICPA membership is small, at only 13,000 in 2003, reflecting the recent implantation of the *public accounting tradition in Japan. However, given the status of the Japanese economy, the JICPA is an influential organization in global accounting: It was a founding member of the *International Accounting Standards Committee (IASC) in 1973, and a JICPA representative chaired the IASC from 1993 to 1995. The JICPA does not set * accounting standards, which are the responsibility of the Accounting Standards Board of Japan. Japan's *Generally Accepted Auditing Standards comprise *auditing standards set by the Business Accounting Deliberation Council, a public sector body, and related JICPA guidelines.

Web site (includes some English-language material): *www.jicpa.or.jp*

Jefferson Wells International A U.S.-based international consulting organization that specializes in internal auditing, accounting, tax, and related areas. Headquartered in Brookfield, WI, Jefferson Wells International was founded in 1995. Originally called AuditForce, it adopted its current name in 2000. Its activities include consulting, training, and project support. It also produces a newsletter titled *In Control*.

Web site: *www.jeffersonwells.com*

job 1. A customer *order to purchase goods or services. The term job often carries connotations of goods or services tailored to a customer's specific requirements. **2.** An employment position.

joint costs Costs incurred in a *manufacturing process prior to a point at which differentiated products can be identified. Joint costs must normally be allocated to the *joint products of a common manufacturing process.

joint products Goods of equal importance produced by a common *manufacturing process. Importance is often assessed in terms of sales *price. For example, leather and beef are considered to be joint products of the cattle industry. Compare *by-product.

joint venture An agreement made between two business enterprises to conduct an activity or operation. Joint venture arrangements are often adopted in high-*risk circumstances. They are also frequently adopted by *multinational corporations to assist in operating in countries with challenging legal, regulatory, or cultural environments

Further reading: Applegate (2001); Groot and Merchant (2000)

journal A manual or computerized register that records accounting *transactions prior to their posting into *general ledger accounts. Journal transaction totals (rather than individual transactions) tend to be posted to general ledger accounts. See also *subsidiary ledger.

journal entry **1.** A *transaction made in a *journal or *subsidiary ledger. **2.** The act of transferring the total of transactions in a *journal or *subsidiary ledger to a *general ledger account.

Journal of Accountancy A U.S. professional accounting magazine. Published monthly by the *American Institute of Certified Public Accountants, the magazine was founded in 1905. Available online, the magazine focuses on professional developments and news in accounting and external auditing, with particular emphasis on the United States.

Web link: *www.aicpa.org/pubs/jofa/joahome.htm*

Journal of Accounting and Economics An international, scholarly accounting journal. Established in 1979, the journal is published in six issues a year by Elsevier Science, in print and online formats. The journal's notes state that it "encourages the application of economic theory to the explanation of accounting phenomena": It covers mainly accounting matters, but auditing topics are also frequently addressed.

Web link: *www.elsevier.nl/inca/publications/store/5/0/5/5/5/6*

Journal of Accounting Literature A U.S. scholarly accounting journal. Established in 1982, the journal is published annually in print format only by the Fisher School of Accounting at the University of Florida. The journal's Web site describes its objective as follows: To "contribute to dissemination of knowledge through publication of (1) high quality state-of-the-art review articles, and (2) papers presented at University of Florida research conferences." The journal frequently reviews auditing-related books.

Web link: *www.cba.ufl.edu/fsoa/schoolinfo/jal.html*

Journal of Accounting Research A U.S. scholarly accounting journal. Established in 1963, the journal is published in five issues a year by the Institute of Professional Accounting at the University of Chicago, in partnership with Blackwell Publishers. It is available in print and online formats. The journal covers a range of scholarly auditing (largely external auditing) topics, in addition to wider accounting matters. The journal focuses on the United States, though there is some international coverage.

Journal Web site: *www-gsb.uchicago.edu/research/journals/jar*
Publisher's Web site: *www.blackwellpublishing.com*

Journal of International Financial Management and Accounting
An international scholarly accounting journal. Established in 1990, the journal is published in three issues a year by Blackwell Publishers on behalf of the *International Association for Accounting Education and Research. It is available in both print and online formats. The journal covers a range of accounting and *corporate governance topics, many of which are of interest to auditors.

Web site: *www.blackwellpublishing.com/journal.asp?ref=0954-1314*

journal voucher A document used to record and explain a *journal entry. The authorization of journal entries is often effected through approval signatures on journal vouchers.

judgment **1.** An informed and educated opinion. The use of judgment is central to the selection and evaluation of *audit evidence. Auditors are continually called on to apply their professional judgment to items that can be open to conflicting interpretation, but the professional frameworks within which auditors work are intended to channel their judgment along rational lines. It has been suggested that judgment "pervades accounting and auditing," yet the judgment of external auditors "should be exercised within the existing accounting framework, not independently of it" (*Cohen Commission Report*, 1978, 16 and 14). **2.** The formal pronouncement of a legal or moral decision.

judgmental sampling The selection of a *sample of data from a *population on the basis of subjective decisions. In judgmental sampling, an auditor may base a sample on knowledge of the *auditee's particular circumstances, or skew a sample toward high-*risk items. Compare *statistical sampling, *stratified sampling, and *random sampling.

junk bond A high-interest *bond or debenture of low credit status. The high *interest rates of junk bonds reflect their high *default *risk. Junk bonds tend to be issued to finance the *takeover of large corporations.

junk mail Unsolicited publicity material sent by physical mail or *e-mail. See also *spam.

just-in-time (JIT) A manufacturing and operating philosophy that aims to supply products to customers in line with fluctuations in *demand. The main advantages of JIT operations include (i) typically low *inventory levels, (ii) simplified *backflush costing methodologies, (iii) efficiency of manufacturing operations, and (iv) responsiveness to customer demand. However, JIT operations carry potentially devastating *risks of failing to supply items on time, in the context of interruption to manufacturing or distribution activity.

Further reading: Fullerton and McWatters (2002)

kaizen The Japanese term for *continuous improvement.

kanban The Japanese term for "ticket" or "card." *Kanban* denotes an operating methodology used to coordinate activity and *inventory movements in the context of *just-in-time production processes.

Key Performance Indicator (KPI) An important performance measurement or statistic relating to an activity. Key Performance Indicators (KPIs) are used extensively for management *control and *risk assessment purposes.

kickback An illegal *commission or *bribe paid for the award of a *contract.

King Reports South African *corporate governance reports. The *King Reports* were named for Mervyn King, the chairperson of the corporate governance committees established by the Institute of Directors in Southern Africa. The first *The King Report on Corporate Governance* (known as the *King I Report*) was issued in 1994, and a second report (*King Report II*) appeared in 2002. Although focused on South Africa, the rigor of the *King Reports* has been greeted with international acclaim.
Further reading: *King Report I* (1994); *King Report II* (2002)
Web site: *www.iodsa.co.za*

Kingston Cotton Mill A landmark British *common law case of 1896 that had repercussions for external auditors throughout the English-speaking world. In the rather quaint language of the day, the case's judicial description of external auditors as "watchdogs" rather than "bloodhounds" established the principle that auditors' duties involve the exercising of reasonable professional care: "What is reasonable skill, care and caution must depend on the particular circumstances of each case. An auditor is not bound to be a detective." The case determined that it was reasonable for the external auditor of the Kingston Cotton Mill to rely on a *management representation of *inventory balances, and the auditor was not held to be liable for failing to detect a *fraud. The legal framework of external auditing has changed significantly since the *Kingston Cotton Mill* case, but its judicial reasoning can be interpreted as an early articulation of the existence of the *expectations gap.

Further reading: *Re Kingston Cotton Mill Company (No.2) [1896] 2 Ch 279 at 288, UK Court of Appeal.*

kiting **1.** The practice of writing checks from one bank account and depositing them in another, in order to temporarily inflate an organization's *cash holdings. Kiting is a *fraudulent use of the time taken by checks to clear through a banking system. **2.** In the United Kingdom, the *fraudulent use of stolen *checks.

know-how Technical knowledge and expertise relating to a *manufacturing operation or other business activity. See also *intellectual capital.

***Koninklijk Nederlands Instituut van Registeraccountants* (Royal NIVRA)** The Netherlands' main professional accounting and external auditing organization. The *Registeraccountant* is the Dutch equivalent of the *Certified Public Accountant, and the institute (commonly referred to as Royal NIVRA) was established in 1967 through the merger of pre-existing accounting institutes. Headquartered in Amsterdam, Royal Nivra had approximately 13,000 members in 2003. It enjoys a high international reputation for its work in both accounting and external auditing, and it is notably open to cosmopolitan influences—the latter may be a reflection of the Netherland's long history of international trade and colonial activity.

Web site (some material in English): *www.nivra.nl*

Korean Institute of Certified Public Accountants (KICPA) South Korea's main professional accounting and external auditing organization. Headquartered in Seoul, the KICPA was established in 1954. In 2003 it had approximately 5,000 members.

Web site (some material in English): *www.kicpa.or.kr*

KPMG International A global accounting, auditing, and professional services firm. One of the *Big Four firms, KPMG was established in its current form in 1987 by the merger of Peat Marwick International and Klynveld Main Goerdeler. The geneology of the firm is complex, with the roots of Peat Marwick International in the United Kingdom and the United States in the nineteenth century, and the roots of Klynveld Main Goerdeler in Germany and the Netherlands in the twentieth century. The firm's name is an acronym of the family names of its founders: Klynveld, Peat, Marwick, and Goerdeler.

Further reading: Matthews et al. (1998)

Web site: *www.kpmg.com*

Kurosawa, Kiyoshi (1902–1990) A Japanese accounting theorist. With fellow modernizer *Iwao Iwata, he was a major figure in the implementation of external auditing requirements in Japan following World War Two. A major auditing landmark was legislation creating the Japanese *Certified Public Accountants profession in 1948. Unlike Iwata, his long life enabled him to fully develop his academic writings on accounting theory: He wrote over 60 books and 600 articles. A major preoccupation in his writings was the need to establish objective, scientific foundations for accounting.

Further reading: Chiba (1994)

labor Work of either a manual or intellectual nature undertaken to create economic *value. See also the *factors of production.

lakh The term used in India for 100,000. See also *crore.

land An area of the earth's surface that can be used for economic purposes. Although land not held specifically for *investment purposes is classified in *property, plant, and equipment, it is not usually subjected to *amortization as it is not a *wasting asset (unless subjected to severe environmental degradation). Land is one of the *factors of production, in which it covers all natural resources, including the sea.

lapping The shifting of accounting entries for *cash receipts between *accounts receivable balances to hide stolen cash. Lapping is possible in cases where a *bookkeeper (i) handles cash receipts from customers and (ii) records cash receipts in accounts receivable balances. An appropriate *segregation of duties between these two functions can assist in preventing lapping. Eventually, lapping catches up with itself: unless stolen cash is replaced (or unless an alternative, fraudulent accounting entry is made), accounts receivable will ultimately be *overstated by the amount of cash stolen.

last-in first-out (LIFO) An *inventory valuation method that assumes inventory is consumed (or sold) in the reverse order in which it is purchased (or manufactured). LIFO methodology, which allocates the most recent inventory costs to *cost of sales, is not acceptable under some forms of *Generally Accepted Accounting Principles. Compare *first-in first-out (FIFO) and *next-in first-out (NIFO).

lead time The time difference between the placing of a customer *order and the fulfilling of the order. Fulfillment can be in the form of the delivery of ordered goods, or performance of ordered services.

learning curve Increases in output and *efficiency as experience and knowledge are gained. In a manufacturing context, the learning curve can be measured by a statistical comparison of increases in cumulative production output with decreases in cumulative inputs. More generally, the learning curve refers to the increasing efficiency and productivity with which an individual or organization deals with an activity. For example, an auditor approaching a new assignment or *auditee may find initial *audit planning and work to be slow, but should experience increasing efficiency as familiarization with the new environment increases.

lease A legal *contract in which one party (a *lessee) hires an asset from another party (a *lessor) for a *rental charge. In accounting and auditing, leases are often categorized into *capital and *operating leases.

ledger A register of accounting transactions. Traditionally ledgers were in the form of books, but in modern usage the term normally refers to computerized recording mechanisms. See also *general ledger and *subsidiary ledger.

Lee, Tom A. (born 1941) A British academic, author, and auditing specialist. Professor Emeritus of Accountancy at the University of Alabama, and Honorary Professor of Accounting at Dundee University in Scotland, Lee's contributions to auditing include the landmark book *Company Auditing* (1972). This was one of the first theoretical studies of external auditing in the United Kingdom, and it developed themes set out a decade earlier in Mautz and Sharaf's *Philosophy of Auditing*. Lee updated and revised *Company Auditing as Corporate Audit Theory* in 1993. Lee has also written many articles of auditing, and he has been a noted critic of external auditing practices. In the aftermath of the accounting scandals at *Enron and *WorldCom, he wrote of the "shame" of the auditing profession (Lee, 2002, 212). He has been equally critical of academic accountants, claiming that they "have fiddled while Rome burned" (Lee, 2002, 212) in neglecting the implications of allegedly declining external auditing standards. Lee's other areas of interest include auditing history and *financial reporting.
　　Further reading: Lee (1972); Lee (1988); Lee (1993); Lee (2001); Lee (2002)

legislation Laws promulgated by a governmental body, in the form of decrees or *statutes. Legislation is sometimes defined as the making of law, but this is an unsatisfactory definition for some legal theorists, who maintain that law can only be discovered, not "made." In English-speaking countries, legislation is often contrasted with *common law. The latter more clearly demonstrates the "discovery" of law on the basis of the accumulated experience of case law.

less developed country (LDC) An alternative term for *developing country.

lessee An individual or organization that acquires the temporary use of an asset from another party (a *lessor) through a *lease contract.

lessor An individual or organization that grants the temporary use of an asset to another party (a *lessee) through a *lease contract.

letter of credit (L/C) A mechanism used in international trade in which a bank *guarantees to settle the cash payment arising from a transaction, once specified conditions have been met.

letter of engagement See *engagement letter.

letter of recommendation An alternative term for *management letter.

letter of representation A formal, written statement made by an *auditee and addressed to an *external auditor, in which the auditee confirms that statements made to the auditor are accurate and complete. Letters of representation also usually define the responsibility of an auditee for the *fair presentation of *financial statements under audit.

leverage **1.** The importance of *debt finance in the capital structure of an organization. Most corporations finance their activities through a combination of debt and *equity finance, and economists devote significant energy to determining the optimal mix of the two forms of finance. Excessive leverage can be *risky to the extent that it obliges a corporation to make high *interest payments to service its debts. High leverage may make a corporation dangerously vulnerable to fluctuations in *interest rates or levels of *income. The *debt-equity ratio and *interest cover are common measurements of leverage. **2.** In a general sense, the *risks of high levels of *fixed costs on an organization.

lex A Latin word meaning "law."

liability A commitment to pay for goods, services, or financing costs. Liabilities possess a number of characteristics: (i) They give rise to transfers of quantifiable economic benefits, in the form of *cash payments or *payments in kind; (ii) they are applicable to a specific individual or organization; and (iii) their existence is certain (other than *contingent liabilities). A liability is recorded as a *credit entry under the conventions of *double entry bookkeeping, and *short-term liabilities are usually referred to as *current liabilities. Contrast *asset.

lien A *creditor's contractual right of possession of an *asset of another party in case of default on a debt or loan. A *mortgage, for example, usually creates a lien over mortgaged property.

limitation of scope See *scope limitation.

limited audit An audit with restricted scope. Agreed limitations on audit work may be determined in reference to (i) specific time periods, (ii) specific activities, or (iii) high *materiality thresholds.

limited liability Legal liability that does not extend beyond the size of an individual's *investment in a *corporation or *partnership. A *stockholder does not suffer liability for a corporation's debts beyond an amount invested in a corporation, while a *limited partner's liability is similarly restricted in a partnership.

limited partner A member of a *partnership who enjoys *limited liability in line with an amount of *capital invested in the partnership.

Limpberg, Theodore (1879–1961) A Dutch auditing theorist and practitioner. Overlapping with *Lawrence Robert Dicksee's later career in the United Kingdom, Limpberg's early life as an external auditor was followed by an academic career in the Netherlands in which he made major contributions to auditing theory. The focus of his work on auditing concerned (i) the discipline's role in society, (ii) its scientific, objective nature, and (iii) links between auditing and economic theory. A major concern in his writings was the need for auditing to transcend routine verification procedures to base itself on procedures tailored to the circumstances of the organization audited. This came to be known as the "sufficient audit"—an audit tailored to particular circumstances, and thereby to be "sufficient" for (or reasonably necessary for) the purpose at hand.

Limpberg also wrote extensively on a theory he described as "inspired confidence." This concerned the importance of the confidence given to a society's economic transactions by the existence of a reputable external auditing profession. He wrote in the context of the economic depressions of the 1920s and 1930s, when many of the practices of the continental European external auditing profession were ad hoc and unsystematic. In the early twenty-first century (in the aftermath of the *Enron and *WorldCom scandals, and with the demise of *Arthur Andersen), it is clear that Limpberg's concerns regarding the importance of the confidence instilled by external auditing remain perennial ones.

Limpberg was influential in the Netherlands and beyond. His Dutch followers came to be known as the "Amsterdam School," and they carried forward his theories into a coherent school of thought. Limpberg's legacy survives in the form of the Netherlands-based Limpberg Institute, a research foundation that has made some of his writings available in English.

Further reading: Camfferman and Zeff (1994); Limpberg (1985)

linear programming (LP) A method for the optimal allocation of scarce resources to alternative activities. The aim of the decision-making process (termed the "objective function") and related constraints are expressed in mathematical terms, and may be plotted graphically in simple scenarios. Typical objective functions include the maximizing of *income and the minimizing of *costs. Linear programming, as its name suggests, is applicable only in contexts where the relationships between elements under consideration are linear in nature.

line of credit See *credit line.

liquid 1. In the form of *cash, or readily convertible into cash with a minimal loss of value. An example of the latter is a marketable *security. *Inventory is not generally considered to be liquid, owing to the time delay typically required to convert it into cash; therefore, inventory tends to be excluded from the *acid test ratio, a key liquidity measure. Contrast *illiquid. **2.** Possessing sufficient cash resources to meet *current liabilities.

liquidation The closing of a business *enterprise and the sale or disposal of its assets.

liquid ratio An alternative term, common in the United Kingdom, for the *acid test ratio.

listed 1. [of securities] Registered and traded on a stock exchange. See also *quoted. **2.** [of goods and services] Enumerated and cataloged in a systematic manner.

loan An asset (usually *cash) lent to an individual or organization, for which the return of the asset or repayment of the cash is anticipated. The cost of a loan is measured by the *interest applied to it. A mortgage is an example of a *long-term loan.

local area network (LAN) The linking of computers within a limited geographical area in order to share and transfer files. An example of a LAN is a network of computers within a building (or group of adjacent buildings).

Local Government Auditing Quarterly A U.S. *public sector auditing magazine. Published quarterly by the *National Association of Local Government Auditors (NALGA), the *Quarterly* is available in print format. Archives of selected articles from 1991 are available online from the NALGA Web site. The NALGA Web site states that the magazine "provides important information about government auditing issues, and articles about local government audit organizations," and that it "describes findings and methods of audits in public safety, social services, revenues, and other important areas."

Web link: *www.nalga.org/qrtly/articles.html*

log A *register that records the use of an *asset, the undertaking of an activity, or other events. An example of a log is a register of individuals who access a room that contains sensitive data or high-value assets.

long-term **1.** Relating to a period of more than one year. **2.** For some loans and debts, the long term may be defined from 5 to 50 years.

loss **1.** An excess of costs over related *sales revenues in a specified time period. Contrast *income. **2.** A decrease in the *net assets of an individual or organization.

low-balling The offering of a very low *sales price to undercut competitors and thereby win a *contract. From the 1980s, external auditors (and the *Big Four firms in particular) have often been accused of low-balling in order to gain audit clients. The low audit fee that results from low-balling can be offset by lucrative *management advisory services.

lump sum A sum of *money paid at a specific point in time rather than in *installments.

maintenance The preservation of the condition and operational functionality of an *asset. Maintenance costs are normally treated as *revenue expenditure in an *income statement. Contrast *betterment.

make-or-buy decision An appraisal of the relative costs and benefits of manufacturing an item or buying it from a *supplier. Both *quantitative and *qualitative considerations may be included in the decision-making process. An example of a qualitative factor is the *risk of reliance on suppliers for essential components in a *production process.

maladministration The incompetent administration of an asset or organization. Maladministration may or may not include *fraud, depending on the intentions of the perpetrators.

Malaysian Institute of Accountants (MIA) Malaysia's regulatory body for accounting and external auditing. Established by legislation in 1967, and headquartered in Kuala Lumpur, the institute had 18,500 members in 2003. Its Web site states that its vision is to be "a globally recognised and respected business partner committed to nation building." Members are known as *chartered accountants, and only chartered accountants with an audit licence issued by the Malaysian Ministry of Finance are permitted to act as *statutory auditors.
  Web site: *www.mia.org.my*

Malaysian Institute of Certified Public Accountants (MICPA) A Malaysian professional accounting organization. Established in 1958 from pre-existing professional bodies that dated back to the British colonial period, the MICPA took its current name in 1964. It adopted the U.S. terminology of *Certified Public Accountant rather than the United Kingdom's *chartered accountant. The MICPA is headquartered in Kuala Lumpur, and in 2003 it had 2,500 members. The MICPA is not Malaysia's regulatory body for accounting and external auditing—that role is filled by the *Malaysian Institute of Accountants (MIA). Both the MICPA and the MIA are full members of the *International Federation of Accountants.
  Web site: *www.micpa.com.my*

175

malpractice Improper, unethical, illegal, or incompetent behavior by a *professional person. See also *negligence.

malpractice insurance Liability *insurance taken by external auditors to cover potential legal action by *auditees (and others) dissatisfied with the auditor's work. From the 1980s the suing of external auditors has become increasingly common, and in addition to malpractice insurance many large audit firms have taken the step of converting from *partnerships to *corporations to reduce the personal liability of individual audit partners.

managed currency A *currency whose *exchange rate is overtly manipulated by a government.

managed risk *Risk that is subjected to *risk management techniques.

management 1. The process of directing, controlling, and *planning in an organization. The main elements of management are commonly thought to include (i) *planning, (ii) organizing, (iii) leading, (iv) employing, and (v) coordinating. Although much management theory is disputed—it has been suggested that "management is too unsystematic to make it a science and its knowledge base is too uncertain to call it a profession" (Sawyer and Vinten, 1996, 18)—the "father" of modern management theory is often held to be Henri Fayol (1841–1925), whose *Administration Industrielle and Générale* appeared in 1916. 2. In an organization, a group of individuals that collectively directs, controls, and makes plans.

management accounting The maintenance, analysis, and reporting of *accounting information related to an organization's costs, revenues, and activities. Management accounting, in contrast to *financial accounting, tends to focus on accounting records for an organization's internal use. Management accounting provides information to an organization's *management for control, planning, and decision-making purposes.

management advisory services (MAS) Services other than external auditing supplied by external auditors. Examples of management advisory services (MAS) include (i) *tax advice, (ii) employee training, (iii) IT systems implementation, (iv) the *outsourcing of internal auditing, and (v) a variety of *consulting projects. (Some users of the term MAS may exclude tax advice from its definition.) Regulators throughout the world have raised concerns in recent years over the levels of MAS supplied by the *Big Four auditing firms, and the alleged extent to which lucrative MAS contracts can compromise the *independence of the external *audit opinion. The term nonaudit services (NAS) is sometimes used as an alternative to MAS.

Further reading: Caswell (1999)

management audit 1. An audit of the extent to which the objectives of an organization are met by the actions of the organization's *management. Flint (1988, 175, n.3) defines the term as follows: An "examination, analysis and evaluation...of the performance of management in regard to the objectives, plans, procedures and strategies of a business enterprise or other organisation, and the expression of an opinion on the effectiveness of management in performance of its responsibilities." Management audits tend to cover both financial and operational matters. 2. An alternative term for *operational audit. 3. [rare or archaic] An alternative term for *internal audit.

Management Audit Ltd A British internal audit consulting firm. Incorporated in 1991 and headed by *Andrew Chambers, Management Audit undertakes consulting, training, and publishing in the fields of internal auditing and *corporate governance.

Web site: *www.management-audit.com*

management by exception The management of an organization through investigation of deviations from expected results. For example, management may concentrate on *variances from *budgeted amounts, and on operational anomalies generated by *exception reports.

management consulting See *consulting.

management information system (MIS) A computer system that generates information of use to an organization's *management. Information generated by an MIS can include (i) *management accounts, (ii) operational data, and (iii) information to support decision-making and investment appraisal.

management letter An *external auditor's report that contains recommendations for improvements in procedures and *internal controls. Alongside an *audit opinion, external auditors normally provide a management letter as a service to *auditees.

management representation A statement made to an auditor by the management of an organization that confirms an item under audit is correct and complete. See also *letter of representation.

manager An individual who undertakes *management duties in an organization. In auditing, managers tend to focus on *audit planning, *risk assessment, supervision of colleagues' work, and determination of an overall *audit opinion, rather than on detailed *fieldwork.

managerial accounting An alternative term for *management accounting.

managerial auditing **1.** An alternative term for *operational auditing. **2.** An alternative name for *internal auditing.

Managerial Auditing Journal A British scholarly auditing journal. Established in 1986, and edited from 1988 by *Gerald Vinten, the journal is published in nine issues a year by MCB University Press in Bradford, England. It is available in print and online formats. The journal combines scholarly and practical analysis on a wide spectrum of auditing topics. Despite its title, the journal's contents are not restricted to managerial, operational, or internal auditing: it frequently includes essays on external auditing. There is strong international coverage, especially for developing countries. The journal's notes describe its mission as follows: to provide "a forum for those with a broad managerial as well as professional interest in audit to explore current practices, ideas and experience; a framework of explanation and guidance on developments and research; and perspectives on professional and career development." It also claims to take its readers "beyond traditional conventions" and look at "the ways in which contemporary auditors are improving both managerial and organizational performance."

Web site: *www.mcb.co.uk*

manufacturing The large-scale *production of tangible items.

manufacturing costs *Costs directly attributable to the *production of tangible items. Administration costs are normally excluded from definitions of manufacturing costs.

margin The difference between the sales *price of a good or service and the cost of manufacturing or supplying it. See also *income (definition 2).

marginal analysis The analysis of the effects of small changes of variable items. For example, *marginal cost looks at the incremental *costs incurred from the manufacture of an additional unit of production. Marginal analysis is important in economic decision-making, as the impact of small changes often determines economic behavior. Economic research suggests that individuals often respond to marginal changes in costs and income.

marginal cost **1.** The incremental increase in total *variable and *fixed costs arising from the manufacture of an additional unit of production. **2.** A British term for *variable cost.

marginal income An alternative term for *contribution.

marginal tax rate The *tax rate paid on the last unit of taxable income, or on an extra unit of taxable income. Under *progressive tax systems, the marginal rate is the highest rate of tax that falls on an individual or organization.

margin of safety The difference between an individual or organization's current operating activity and a critical performance measure like a *break-even or *insolvency point. A margin of safety can be measured in *values, *volumes, or *percentages, and the concept is an important consideration in *risk management.

markdown A reduction in the selling price of a product.

market An arrangement or context in which goods and services are *exchanged. *Money is the most efficient means of facilitating exchange. *Prices in an unregulated or *free-market economy are established by the interplay of the decisions of buyers and sellers in achieving the *equilibrium of *supply and *demand. Markets can be subverted by *cartels and *monopolies, and are often subjected in practice to complex *regulations. See also *black market, *common market, *efficient market hypothesis, *over-the-counter market, and *spot market.

market capitalization An alternative term for *capitalization (definition 2).

market price The *price of a good, service, *commodity, or *security negotiated between buyers and sellers in a *free market. Compare *book value and *fair market value.

market share The proportion of the activity in a *market attributable to a specific organization, activity, or product. Market share can be expressed in terms of *value, *volume, or *percentage.

market value An alternative term for *fair market value.

markup An amount added to a product's selling price. A markup may be calculated by reference to a product's costs, or to a product's previous selling prices. See also *cost-plus pricing and *markdown.

matching **1.** The financial reporting of sales and expenses in line with the *accruals basis of accounting. **2.** The allocation of *cash receipts to individual balances within *accounts receivable.

materiality The importance and relevance of an item in an auditing context. The concept of materiality permeates auditing processes, and it has been described as "multidimensional" (Lee, 1994, 178): It affects *audit planning, the selection of *audit evidence, the testing of *samples, and the preparation of *audit reports. Materiality is often judged on the basis of its potential impact on an activity, individual, or organization. In the context of external auditing, for example, the potential impact of the omission or *misstatement of an item on a reader's interpretation of published *financial statements drives materiality considerations.

Some forms of materiality may be assessed *quantitatively, and this approach is often taken by external auditors. For example, the materiality of a *balance sheet item may be calculated in relation to a defined percentage of *net assets, or the materiality of an *income statement item may be calculated in relation to a defined percentage of sales or *net income. An auditor may only review items that fall within such defined materiality categories. However, some items may be material whatever their size. A *bribe, for example, may only be small in relation to balance sheet values, yet its intrinsic nature may make it material. Materiality therefore usually comprises a mixture of qualitative and quantitative considerations.

maturity date The date at which a debt, the *principal (definition 2) of a loan, or an *insurance policy becomes due for payment.

Mautz, Robert Khun (born 1915) A U.S. academic, author, and specialist in auditing and accounting. Professor Mautz coauthored *The Philosophy of Auditing*, a landmark book of 1961 that set out the famous *postulates of auditing. Mautz's career has involved both professional experience as a *Certified Public Accountant and a distinguished academic profile. After several years in *public accounting he started his academic career at the University of Illinois in 1948. He left university life in 1972 to join the accounting firm Ernst & Whinney (now part of *Ernst & Young) as a partner, and in 1978 returned to academic life. Other than *The Philosophy of Auditing*, Mautz's achievements include (i) the authorship of a number of books on auditing, including *Fundamentals of Auditing* (1954), (ii) the founding editorship of the journal *Accounting Horizons,* (iii) awards for professional service from the *American Institute of Certified Public Accountants, and (iv) induction in 1978 into the *Accounting Hall of Fame.
Further reading: Mautz (1954); Mautz and Sharaf (1961)

Mc2 Management Consulting A U.S. internal auditing and *risk management consulting practice. Founded in 1991 by *David McNamee as Management Control Concepts, the practice adopted its current name in 2000. It undertakes consulting and training in internal auditing, *corporate governance, risk management, and related areas.
Web site: *www.mc2consulting.com*

McKesson and Robbins Inc. A U.S. corporation whose *financial reporting practices were investigated in the 1930s by the *Securities and Exchange Commission (SEC). The SEC investigation was a landmark event in the evolution of external auditing: it drew attention to the requirement for auditors to seek *audit evidence outside a client's accounting system in order to support accounting balances. McKesson and Robbins Inc. inflated their *inventory and *accounts receivables balances by $19 million, and the external auditor (Price Waterhouse & Co.) failed to detect the *fraud. The SEC investigation "arguably more than any other in the history of corporate auditing, had the effect of changing generally accepted auditing practice almost instantly—especially with respect to *evaluating evidence from a reliable source" (Lee, 1993, 133).

Further reading: McKesson and Robbins Inc. (1982)

McNamee, David (born 1945) A U.S. internal auditing author and practitioner. McNamee spent 22 years with Pacific Telesis / Pacific Bell before founding in 1991 an international consulting practice, Management Control Concepts (later renamed *Mc2 Management Consulting). A prolific author, McNamee has written many articles and books on internal auditing, *risk management, and related subjects. His books include *Risk Management: Changing the Internal Auditor's Paradigm* (1998), coauthored with Georges M. Selim, and *Business Risk Assessment* (1998).

Further reading: McNamee (1998); McNamee and Selim (1998)

mean 1. [noun] A measure of central tendency of a *population of data. The arithmetic mean is popularly referred to as the *average, and it is calculated by adding together the values of individual items in a set of numbers and dividing the total by the number of items. For example, the mean of five individual sales transactions of $5, $10, $15, $20, and $30 is calculated as $16 (i.e., 5 + 10 + 15 + 20 + 30 divided by 5). In this example, the substitution of the $30 sale by one of $150 would distort the mean by skewing it toward the size of the single, large transaction, with a potentially misleading mean of $40. Compare *median, *mode, and *weighted average. **2.** [adjective] Miserly, ungenerous.

median The midpoint of a *population of data arranged in ascending or descending order. The median is calculated by taking the item of a set of numbers at which there is an equal number of items with a value above it as below it. For example, the median of five individual sales transactions of $5, $10, $15, $20, and $30 is $15, as there are two items above it ($20 and $30) and two items below it ($10 and $15). The median differs from the *mean in that it is less affected by large items. If, in our example, the sale of $30 were replaced by one of $150, the median would be unchanged. See also *mode.

memorandum account A record of *transactions for an *asset, *liability, or area of *revenue or *expenditure that is kept separate from a system of *double entry bookkeeping. Memorandum accounts serve as reference sources for, among other things, *obsolete fixed assets and old *inventory with no monetary value. They are not included in *financial statements, and are normally maintained only for information or perhaps operational purposes. However, *Generally Accepted Accounting Principles in some countries (e.g., in Italy) have traditionally required *disclosure in financial statements of some memorandum accounts.

merger The combining of two (or more than two) organizations that results in the creation of a new legal and economic entity. In contrast to an *acquisition, a merger generally implies a voluntary combination by both parties. Following a merger, a new organization emerges that tends to reflect the character of both premerger organizations, and the *stockholders of merging corporations tend to share on an equal footing the risks and rewards of the newly created entity. However, in practice, one party to a merger often dominates a merger arrangement.

Most forms of *Generally Accepted Accounting Principles (GAAP) tend to strictly differentiate mergers from *acquisitions, and under most forms of GAAP the accounting treatment of mergers does not normally give rise to *goodwill. In many jurisdictions, large corporate mergers that concentrate market power and reduce *competition are frequently reviewed by regulatory authorities. Mergers have been common among large accounting firms in recent years. In 1998, for example, Coopers & Lybrand merged with Price Waterhouse to create a new firm, *PricewaterhouseCoopers.

Further reading: Davison (2001); Selim et al. (2002)

Milne, Robert B. (d. 1964) A U.S. internal auditing pioneer. Milne was one of three "founding fathers" of the *Institute of Internal Auditors (IIA), along with *Victor Z. Brink and *John B. Thurston. An early internal auditing pioneer with the Columbia Engineering Corporation, he was elected the IIA's second president in 1942.

Further reading: Flesher (1991)

minority interest *Equity ownership in a corporation controlled by another, dominant stockholder. Minority interests are rewarded by *dividend income and *appreciation in the value of *common stock, but they are normally unable to determine the strategic policies of a corporation, as they are outnumbered in voting power.

minute An official summary of discussions at a meeting. The meetings of *boards of directors and their committees are normally minuted.

mission statement A formal, written declaration of high-level objectives and strategies.

misstatement The inaccurate valuation of an item in *financial statements or in a *general ledger account.

Mitchell, Austin (born 1934) A British Member of Parliament and commentator on accounting and auditing issues. Mitchell, who represents the constituency of Grimsby in the north of England, is a high profile personality in the *critical accounting movement in the United Kingdom, through his journalism, media appearances, and monographs. He is a trustee of the *Association for Accountancy and Business Affairs. His written output is prolific. In addition to numerous articles in the professional and academic press, he has coauthored several monographs, including *Accounting for Change: Proposals for Reform of Audit and Accounting* (Mitchell et al., 1991) and *Auditors: Holding the Public to Ransom* (Cousins et al., 1998). One of Austin Mitchell's main areas of interest is *regulation of the external auditing profession, and (as can be gauged by the titles of his monographs) he is something of a thorn in the side of the British external auditing establishment.

Further reading: Cousins et al. (1998); Mitchell et al. (1991); Mitchell et al. (1998); Mitchell and Sikka (2002)

Web site: *www.austinmitchell.org*

mixed cost An alternative term for *semi-variable cost.

mixed economy An economy in which the *private and *public sectors coexist. Most economies are mixed to a greater or lesser extent, though one or two overwhelmingly *command economies still exist in the early twenty-first century.

mode The item that occurs most frequently in a set of numbers. For example, if 10 sales are made at $5, 20 sales at $10, and 8 sales at $15, the mode is the more frequently occurring $10 sale. Compare the calculation of the *mean and the *median.

modem A device that connects a computer to a telephone line in order to transfer data and files. The word derives from the initial letters of the words modulator and demodulator.

money 1. A generally accepted medium of *exchange. Money has several functions—it (i) facilitates transactions (compare *barter), (ii) stores value and thereby permits saving, (iii) permits *credit, and (iv) offers an easy means of *quantification and accounting. A system of money in a specific country or region is known as a *currency, and *liquid forms of money are referred to as *cash. **2.** An informal term for *income or *salary.

money laundering The transferring of *money derived from illegal activities into legal or legitimate channels. Money laundering is intended to conceal the illegal origins of funds, and it is commonly associated with drug trafficking and *smuggling. In the United States, anti-money laundering legislation was significantly enhanced by the provisions of the Patriot Act of 2001. Auditing techniques designed to investigate illegal activities like money laundering are often referred to as *forensic auditing.
    Further reading: Quinn (2002)

monitoring The surveillance and review of an activity or asset over time. Monitoring (as suggested in *Internal Control—Integrated Framework or the COSO Report) is an essential means of ascertaining and reporting on the effectiveness of organizational controls. Monitoring is also an important means of obtaining *audit evidence. See also *oversight.

monopoly A *market that has only one *supplier. The sole supplier in a monopolistic market may be in a position to (i) unduly influence the *price of the goods and services it provides, (ii) make excessive profits by manipulating prices and supply, and (iii) prevent *competition by erecting *barriers to entry to the market. Regulations and *antitrust laws are designed to combat the effects of monopoly. See also *cartel and *oligopoly.

Montgomery, Robert Hiester (1872–1953) A U.S. auditing practitioner, academic, and author. After an early career in law and *public accounting, and active participation in the *American Institute of Certified Public Accountants (for which he helped to establish the *Journal of Accountancy), Montgomery was appointed a professor at Columbia University in 1919. He was a prolific author of authoritative books on auditing. His works included the editing of the U.S. edition of *Lawrence Robert Dicksee's Auditing in 1904, and the authorship of Auditing Theory and Practice in 1912. The latter book is still in print, in its 12th edition, revised by other authors under the eponymous title Montgomery's Auditing. Colonel Montgomery (the military rank was awarded in World War I) was an avid collector of rare books on auditing and accounting, and he donated his collection to Columbia University. In 1950 he was inducted into the *Accounting Hall of Fame.
    Further reading: Montgomery (1912); O'Reilly et al. (1998)

moonlighting The undertaking of work in addition to one's main occupation. The term carries connotations of secrecy, irregular hours, and cash *wages.

mortgage The granting of a property as *collateral against a *loan. The loan is often taken for the express purchase of financing the purchase of the mortgaged property. See also *lien.

multinational 1. [noun] An alternative term for *multinational corporation. 2. [adjective] Involving two or more countries or nationalities.

multinational corporation (MNC) At the simplest level, the term MNC refers to a corporation with activities in two or more countries. Alternative definitions include the following: (i) a corporation with "a worldwide view of production, the sourcing of raw materials and components, and final markets" (Radebaugh and Gray, 1997, 24); (ii) a corporation producing at least 25 percent of its output outside its country of origin (which may or may not be the country where the MNC is legally based).

To bring coherence to their sprawling operations, and to manage the vast array of *risks they face, many MNCs introduce standardized internal procedures, as far as this is compatible with local laws, regulations, and cultural practices. The risk of contravention of the *Foreign Corrupt Practices Act* is a major concern for U.S. MNCs. Factors such as these present unique challenges to MNCs' internal and external auditors, who often play a key role in the verification of global *controls, *procedures, and risk management programs.

multinational enterprise (MNE) An alternative term for *multinational corporation (MNE). The term "multinational enterprise" explicitly extends the term's reference to noncorporate organizations, like partnerships.

mutual fund A professionally managed *portfolio of *securities. For *investors, mutual funds offer (i) the *diversification of *risk for relatively modest levels of investment and (ii) the expertise of professional management.

National Association of Corporate Directors (NACD®) A U.S. organization for corporate *directors, *boards of directors, and their advisors. Established in 1977 and headquartered in Washington, DC, the NACD Web site describes the organization as "the premier educational, publishing and consulting organization in board leadership" and "an authoritative voice and vital forum on matters of policy and practice." The NACD's activities include highly respected research into aspects of *corporate governance through the reports of its *Blue Ribbon Commissions.

Further reading: NACD (1996); NACD (2000); NACD (2001)

Web site: *www.nacdonline.org*

National Association of Local Government Auditors (NALGA) A U.S. organization for *public sector auditors. Established in 1989 and headquartered in Lexington, KY, NALGA focuses on local government auditing. On its Web site, NALGA states that it "disseminates information and ideas about financial and performance auditing, provides training, and offers a national forum to discuss auditing issues." The NALGA publishes the *Local Government Auditing Quarterly* and in 2003 the association had in excess of 500 members, comprising both individuals and organizations.

Web site: *www.nalga.org*

National Association of State Boards of Accountancy (NASBA) A U.S. accounting organization. Established in 1908 and headquartered in Nashville, TN, NASBA is an umbrella body for the United States' 54 boards of accountancy. It was originally called The Association of CPA Examiners until it adopted its current name in 1967. The individual states' boards of accountancy set out the requirements for licensing *Certified Public Accountants, and links to individual states' licensure requirements are available at the NASBA Web site.

Web site: *www.nasba.org*

National Audit Office (NAO) The British agency for central government auditing. The NAO is the United Kingdom's *Supreme Audit Institution, and it is the equivalent of the U.S. *General Accounting Office. On its Web site, the NAO describes its activities as follows: "We audit the accounts of all government departments and agencies as well as a wide range of other public bodies, and report to Parliament on the economy, efficiency and effectiveness with which government bodies have used public money."

Web site: *www.nao.gov.uk*

nationalization **1.** The transfer to government control of *private sector economic activity and organizations. Contrast *privatization. **2.** The reinforcement of the national characteristics of an activity or organization. In some countries, organizational quotas ensure a defined level of involvement of certain ethnic groups in *public and *private sector institutions. In Malaysia, for example, *Bumiputra* ("sons of the soil") laws establish racial quotas of this nature in favor of ethnic Malays.

negative assurance **1.** A weak form of external *audit opinion in circumstances when an auditor does not follow *Generally Accepted Auditing Standards (GAAS). Negative assurance is offered by external auditors to support specific transactions like *flotations, and in circumstances when standard audit opinions are inappropriate or impractical. The thrust of negative assurance is a statement that the auditor is unaware of any problems with *financial statements or *transaction under consideration. Negative assurance does not carry the authority and weight of a standard audit opinion issued in line with GAAS. **2.** A means of obtaining *audit evidence by sending written requests to *third parties to confirm the existence and accuracy of items in *financial statements. With negative assurance, a third party is requested to reply only if a stated *balance is incorrect or disputed. The technique is often used in *circularizations.

negative goodwill **1.** In an *acquisition, the excess of the *fair value of acquired *net assets over the *consideration paid by an acquiring company. Contrast (positive) *goodwill. **2.** The low esteem in which an organization's reputation and *brands are held. **3.** An unfavorable or unfriendly disposition toward an individual or organization.

negligence A failure to exercise proper care in the performance of an activity that leads to injury or loss to another party. In an external auditing context, negligence refers to an audit conducted without the due care and attention one would expect from *professional auditors, and perhaps also conducted in contravention of *Generally Accepted Auditing Standards. See also *malpractice insurance.

net An amount stated after the deduction of *allowances, *discounts, *taxation, or other items. Contrast *gross.

net assets The difference between the total *assets and total *liabilities of an organization or individual.

net income Total revenues less total *expenses in an *income statement. Contrast *gross income.

net off, to To deduct *allowances, *discounts, *taxation, or other items from an amount.

net present value (NPV) The value of an investment derived from comparisons of costs with the present value of anticipated future, incremental *cash flows. The *present value of cash flows is calculated by applying an appropriate *cost of capital rate to each period's cash flows. This approach recognizes the *time value of money. See also the *internal rate of return.

net profit An alternative term for *net income.

net realizable value (NRV) 1. The expected sales *price of an *asset or item of *inventory after the deduction of relevant selling, distribution, and other incidental expenses. **2.** The expected recoverable value of *accounts receivable balances. The NRV of accounts receivable is stated after the deduction of an appropriate *allowance for bad debts.

net risk A *risk after the application of *risk management procedures. Contrast *gross risk.

net sales Sales after the deduction of *discounts, *rebates, *allowances for bad debts, and *customer returns.

next-in first-out (NIFO) An *inventory valuation method that allocates replacement or *current costs to *cost of sales. NIFO is unacceptable under most forms of *Generally Accepted Accounting Principles, though it may be a valuable costing technique in times of high *inflation. Compare *first-in first-out (FIFO) and *last-in first-out (LIFO).

Nolan Principles A popular name for a British *public sector corporate governance report of 1995. The Committee on Standards in Public Life—popularly named for its chairperson—was established in 1994 by the British government to elaborate governance standards following allegations of bribes and abuse of office by members of the British parliament. The committee's 1995 report identified seven "principles of public life": (i) selflessness, (ii) integrity, (iii) objectivity, (iv) *accountability, (v) openness, (vi) honesty, and (vii) leadership.
Further reading: *Nolan Principles* (1995)

nominal ledger A rather archaic British term for *general ledger.

nominal value The monetary amount of an individual *security or other *financial instrument. The *par values of *common stock and the *face values of *bonds are examples of nominal values, which can differ significantly from their *market values.

nonaudit services (NAS) An alternative term for *management advisory services.

nonexecutive director (NED) The British term for *outside director.

nongovernmental organization (NGO) A *private sector organization dedicated to assistance and development in the fields of economics, finance, health, political governance, humanitarian relief, and related areas. Nongovernmental organizations are often active in *developing countries.

nonprofit organization An alternative term for *not-for-profit organization.

nonrecurring [of items in financial statements] Infrequent or unusual. See also *exceptional.

nonstatistical sampling An alternative term for *judgmental sampling.

normal distribution A *probability distribution model based on large *samples of items that cover a range of values in a *population. When plotted graphically, a normal distribution has a bell-shaped curve that is symmetrical around the *mean. The *standard deviation of the mean is used to measure fixed proportions of items in the population that vary from the mean. The normal distribution is a model, based on the so-called central limit theorem, and in practice it has been shown to more or less accurately reflect large random samples. If the sizes of adult males in a population are plotted graphically, for example, the pattern tends to approximate to the classic bell-shaped curve.

normal spoilage Unavoidable waste, *scrap, and defective goods arising from manufacturing processes. Unlike *abnormal spoilage, normal *spoilage is considered to be inherent in a *production process. It is generally viewed as uncontrollable in the short run, as it is driven by technological aspects of production that can be altered only in the long term. The costs of normal spoilage are therefore treated as acceptable production costs, rather than as items to be expensed as incurred.

North, the A collective term for economically *developed countries. The term derives from the fact that most of the world's wealthy countries (in North

America, Western Europe, and the Pacific Rim) are located in the northern hemisphere. Contrast the *South.

note payable A written, *contractual obligation to pay *money at a specified, future date. See also *promissory note.

note receivable A written, *contractual right to receive *money at a specified, future date.

not-for-profit organization An institution that undertakes an activity without a *profit-seeking motive. Examples of not-for-profit organizations include charities, government institutions, and educational establishments—they (and their donors) often enjoy exemption from some forms of *taxation. In not-for-profit organizations, *income in excess of expenses is often referred to as a *surplus rather than as a profit. Organizations of this type are not motivated primarily by profits—they aim to achieve their declared objectives while maximizing the *Three E's of *economy, *efficiency, and *effectiveness.

objective **1.** [noun] See *audit objective. **2.** [adjective] Impartial, without bias. Objectivity is fundamental to the credibility of auditing, owing to the importance of auditor *judgment. The *reasonableness of an objective judgment is often assessed on the basis of the likelihood of the same judgment being reached independently by another auditor.

observation **1.** A systematic *examination or analysis of an activity or procedure. Observation is a key method of obtaining and *evaluating *audit evidence, and it includes *inspections of the performance of *internal control procedures. **2.** The following or obeying of laws, rules, and regulations.

obsolescence A reduction or ending of an asset's *useful economic life (or sales value) through technological or other changes. Obsolescence is an important factor in the *amortization of *long-term assets and the valuation of *inventory. The operational effectiveness of an item of plant and equipment can end for many reasons: (i) the inability to obtain spare parts, (ii) the diminishing availability of maintenance engineers, and (iii) inefficiency in comparison to other assets available in the marketplace. If an asset becomes obsolete before the end of its amortization period, it is normally subject to immediate *write-off (less any *scrap value). For items of inventory, changing fashions and shifts in customer demand can signal a drastic reduction in sales value. Many manufacturers rely on planned obsolescence of their products to maintain ongoing demand.

off-balance sheet (OBS) A *liability or other item that is not included in a *balance sheet. *Creative accounting techniques often aim at manipulating *financial statements through off-balance sheet *transactions, "in which significant corporate resources, *income or *cash flow are never brought into... audited *financial statements because of the terms in which the relevant *contracted *transactions are written (for example, *leases, *quasi-subsidiary companies, *joint ventures, and *contingent contracts)" (Lee, 1993, 144). *Generally Accepted Accounting Principles around the world have increasingly narrowed the scope for off-balance sheet activity. See also *substance over form.

Office of Internal Oversight Services (OIOS) The main *internal auditing and *oversight body of the United Nations. On its Web site, the OIOS states its mission to be as follows: "To provide internal oversight for the United Nations that adds value to the Organization through independent, professional and timely internal audit, *monitoring, *inspection, *evaluation, management *consulting and *investigation activities. To be an agent of change that promotes responsible administration of resources, a culture of *accountability and *transparency and improved programme performance." This mission statement reflects modern concepts of internal auditing in its careful balancing of *compliance testing and consulting activity.

Web link: *www.un.org/Depts/oios*

offset, to To classify an amount so that it reduces or eliminates another amount. In a *general ledger, for example, *amortization *accounts are offset against *property, plant, and equipment accounts to calculate the net *book value of *fixed assets.

offshore 1. [of corporations and investments] Located in a *tax haven, typically a small, island nation. 2. [in the oil and gas industry] Extracted from the seabed.

oligopoly A *market in which a small number of *suppliers provide the bulk of activity. The leading suppliers in an oligopolistic market may have the potential opportunity to act together to influence the *prices of their products and services. Regulations and *antitrust laws are designed to combat the anti*competitive effects of oligopolistic markets. See also *cartel and *monopoly.

operating expenses 1. *Costs that relate to an organization's normal activities. Examples of operating expenses include administrative, *manufacturing, and selling costs. 2. *Costs incurred by an organization that do not relate directly to *manufacturing activity.

operating lease A *lease whose contractual terms and economic effects do not involve the transfer of the *risks and *rewards of a leased asset. Under most systems of *Generally Accepted Accounting Principles, a *lessee does not *capitalize an asset obtained through an operation lease—ownership remains with a *lessor. Contrast *capital lease.

operational auditing 1. The auditing of an organization's operational and *managerial activities, as opposed to its accounting transactions. The first use of the term is widely attributed to Frederic E. Mints in 1954 (Flesher, 1991, 5) prior to which the term nonaccounting had been used in place of operational.

Operational auditing often focuses on the *Three E's of the *economy, *efficiency, and *effectiveness of activities. Compare *compliance audit and *management audit. **2.** In a wider and looser sense, the term is often used as an alternative name for internal auditing.

Further reading: Cadmus (1964); Chambers and Rand (1997); Flesher (1982); Mints (1954)

opinion See *audit opinion.

opportunity cost The *cost arising from a decision not to pursue a course of action. Opportunity cost is often measured in terms of the *reward foregone by choosing a next best course of action. For example, if an organization purchases a productive asset for $100, the opportunity cost is calculated as the most rewarding alternative use to which the $100 could have been put. The alternative action may include investing the amount at a bank to earn *interest. See also *cost-benefit analysis.

option The right to buy or sell an *asset or *security at a specific *price within a defined time period. The option confers a right rather than an obligation. See *call option and *put option.

order **1.** A contractual commitment to purchase a good or service. **2.** An instruction or command. **3.** A logical arrangement or structuring of items. **4.** A document instructing a bank to pay a sum of *money to a specified individual.

Ordre des Experts-Comptables A French professional accounting and external auditing organization. The *expert-comptable* is the French equivalent of the *Certified Public Accountant, but the *public accounting profession is less extensive in France than in the English-speaking world. The *Ordre* had around 16,000 members in 2003, with a significant overlapping of membership with the French body that supervises external auditing, the *Compagnie Nationale des Commissaires aux Comptes* (CNCC).

The *Ordre*'s current name dates from 1994, but its predecessor organizations trace their origins to the nineteenth century—the most recognizable antecedents were set up in the 1940s. The *Ordre* is headquartered in Paris, and its activities include a French-language publishing program, including a monthly magazine, the *Revue Française de la Comptabilité*. It has no direct standard-setting responsibilities, but it participates in the activities of the national French *accounting standards-setting body, the *Comité de la Réglementation Comptable*. (French *auditing standards are set by the CNCC.)

Web site (some material in English): *www.experts-comptables.org*

organizational governance An alternative term for *corporate governance. The term organizational governance explicitly extends the theories of corporate governance to all noncorporate organizations like partnerships.

organization chart A diagrammatic portrayal of the structure of an organization. Organization charts tend to focus on *reporting and *accountability relationships between employees, and on the hierarchical links between branches and operational entities.

Organization for Economic Co-operation and Development (OECD)

A Paris-based international organization representing 30 nations. The OECD was established in 1961, and it superseded the Organization for European Economic Co-operation which administered U.S. aid under the Marshall Plan following World War II. The OECD's activities include the production of economic statistics, technical assistance for developing countries, and an extensive publications program. The OECD describes itself (on its Web site) as an organization of nations that share "a commitment to democratic government and the market economy." It also states that the organization "has been called a think tank, a monitoring agency, a rich man's club and an unacademic university. It has elements of all, but none of these descriptions captures the essence of the OECD."

The OECD's areas of interest include (i) the promotion of the institutional framework for *globalization, (ii) the curbing of international *bribery, (iii) the monitoring of *tax havens, and (iv) the enhancement of international *corporate governance. On the latter topic, the OECD undertakes a vigorous program of publications and policy statements: Its *OECD Principles of Corporate Governance*, finalized in 1999, are nonbinding but are widely considered to be authoritative. The OECD's publications also include guidelines for the conduct of *multinational enterprises in areas like environment practices and anti*corruption measures. All these policy documents and guidelines are available from the OECD Web site. The organization also participates in the *International Forum on Accountancy Development.

Web site: *www.oecd.org*

organization man (or woman) A human character molded by the impersonality of large-scale organizational management, and characterized by conformity, mediocrity, and a mechanistic nature. The term was coined by William H. Whyte in 1956, in a book of the same title, to denote the suppression of individuality and personal morality by the ideologies of modern bureaucratic organizations.

Further reading: Whyte (2002)

outside director A member of an organization's *board of directors who is not an employee of the organization. Outside directors are expected to bring to a board of directors an independent perspective of performance and standards of conduct, and to share best practices observed in other organizations.

outsourcing The obtaining of goods and services from an external *supplier, rather than from internal resources. The outsourcing of internal auditing services by external auditing firms grew in importance at the close of the twentieth century. Advantages of outsourcing internal auditing services include (i) access to expertise and *know-how, (ii) the flexible use of audit resources, and (iii) reductions in the size of an in-house *internal audit function. Disadvantages include (i) an organization's dependence on its *suppliers, (ii) a loss of control to outside consultants, (iii) security risks as suppliers gain access to confidential or sensitive information, and (iv) a potential loss of collective organizational memory of audit-related areas.

Further reading: Figg (2000b); Rittenberg (1997); Rittenberg and Covalski (2001)

outstanding 1. Of exceptional quality. 2. Still unresolved. 3. Still unpaid.

overdraft A deficit in a bank account. An overdraft may or may not be in accordance with an agreed *credit line.

overhead An administrative or *indirect cost that is not directly related to a *manufactured product or a revenue-generating service. Contrast *cost of sales.

oversight 1. The *monitoring of an activity or asset over time. Auditing is central to oversight in *corporate governance: The United Nations, for example, has institutionalized its internal auditing activity within its *Office of Internal Oversight Services (OIOS). 2. A failure to notice an event or to perform an action.

overstatement The exaggerated quantification or description of an item. The term is often used in the context of incorrectly stated accounting *balances. Contrast *understatement.

over-the-counter (OTC) market A market for *securities that are not listed on a stock exchange. The term dates from the nineteenth century, when securities of this type were traded in banks and physically handed to *investors across bank counters.

overtrading The undertaking of business activity that results in *cash flow problems and potential *insolvency. Overtrading is characterized by *working capital problems arising from the simultaneous (i) slow receipt of cash receipts relating to *accounts receivable and (ii) pressing demands for payments to *suppliers.

Pacioli, Luca (1445–1517) An Italian monk and mathematician. Although considered by many to be the "founder" of *double entry bookkeeping, Pacioli is best described as the first individual in Europe to systemically set out double entry accounting principles. His famous Italian-language treatise *Summa de Arithmetica, Geometria, Proportioni et Proportionalità* (1494) dealt principally with mathematics, but it included a section devoted to accounting techniques. Very much a man of the Italian Renaissance, the multi-talented Pacioli obtained his bookkeeping knowledge from contemporary Venetian merchants' practices. Some accounting historians have tended to exaggerate Pacioli's standing as a major Renaissance thinker, perhaps (by extension) to enhance the standing of accounting theory itself. However, Pacioli was only a minor figure in the Renaissance, and many standard works on the subject only mention him in passing: Some Italian Renaissance histories (e.g., Stephens, 1990) do not mention him at all.

Further reading: Brown (1984); Lee et al. (1996)

Pacioli Society An Australian accounting organization. Founded in 1968 by *Raymond John Chambers as a forum for accounting debate, the society now operates as part of the University of Sydney's *Accounting Foundation, and it is linked to the academic journal *Abacus.

Web link: *www.econ.usyd.edu.au/content.php?pageid=1983*

paid-in capital Stockholders' *equity that has been issued and paid in cash. There are several aspects of paid-in capital, including (i) the *par value of *common stock, (ii) a *premium (definition 2), and (iii) common stock received from donations.

paperless office A term used to denote an environment in which computerized, on-screen information minimizes the level of paper documentation. In recent years, sophisticated information technology systems have reduced the need for extensive, paper-based documentation. The reduction in *hard copy records has not been met without reservations, however, by those (including regulatory authorities) who prefer to see an adequate level of physical documentation to support *audit trails. On this theme, a humorous comment that circulated in the late twentieth century: "The paperless office is about as useful as the paperless toilet" (*anon.*).

paper profit *Income (definition 2) that is not mirrored in underlying *cash flow. See also *unrealized gain.

parent organization A corporation or other entity that controls one or more *subsidiary organizations. Control can be effected through either a majority of *common stock voting rights or through dominance influence on a subsidiary's management or operating policies. See also *holding company.

pari passu A Latin expression meaning "with an equal rate of progress," "equally," or "side by side." The term is commonly used in economic literature.

partnership An unincorporated business entity in which two or more individuals (known as partners) agree to share the *risks and *rewards of an activity. Unlike a *corporation, a partnership does not have a separate legal personality— partners essentially act as *agents for one another, and individual partners have unlimited personal liability for the debts of the business. (The liability of so-called "limited partners" is restricted to the value of their investment in the partnership.) The advantages of partnerships include (i) a low level of administrative costs, (ii) a low level of regulations, and (iii) flexibility to admit new partners. The main disadvantage of partnerships is the unlimited liability of individual partners.

par value The nominal, monetary amount of an individual share of *common stock. Par value tends to be the legally protected minimum value of stock for creditor protection purposes and it is usually established when stock is issued. In practice, common stock market values tend to significantly exceed their historic par values, and common stock is often issued at a *premium (definition 2). See also *face value.

password A string of characters that permits access to a computerized information system. Password access is designed to increase the confidentiality of information, and to enforce *authorization limits. Password control is strengthened by (i) the maintenance of secrecy, (ii) their regular changing, and (iii) the inclusion of nonalphanumeric characters that make decipherment more difficult.

patent **1.** [noun] A license granted by a government that gives rights over an activity for a defined time period. A patent is an *intangible asset. Typical activities covered by a patent are the manufacture and sale of *products. See also *trademark. **2.** [adjective] Obvious.

payback period **1.** A period of time over which the costs of an investment are recouped by cash flows the investment generates. To take a simple example, a

$12,500 investment that is expected to result in annual, net cash inflows of $5,000 has a payback period of 2.5 years. In practice, payback calculations are complicated by uncertainty over cash flows and the effects of the *time value of money. The latter issue is usually addressed by *discounting future cash flows to their *present values. **2.** A period of time over which a loan should be reimbursed.

payment in kind The transfer of economic benefits in the form of goods and services, rather than in the form of *money. See also *barter.

payroll A list of an organization's employees and their *remuneration details.

peer review The review of an auditor's work by another auditor. Peer review is a form of self-regulation and *quality control in the external auditing profession.

pension plan An arrangement to fund regular payments and other benefits to individuals who no longer work. Pensions can be paid by a government on the basis of age, or by employers on the basis of a period of employment. Most pension schemes require contributions from members during their active or working lives, through the form of *taxation (for government pension plans) or *payroll deductions (for occupational pension plans), but some pension plans are non-contributory. Pensions are often classified into *defined benefit and *defined contribution plans, and their complex funding requirements are determined by *actuaries. In the early twenty-first century many pension plans were under severe funding pressure as a result of (i) demographic changes and (ii) poorly performing *equity investments. Pension funds are among the largest *institutional investors.

per annum A Latin expression meaning "annually." Compare *per diem*.

per capita Latin expression meaning "by head" (of population). The phrase is commonly used in the context of economic statistics: Examples are "per capita *Gross Domestic Product (GDP)" and "per capita *consumption."

percentage A number or rate expressed as a proportion of 100.

per diem A Latin expression meaning "daily." The phrase is common in accounting and auditing, in which it is used to denote daily travel subsistence allowances and the charging of professional fees. Compare *per annum*.

performance audit An audit of an activity or operation with reference to adherence to *policies, *procedures, *regulations, and defined objectives.

Performance auditing is an aspect of *management auditing and *operational auditing, and it is often associated with *public sector organizations.

Further reading: Dittenhofer (2001); Morgan and Raaum (2001)

periodic Occurring from time to time. The term is used in relation to both regular and irregular time intervals.

permanent difference A difference between *income (definition 2) calculated under *Generally Accepted Accounting Principles and income calculated according to *taxation rules. Permanent differences are never resolved or reversed. Contrast *temporary difference.

permanent file Audit documentation that records information of a *long-term nature. The records of *audit tests for specific assignments are normally maintained separately from a permanent file. A permanent file typically includes the following information on an *auditee: (i) Organization charts and charters, (ii) *policies and *procedures, (iii) details of *internal controls, and (iv) *minutes of *board meetings.

perpetual inventory (PI) A system of *inventory control that regularly updates inventory quantities. A PI system may be *real time, or there may be a slight delay between inventory movements and the updating of inventory balances. Auditors often place reliance on PI systems through periodic verification of their correct functioning. In such cases, auditors frequently dispense with traditional *physical inventory counts at financial period-ends, as they can obtain *audit evidence on the accuracy of inventory balances at any time (thereby minimizing disruption to warehouse operations). Under a continuous stocktaking exercise, all locations or products within a warehouse can be gradually audited over a defined time period.

perpetuity An *annuity that continues indefinitely, with no specified *maturity date. The *present value of a perpetuity is calculated by dividing the perpetuity's periodic, constant payment by an appropriate *discount (definition 2) rate.

Petroleum Accounting and Financial Management Journal A U.S. industry-specific accounting journal. Established in 1982, the journal is published three times a year by the Institute of Petroleum Accounting at the University of North Texas. It is available in print format only, but content summaries are available online. The journal contains a mix of academic and practitioner articles, and its contents are of value for auditors in the petroleum sector. It frequently covers auditing and *corporate governance issues, and its scope is international.

Web site: *www.unt.edu/ipa/journal.htm*

petty cash   Small amounts of *cash (definition 1) kept for minor, day-to-day expenses. Although not *material, *internal controls over petty cash tend to be strong in most organizations. Typical controls include (i) a secure storage location, (ii) the *accountability of specific individuals for cash custody and handling, (iii) authorization procedures to support disbursements, (iv) documentary evidence to support disbursements, and (v) periodic counts to verify the cash balance held.

phantom employee   A fictitious employee included in a *payroll register. Phantom employees are normally created for *fraudulent purposes, as *compensation nominally paid to the "phantoms" can be illegally diverted elsewhere.

phantom ticking   The falsification of audit *work papers through the documentation of misleading or bogus *audit tests. The term derives from the *ticking procedures used in manual audit work papers.

Philippine Institute of Certified Public Accountants (PICPA)   The Philippines' main professional accounting and external auditing organization. Established in 1929, the PICPA is headquartered in Manila. In 2003 it had approximately 76,000 members, a significant minority of whom were based outside of the Philippines (e.g., in the Mideast). The PICPA issues Philippine *auditing standards, and it has encouraged the country's *accounting standards-setter to adopt *International Accounting Standards.
   Web site: *www.picpa.com.ph*

Philosophy of Auditing, The   A landmark study of auditing's theoretical underpinnings. Coauthored by *Robert Khun Mautz and Hussein A. Sharaf, and published by the *American Accounting Association, *The Philosophy of Auditing* first appeared in 1961. Among the book's contributions to the development of auditing theory was its elaboration of *postulates of auditing.
   Further reading: Mautz and Sharaf (1961)

physical inspection   The careful *examination of a *tangible asset. Physical *inspection is an important means of gathering and *evaluating *audit evidence for *inventory, *property, plant, and equipment, and other assets. It is a form of *substantive testing. The term is often used synonymously with *physical verification.

physical inventory   **1.** Audit procedures devised to obtain evidence of the existence, condition, and physical quantities of *inventory. The counting of inventory quantities is normally performed on a sample basis, especially when the volume of inventory makes a full count unfeasible. The results of sample counting may be extrapolated to the entire inventory *population, provided that *compliance testing suggests the satisfactory operation of relevant *internal controls. Physical inventory tests may range from counts performed annually to periodic (or *continuous) verifications of the accuracy of *perpetual inventory data, or a combination of the two. Obtaining evidence of the accuracy of inventory balances stated in financial statements has been of immense importance to auditors since the *great salad oil swindle of the early 1960s. **2.** Audit procedures devised to obtain evidence of the existence, condition, and physical quantities of *property, plant, and equipment.

physical verification The *examination of a *tangible asset in order to obtain evidence of its existence and condition. The term is often used synonymously with *physical inspection. See also *verification.

plan comptable général (PCG) The national *chart of accounts used in France as well as in some other countries (e.g., in West Africa) influenced by French culture. Roughly translated as "general accounting plan," the *PCG* exists in different forms for different industries. It is characterized by the use of standardized general ledger account numbers, which facilitates tax assessments and the gathering of national economic statistics. The *PCG* also gives guidance on the accounting treatment of the items it covers. The *PCG* was introduced to France during the 1940s, and early drafts during World War II were based on German models.

Further reading: Colasse and Durand (1995); Nobes and Parker (2002), 215–238

planned economy An alternative term for *command economy.

planning The establishment of objectives and intentional strategies for the achievement of objectives. Planning is considered to be one of the main functions of organizational *management, and it is often analyzed into *short-term and *long-term aspects. See also *audit planning.

point of sale (POS) **1.** A computerized retail system that captures sales *transactions at the location and moment of customer payment. **2.** The principle, in accordance with the *accruals basis of accounting, that *revenue is *recognized in financial statements only in the accounting period to which it relates. The point of sale for tangible products is usually based on the date of dispatch of goods to customers, and for services on the date at which a service is performed.

poison pill A damaging tactic adopted by a corporation as a deterrent to an unwelcomed *takeover bid. An example of a poison pill is the sale of an attractive asset in order to make a corporation a less attractive takeover target.

policy 1. A formal rule of conduct in an organization. Policies often describe (i) essential administrative *procedures, (ii) limits of *authority, and (iii) required adherence to *regulations. See also *procedure. 2. An *insurance contract.

pooling of interests An accounting method used for *business combinations in cases when an acquiring corporation issues *common stock in exchange for the *acquisition of the common stock of another corporation. The acquired corporation's *net assets are brought into consolidated accounts at *book value, and *net income is consolidated for an entire *fiscal year, irrespective of the date of the acquisition. *Generally Accepted Accounting Principles set strict criteria for the use of pooling of interests accounting.

population A set of data from which a *sample may be extracted. Auditors frequently make judgments on *audit evidence by *extrapolating the findings of samples to entire populations of data. See also *judgmental sampling, *random sampling, *stratified sampling, and *statistical sampling.

portfolio 1. A combination of *securities or other investments. Portfolios can *diversify risk by containing assets with different risk profiles. *Portfolio theory analyzes the composition of efficient portfolios. 2. A bank's list of its *loans to customers.

portfolio risk The risk that an actual *return on an investment (or on a *portfolio of investments) differs from an expected return. See *portfolio theory.

portfolio theory A branch of financial economics associated with Harry M. Markowitz (born 1927) that analyzes the *diversification of *risk through the holding of a *portfolio of investments. A major assumption underlying portfolio theory is that investors are *risk-averse by nature, yet they desire high *returns on their investments. Investors therefore expect higher *returns from higher risks, and they aim to hold efficient portfolios of investments in line with their *risk appetites. An efficient portfolio of investments is one that gives the highest possible return for a specific level of risk, or the smallest possible level of risk for a specific expected return. Efficient portfolios of investments generally benefit from the spreading of risk through *diversification, but in any portfolio there is an element of risk that cannot be diversified away: this is known as *systematic risk.

post-audit period In external auditing, the period of time between the end of detailed *audit testing and the formal issuing of an *audit opinion. The external auditor is obliged to consider the impact on audited *financial statements of any *material events during this period. See also *event after the balance sheet date.

post balance sheet event An alternative term for an *event after the balance sheet date.

post balance sheet review An external auditor's review of *events after the balance sheet date.

post-dated check A *check that can be honored only on a specified date later than the date on which the check is issued.

posting The recording of an accounting *transaction or *journal entry. Some users restrict the term to one of two contexts: (i) the recording of an item directly in a *general ledger account and (ii) the transfer of *subsidiary ledger totals to a general ledger account. In practice, however, the term is often used freely in both contexts.

postulates of auditing Theoretical principles and assumptions that purport to define the basis of auditing. *Robert Khun Mautz and Hussein A. Sharaf elaborated eight "tentative" postulates of auditing in *The Philosophy of Auditing* (1961, Chapter 3):

1. *Financial statements and *financial data are verifiable.
2. There is no necessary *conflict of interest between the auditor and the *management of the enterprise under audit.
3. The financial statements and other information submitted for *verification are free from *collusive and other unusual *irregularities.
4. The existence of a satisfactory system of *internal control eliminates the *probability of irregularities.
5. Consistent application of generally accepted principles of accounting results in the *fair presentation of *financial position and the results of operations.
6. In the absence of clear evidence to the contrary, what has held true in the past for the enterprise under examination will hold true in the future.
7. When examining financial data for the purpose of expressing an *independent opinion thereon, the auditor acts exclusively in the capacity of an auditor.
8. The *professional status of the independent auditor imposes commensurate professional obligations.

Mautz and Sharaf's postulates were developed in the context of external auditing, and have been debated and criticized at length, not least by critics of some of the postulates' apparently "optimistic" nature. Some theorists (e.g., Flint, 1988, and Lee, 1993) have attempted to develop and refine the postulates. Nearly half a century after their formulation, however, the postulates remain highly relevant: For example, postulates 7 and 8 go to the heart of concerns over the independence of external auditors, a topic that has dominated *corporate governance following the demise of *Enron in 2001 and that of the auditing firm *Arthur Andersen in 2002.

Further reading: Mautz and Sharaf (1961)

Power, Michael (born 1957) A British academic, author, and auditing specialist. A professor of accounting at the London School of Economics and Political Science, Power is best known for his book *The Audit Society: Rituals of Verification* (1997), in which he popularized the controversial concept of the *audit society. Power's thoughts on the audit society were adumbrated in some of his earlier writings, including the 1994 monograph *The Audit Explosion*, and have been refined in his subsequent writings (Power, 2000).

Power is an articulate critic of received ideas of the practice and theory of auditing, and his arguments owe something to the *critical accounting movement. He has drawn attention to the theoretical uncertainties of auditing, referring to the discipline's "essentially elusive epistemological character" (Power, 1997, 11), and has claimed that "there is no robust conception of 'good' auditing independent either of auditor judgements or of the system of knowledge in which those judgements are embedded and against which particular audits could be judged" (Power, 1997, 29). He has also claimed that "a certain proceduralization of the audit process acts as compensation for its essential obscurity" (1997, 81), thereby casting doubt on the "official" explanations of auditing promoted by *professional associations. Clearly, such arguments are controversial, and there is an entire literature devoted to analyzing, criticizing, and defending Power's arguments. His other areas of interest include financial regulation, *risk management, and the links between science and accounting.

Further reading: Power (1994a); Power (1994b); Power (1994c); Power (1997); Power (2000); Power (2003)

***Practical Accountant*®** A U.S. accounting magazine. Founded in 1968, *Practical Accountant* is published monthly by the Accountants Media Group, a division of Thomson, as part of the *WebCPA framework. Its primary audience comprises *Certified Public Accountants in the United States.

Web site: *www.webcpa.com/practicalaccountant*

Practicing CPA, The A U.S. professional accounting newsletter. Published ten times a year by the *American Institute of Certified Public Accountants, the newsletter is available online. It focuses on professional developments and news of relevance to *Certified Public Accountants. Topics covered by the newsletter include the management of *public accounting firms.

Web site: *www.aicpa.org/pubs/tpcpa/index.htm*

predatory pricing A sales *pricing policy intended to undercut competitors' prices. Predatory pricing can be undertaken to achieve any or all of the following objectives: (i) to maintain or increase *market share, (ii) to drive competitors out of a *market, and (iii) to erect *barriers to entry to a market.

preference shares A British term for *preferred stock.

preferred stock An ownership share in a corporation that has preference over *common stock in the distribution of earnings. Preferred status over common stock also often relates to payments arising on a corporation's liquidation. Preferred *stockholders take on less risk than common stockholders, as their dividend income is usually based on a fixed percentage. The owners of preferred stock do not normally enjoy voting rights, or may have only restricted voting rights.

preliminary audit An audit performed in advance of a main audit. In external auditing, preliminary audits often take place during an *auditee's *fiscal year, and they focus on *audit planning and *compliance testing. In contrast, final audits tend to concentrate on *substantive testing.

premium 1. [noun] A regular payment of *money to pay for an *insurance policy. A premium is a form of *consideration. **2.** [noun] An amount added to a basic or established *cost or *price. Examples include (i) an excess paid over the *par value of *common stock, (ii) an excess paid over the *face value of a *bond, and (iii) an increase in the sales *price of a product. **3.** [adjective] Of high or exceptional quality.

prepaid expenses Expenses not yet incurred in a *financial reporting period, but for which cash payment has already been made. In line with the *accruals basis of accounting, prepaid expenses are recorded as a *current or *long-term asset in the *balance sheet, and are released to expenses in the accounting periods to which they relate. Typical prepaid expenses include *insurance and rental costs.

present fairly, to See *fair presentation.

present value The value at the present time of future *cash flows. The *time value of money implies that units of *money are worth more at present than in the future, owing to the erosion of monetary value caused by *inflation. Present values are thereby calculated by restating future cash flows in current terms by the use of an appropriate *discount rate (normally an organization's *cost of capital). See also *net present value.

preventative control An *internal control designed to anticipate and block the occurrence of an unwanted event. Compare *corrective control and *detective control.

price 1. The rate at which a good or service can be exchanged for *money. Price mechanisms are driven by competitive pressures in capitalist or *mixed economies in the regulation of *supply and *demand, and they facilitate distribution and exchange. Price controls are often used by governments in attempts to regulate and control markets. **2.** The *rate of exchange between two goods. See also *barter arrangements.

price discrimination A sales *pricing policy in which different prices are established for different buyers. Price discrimination is only possible in a *market that can be segmented in some manner. For example, a transport business may set different prices at different times of the day, and a *multinational corporation may set different prices for a *product in different countries.

price/earnings (P/E) ratio The ratio of the *market price of a share of a corporation's *common stock to *earnings per share. The P/E ratio is a fundamental investment statistic used to appraise a corporation's *securities.

price sensitive information Information likely to affect the *market value of a *listed *security. See also *insider dealing.

PricewaterhouseCoopers (PwC) A global accounting, auditing, and professional services firm. One of the *Big Four firms, PwC was established in its current form by the merger of Price Waterhouse and Coopers & Lybrand in 1998. (The merger was an important stage in the ongoing consolidation of the large accounting firms, and at the time it reduced the Big Six to the *Big Five.) The origins of both Price Waterhouse and Coopers & Lybrand are traced to the United Kingdom in the nineteenth century.
    Further reading: Allen (1990); Jones (1995); Matthews et al. (1998)
    Web site: *www.pwcglobal.com*

prima facie A Latin term, used extensively in legal contexts, meaning "at first sight" or "as it first appears." For example, to describe evidence as *prima facie* indicates that the weight of the evidence appears to be overwhelming.

prime cost 1. *Direct costs in a manufacturing process. Prime costs usually exclude *overheads. **2.** An alternative term for *conversion cost.

principal 1. [noun] An individual who, in *agency theory, delegates responsibilities to an *agent. A principal can be remote from the actions of an agent in both physical terms (i.e., geographical distance) and intellectual terms (i.e., an inability to understand the complexity of an activity). **2.** [noun] The base amount of a financial instrument on which *interest accrues. **3.** [adjective] Main, or most important.

principal–agent problem See *agency costs.

principal auditor An alternative term for *Chief Auditing Executive.

prisoner's dilemma A branch of *game theory that systematically analyzes strategies for the optimal selection of alternative courses of action in competitive conditions. The prisoner's dilemma focuses on the complexities of making competitive choices. In a simplified version of the game, two criminal accomplices are held in separate prison cells, without means of communicating between one another. They face charges of either homicide or theft, according to the following options: (i) If both prisoners confess to homicide, then both will be sentenced for homicide, but with reduced prison sentences; (ii) if neither prisoner confesses to homicide, then both prisoners will be sentenced for the lesser charge of theft; or (iii) if one prisoner confesses to homicide, then he or she will be freed and the accomplice alone will be sentenced for homicide. It is clearly against the interests of the prisoners for both of them to confess, but this is a likely outcome arising from suspicion of the other's motives. Prisoner's theory is often applied to the decisions facing individuals in economic and social contexts.

private sector In *mixed economies, the parts of economic life not under direct government control. The term refers both to organizations (listed *corporations and *not-for-profit entities) and economic *transactions between individuals.

privatization The transfer from government control to the *private sector of economic activity and organizations. Privatization covers a variety of matters: (i) the denationalization of government-controlled *corporations, (ii) the *deregulation or liberalization of economic sectors, and (iii) the subcontracting to the private sector of traditionally *public sector activities. Contrast *nationalization.

probability The likelihood of the occurrence of an event, measured by the ratio of likely occurrences to the total number of possible occurrences. Probabilities can be expressed as (i) *percentages, (ii) decimals between 0 and 1, (iii) fractions, and (iv) qualitative estimates (e.g., high, medium, and low). Using percentages, a probability of 0 percent suggests that an event will never occur, while a probability of 100 percent suggests that an event will occur with *certainty. See also *expected value, *risk, and *uncertainty.

procedural audit An audit of an organization's *procedures, *internal controls, and related areas. An example of a procedural audit is a review of the adherence by an organization's employees to a *disbursements *authorization procedure.

procedure A formal, detailed rule of conduct in an organization. The terms procedure and *policy are often used interchangeably, but careful users restrict the former to detailed administrative rules, and the latter to more general statements on organizational conduct.

proceeds *Money received as a result of a *transaction.

process **1.** [noun] An intentional, sequential series of actions to achieve a defined purpose. See also *business process re-engineering. **2.** [noun] A court action. **3.** [verb] The sorting, analysis, and reporting of *data, especially by a computer. See *data processing.

process costing A costing method that uses an organization's manufacturing *processes to allocate costs to *products. Typically used in the large-scale production of identical items (e.g., in the chemicals industry), process costing uses activity levels in *cost centers to determine cost *absorption.

product An item created as a result of a *production process. See also *consumer good.

production **1.** The creation of tangible items from *raw materials and other inputs. See also *by-product, *joint product, and the *factors of production. **2.** The display or showing of something.

productivity A measure of the rate of output from the use of defined quantities of inputs. Based on the use of *factors of production, the concept is typically applied to labor productivity and capital productivity, and it is often measured by ratios and indexes.

profession A skilled occupation that requires a high level of expertise and that fulfills a public service. The three traditional "learned professions" are divinity, law, and medicine, but from the nineteenth century a number of new professions arose, including accounting and auditing. Elements of a profession typically include (i) provision of a service that is "essential to the public" (Flint, 1988, 88), (ii) mastery of a body of formal knowledge, (iii) certification as a means of obtaining exclusive or *monopolistic rights, (iv) an institutional framework, (v) written standards for work performance, personal conduct, and ethics, and (vi) a commitment to exercise due care in the performance of duties. That the responsibilities of external auditors derive from their *professional status was one of the *postulates of auditing developed by *Robert Khun Mautz and Hussein A. Sharaf. Internal auditing has become increasingly professionalized since the founding of the *Institute of Internal Auditors in 1941.

Further reading: Abbott (1988); Friedson (1986); Larson (1977); Lee (1993), 87–92; O'Regan (2001)

Professional Practices Framework (PPF) The professional framework for internal auditing established by the *Institute of Internal Auditors.

Further reading: Chapman and Anderson (2002); IIA (1999)

profit See *income (definitions 2 and 3).

profitability The capacity of an activity or organization to generate *income (definition 2).

profit and loss account An alternative term for *income statement that is commonly used in the United Kingdom and in other countries with significant British influence.

profit center An activity, unit, or individual within an organization with which *income can be identified. Compare *cost center.

profit margin 1. The ratio of *net income to *net sales. 2. The ratio of *gross income to *net sales.

profit-seeking Motivated primarily by the generation of *income (definitions 2 and 3).

profit-sharing A *contractual arrangement to share the *net income of an organization between two or more parties. Contexts in which profit-sharing occurs include (i) employee *compensation schemes, (ii) *partnerships, and (iii) *joint venture arrangements.

profit-taking The sale of an investment or asset to *realize an *appreciation in value.

pro forma A Latin expression meaning "for form's sake" or "as a matter of form." For example, *pro forma* financial statements contain assumed or estimated amounts, and *pro forma* invoices are sent to customers to elicit payments in advance of the dispatch of the related goods.

program evaluation and review techniques (PERT) See *critical path analysis.

progress billing The raising of *sales invoices and the *recognition of revenue in accordance with the progress of a *long-term sales *transaction.

progressive tax A *taxation system in which *tax rates increase with higher levels of taxable income. Contrast *regressive tax.

project An undertaking to achieve defined objectives. The accounting treatment of projects is driven, in accordance with the *accruals concept, by the distribution of costs and revenues over the *short and *long terms.

promissory note A *contractual document that contains a promise to pay a specified sum of *money at a specified date. Some forms of promissory note are traded.

property, plant, and equipment *Long-term, *tangible assets used for operational or administrative purposes. The term does not normally refer to assets held principally for investment or trading purposes. It typically refers to land, buildings, machinery, and office equipment. Other than land, assets in this category are normally subjected to *amortization under most systems of *Generally Accepted Accounting Principles. Contrast *current asset.

pro rata A Latin expression meaning "on a proportional basis." The term is used to describe the proportional *allocation of costs and revenues to activities, assets, liabilities, or time periods.

prospectus A document that promotes the sale of an asset or service. In particular, the term is used in the context of corporate documents to promote the issuing of new *securities.

Protiviti® A U.S.-based international consulting firm specializing in internal auditing and *risk management. Protiviti is a subsidiary of Robert Half International Inc., and its activities include *KnowledgeLeader*, a subscription-based Web site with risk management and internal auditing resources.
  Web site: *www.protiviti.com*

provision **1.** A *liability arising from the accounting treatment of *accrued expenses. A provision is shown as either a *short-term or *long-term liability in a *balance sheet, depending on the nature of the underlying circumstances that give rise to the provision. **2.** An amount *recognized in an accounting period for a reduction of the value of an *asset, in line with the *accruals basis of accounting. An example of a provision is an *allowance for bad debts. See also *reserve. **3.** A legally binding condition or *contractual clause.

provision for doubtful debts A British term for *allowance for bad debts.

proxy The authority to represent another individual, or to vote on that individual's behalf. Proxy voting arrangements are common at corporate *stockholders' meetings.

prudence The exercise of care and restraint. In accounting, prudence underpins the *accruals concept in which *revenues and *expenses are *recognized only in the periods in which they are earned or incurred. Prudence discourages the anticipation of revenues and the deferment of expenses. In auditing, prudence refers to the exercise of careful *professional judgment. A prudent auditor is considered to exhibit "knowledge, skill, caution, and responsiveness" (Mautz and Sharaf, 1961, 139).

public accountant An individual licensed to perform defined accounting and auditing activities for the public. The range of activities undertaken by modern public accountants includes (i) the giving of *external audit opinions, (ii) the provision of financial accounting and taxation services, and (iii) other *management advisory services. The history of public accounting has been succinctly summarized as follows: Public accounting "was born through *bankruptcies, fed on failures and *fraud, grew on *liquidations and graduated through audits" (quoted in Matthews et al., 1998, 93). See also *Certified Public Accountant.

Public Company Accounting Oversight Board (PCAOB) A panel established in 2002 by the *Securities and Exchange Commission (SEC) as a result of the *Sarbanes-Oxley Act. The board consists of a five-member panel and its duties are centered on the oversight of the external auditing of public corporations' financial statements. On its Web site, the PCAOB describes its mission as follows: To "protect investors in U.S. securities markets and to further the public interest by ensuring that public company financial statements are audited according to the highest standards of quality, independence, and ethics." The PCAOB also has authority to discipline external auditors.

Web site: *www.pcaobus.org*

public sector In *mixed economies, the parts of economic life that are under government control. This sector includes government departments and nationalized *corporations, and in most countries it is subjected to extensive auditing. See also *Supreme Audit Institution.

Further reading: Normanton (1966)

public utility An organization that provides resources or services considered essential for the public good. Typical examples of public utilities include (i) electricity, gas, and water supplies, (ii) refuse collection, (iii) postal services, and (iv) certain forms of transport. Public utilities often enjoy government-sanctioned *monopoly rights.

put option   The right to sell an *asset or *security at a specific *price within a defined time period. Contrast *call option.

pyramid scheme   A high-*risk *investment system based on small, initial sums of *money. Pyramid schemes are often *fraudulent. They function like chain letters, depending on ever-increasing numbers of money-paying participants to join the scheme: Investors are promised high *returns, and the *cash flow to pay the returns is dependent on the new investors' contributions. When the pool of new investors eventually dries up, the system collapses under the weight of its own mathematics, and participants can lose all or part of their investment. In Albania in the 1990s, a series of large-scale pyramid schemes robbed thousands of people of their life savings, causing serious street unrest and a political crisis.

qualified opinion An external auditor's opinion that, except for a stated limitation, an entity's financial statements conform with *Generally Accepted Accounting Principles, and offer a *fair presentation of the entity's financial position, the results of its operations, and changes in cash flows. Qualified opinions normally arise from a limitation in the scope of the audit work, and under most systems of *Generally Accepted Auditing Standards external auditors are obliged to explain the reasons for issuing a qualified opinion. Compare *adverse opinion, *disclaimer, and *unqualified opinion.

qualitative Relating to measurement by nonmonetary or nonquantitative methods. Examples of qualitative considerations include (i) customer satisfaction, (ii) employee morale, and (iii) the aesthetic appeal of products. Contrast *quantitative.

quality 1. The conformity of an item or activity to an objective standard. The objective standard may be derived from the characteristics displayed by similar items or activities. **2.** Excellence.

quality audit The auditing of activities and operations with focus on adherence to the principles of *total quality management. Contrast *audit quality.

quality control Systems or procedures that aim to maintain high standards in *manufacturing processes or in the supply of services. The control of *quality is maintained through the *sample testing of the activity under consideration: The quality control of external auditing, for example, is partially effected through *peer review of a sample of audits.

quality of earnings The extent to which *net income reflects and portrays underlying economic circumstances. External auditors review the quality of earnings of *auditees, to obtain evidence that *financial statements have not been distorted by *creative accounting or other types of manipulation.

quality management See *total quality management.

quantitative Relating to measurement by quantity or monetary methods. Sales expressed in dollars or units are examples of quantitative measurements. Contrast *qualitative.

quasi A Latin word meaning "almost" or "as if." The word is encountered in terms like quasi-*contract, quasi-military, and quasi-official.

questionable payment A potentially illegal or improper payment. Examples of improper payments include *bribes and other cash *disbursements made for *corrupt purposes. See also *facilitating payment and the *Foreign Corrupt Practices Act*.

questionnaire A document that contains a structured series of questions. Questionnaires are often used in auditing and *internal control survey. In particular, *Control Risk Self Assessment techniques are frequently based on questionnaires. The limitations of questionnaires have often been emphasized by critics: for example, they have been called "subjective and easy to manipulate" (Toffler and Reingold, 2003, 144). However, they offer the advantage of being a cost-effective means of obtaining information in large organizations. See also *checklist and *box-ticking approach.

quick ratio An alternative term for the *acid test ratio.

quoted **1.** [of securities] Registered and traded on a stock exchange. See also *listed. **2.** [of a *price] Suggested prior to the formalizing of a *contract.

R

Radde, Leon R. (d. 1986) A U.S. internal auditing practitioner and educator. Radde was active in the *Institute of Internal Auditors from the 1960s to the 1980s, and he played a major role in the foundation of the *Certified Internal Auditor program. He taught internal auditing at the University of Minnesota. Following his death the IIA established an award in his honor: the Leon R. Radde Educator of the Year Award, that is given for the promotion of internal auditing education.

Further reading: Flesher (1991); Radde (1982)

rainy day reserves An alternative term for *cookie jar reserves.

random sampling The selection of a *sample of data from a *population on the basis that each item in the population has an even chance of being selected. In random sampling, there is no *judgmental element to skew the sample. See also *stratified sampling and *statistical sampling,

random walk The theory that the *market prices of *common stock (and other items, like *commodities) exhibit unpredictable patterns, and do not reflect historical trends. The theory argues that stock prices behave unpredictably because stock markets are inefficient. The market value of a security or commodity is independent of its *historical prices, and any new data affecting its value is immediately reflected in its price.

Rapport Viénot See *Viénot Report.

rate of exchange See *exchange rate.

rate of interest See *interest rate.

rate of return *Income derived from investments expressed as a percentage of an amount invested.

ratio A *quantitative relationship between two amounts. A ratio is calculated by dividing one amount by another, to see how many times the value of one item is contained in the other. See *ratio analysis.

ratio analysis The analysis of *financial statements through the investigation and interpretation of *ratios. Examples of important ratios include (i) the *acid test ratio, (ii) the *current ratio, (iii) the *debt-equity ratio, (iv) the *interest coverage ratio, and (v) the *price/earnings ratio. Financial statement ratios are often assessed in comparison with sector averages.

raw materials *Factors of production, typically natural resources, that have not yet been subjected to a *manufacturing process. During a manufacturing process, raw materials are normally referred to as *work-in-process until their conversion into *finished goods.

realization **1.** The conversion of an item into *cash. **2.** The *recognition of a *gain or *loss in an *income statement, in accordance with *Generally Accepted Accounting Principles.

real time The immediate (or almost immediate) processing and updating of information in computerized accounting systems.

real time auditing Auditing in the context of the *real time processing of information in computerized accounting systems. Future possible moves toward real time corporate reporting may further encourage the development of real time auditing.
   Further reading: Wilks (2002)

reasonable **1.** Fair, logical, and justifiable. Auditors are normally required, through the assessment of *audit evidence, to judge the reasonableness of matters under review: These may range from *financial statement items to operational *procedures to *internal controls. For example, *analytical reviews focus on the reasonableness and logic of relationships between items in financial statements. **2.** Inexpensive, or good value.

rebate **1.** A partial *refund of a sum of *money. **2.** An alternative term for *discount.

receipt **1.** A document that records or acknowledges the occurrence of an event. Examples include (i) *invoices and bills for expenditure, (ii) confirmation of *cash payments, and (iii) *product delivery documentation. **2.** The act of taking delivery of cash or an asset. **3.** [plural] An alternative term for *sales.

receivables Amounts of *money owed to an organization or individual. Trade receivables are referred to as *accounts receivable and nontrade receivables range from employee *advances to *taxation rebates. See also *debtor.

recession A slowdown in economic activity in a *market or territory. See also *depression.

Recognised Qualifying Body (RQB) A statutorily recognized organization for the licensing of external auditors in the United Kingdom. Based on the provisions of the United Kingdom's Companies Act 1989, the British Department of Trade and Industry is responsible for designating professional bodies as RQBs. There were five such bodies at the time of this writing: The *Institute of Chartered Accountants in England and Wales, the *Institute of Chartered Accountants in Scotland, the *Institute of Chartered Accountants in Ireland, the *Association of Chartered Certified Accountants, and the *Association of International Accountants. Membership of an RQB does not in itself license individuals to conduct external audits. The normal criteria for an individual to register as an external auditor through an RQB is success in a certification program followed by a period of relevant, supervised work experience.

recognition 1. The recording or capture of a *transaction in a *general ledger or set of *financial statements. The recognition of expenses and revenues is driven by the *accruals basis of accounting. See also *realization (definition 2). 2. The public or official acceptance of the credibility and *professional status of an individual or organization.

reconciliation An *internal control procedure to identify differences between two *balances. Common reconciliations include *bank reconciliations and *general ledger to *subsidiary ledger reconciliations.

red, in the To make a *loss or to have negative *cash flow. Contrast the phrase "in the *black."

redemption 1. Payment of a *liability on or before a *maturity date. 2. The exchange of a *coupon for *cash or for an *asset. 3. The fulfillment of a pledge or promise. 4. Atonement for poor past behavior or performance.

reducing balance method A British term for *accelerated method.

re-engineering See *business process re-engineering.

refund The paying back of a sum of *money. See also *rebate.

register 1. A formal document that lists items. See also *log and *risk register. 2. A degree of linguistic formality.

regressive tax 1. A *taxation system in which *tax rates decrease with higher levels of taxable income. Contrast *progressive tax. 2. A *taxation system which is considered to favor the wealthy and cause hardship to poorer individuals. For example, a taxation regime that derives a large proportion of its revenues from *sales taxes may be described as regressive, in that the burden of sales taxes falls most heavily on poorer individuals.

regulation A rule established and enforced by an institution with legal, *quasi-legal, or moral *authority. See also *policy and *procedure.

related party Two individuals or organizations whose relationships involve the exercise of *control, dominance, or influence. It is assumed that *transactions between related parties may not be made at *arm's length, and the *disclosure of transactions of this nature in *financial statements is required under most systems of *Generally Accepted Accounting Principles.

relevant cost A *cost that has a bearing on a decision-making process or that is affected by a decision-making process. See also *avoidable cost, *controllable cost, and *discretionary cost.

reliable Trustworthy, safe, or free from error. Reliable *audit evidence has the qualities of completeness and representational faithfulness, and it is capable of independent *verification.

remote operating unit An alternative term for *branch.

remuneration **1.** *Salaries and *wages paid to an organization's employees. **2.** *Fees paid to an individual for the performance of services.

remuneration committee A committee of a *board of directors (or similar governing body) that oversees an organization's *executive remuneration policy. Remuneration committees are often comprised of *outside directors to encourage *independence and to minimize potential *conflicts of interest.

rent **1.** The cost of *leasing or hiring an asset. **2.** In economic theory, the difference between the *return made by a *factor of production and the return required to keep the factor of production in its current use. For example, an auditor who earns a salary of $80,000 and who could take alternative employment as a teacher at $50,000 earns an economic rent of $30,000. Economic rent is usually only possible when there is a shortage of the supply of a factor of production.

reperformance The repetition of an activity to observe whether the original activity was undertaken in accordance with established *policies and *procedures. Reperformance is a common *audit test—for example, auditors may recalculate an asset's *amortization expenses, or perform a *walk-through test of a *sales *transaction.

replacement cost See *current cost.

reporting 1. The providing of information to others. Reporting is central to *management functions like *planning and *control. See also *audit report and *financial reporting. 2. The channeling of *accountability relationships between individuals in an organization through the hierarchy of a *chain of command.

representation letter A document signed by the management of an organization and addressed to an external auditor that states financial statements are fairly presented and free from *fraud, *misstatements, or other *irregularities. Representation letters can cover individual items in financial statements, or financial statements as a whole. Representation letters can also occur in an internal auditing context. For example, in reviews of compliance with the *Foreign Corrupt Practices Act, an internal auditor may request management confirmation of (i) the nonexistence of *conflicts of interest, (ii) the nonpayment of *bribes, and (iii) the operation of satisfactory *internal controls.

reputation risk The *risk of damage to an organization's image and *brand. Reputation risk can be addressed by appropriate management of an organization's relationships with its stakeholders, including its customers, investors, and the wider public. See also *corporate social responsibility.

requisition 1. A decision by a government to make use of, or take ownership of, an *asset. The requisitioning of assets often takes place during wartime or during a forced *nationalization process. 2. A written demand or request to purchase or take possession of an item or for the performance of an activity. An example of a requisition is a request for the withdrawal of an item from *inventory.

research and development (R&D) Investigations of a *long-term (and often scientific) nature intended to develop new *products and services. Depending on the specific circumstances of R&D activity, *Generally Accepted Accounting Principles around the world set strict criteria for the treatment of R&D costs as either *revenue expenditure or items to be *capitalized and *amortized.

reserve 1. An alternative term for *provision (definitions 1 and 2). 2. Additional amounts of *inventory, *money, or other items maintained for operational or *investment purposes. 3. An alternative term for *retained earnings. 4. The setting aside of *retained earnings for a specific purpose.

residual risk The *risk remaining after the application of *risk management techniques and *internal controls. It is often impossible to eliminate risks entirely; but risks can be managed to levels that an organization's managers deem to be acceptably low. The culture of an organization (its *risk appetite) tends to determine levels of acceptable residual risk. See also *net risk.

residual value 1. The value of an asset at the end of its *useful economic life. Residual values tend to be based on resale or *scrap values, less any disposal or selling costs. The costs of assets subjected to *amortization normally exclude residual values. 2. The value of an asset, less amortization charges, at any stage of its useful economic life.

responsibility accounting A system of *management accounting in which *individual managers are held *accountable for operational and financial performance. See also *accountability.

restatement The revision of an *accounting or *financial statement item to incorporate specific changes.

retained earnings Accumulated *net income recorded as *stockholders' *equity in a corporation's *balance sheet. Retained earnings are normally available for distribution as *dividends.

return 1. *Income derived from investments. Returns from investments can be in the form of *cash or *appreciations in *asset values. For example, investors in a corporation's *common stock hope for returns from both *dividend income and *appreciations in the market value of the stock. 2. An abbreviated term for *customer return. 3. The submission of a formal report or document, such as a *taxation calculation.

revaluation 1. An increase in the *value of an *asset that is *recognized in *financial statements. Revaluations are normally made to bring an asset's *book value into line with its *market value. 2. An increase in the value of a *currency in relation to other currencies, usually resulting from an intentional government policy. Contrast *devaluation.

revenue See *income.

revenue expenditure Expenditure on *short-term expenses that is charged to an *income statement in the period in which it is incurred. Contrast *capital expenditure.

review 1. A formal assessment of an activity with the intention of suggesting or implementing changes. In the context of external auditing, a review implies an audit-type investigation that does not meet the full requirements of *Generally Accepted Auditing Standards. **2.** An abbreviated term for *analytical review.

Revue Française de la Comptabilité A French-language accounting magazine. Published monthly by the *Ordre des Experts-Comptables* in France, and available in print and online formats, the *Revue* contains news and professional developments in accounting and external auditing, with particular focus on France and the European Union.
   Web link: *www.experts-comptables.org/html/pub/publi/rfc.html*

reward An increase in wealth through *income, the transfer of *cash, or the *appreciation of an asset. The term reward is often used in contrast to *risk—for example, "the partners all accepted the risks and rewards of the transaction."

Ridley, Jeffrey (born 1930) A British internal auditing academic, author, and practitioner. Since 1991 Ridley has been Visiting Professor of Auditing at South Bank University in London. Along with *Andrew Chambers and *Gerald Vinten, Ridley has been one of the United Kingdom's leading advocates of internal auditing. A former president of the *Institute of Internal Auditors UK and Ireland, he is the author of many articles on internal auditing, and of the books *International Quality Standards: Implications for Internal Auditing* (1996), coauthored with Kystyna Stephens, and *Leading Edge Internal Auditing* (1998), coauthored with Andrew Chambers. In addition to internal auditing, his other areas of interest include *corporate governance and *quality management.
   Further reading: Ridley and Stephens (1996); Ridley and Chambers, A. (1998)

right A legal or moral entitlement to something.

right of return A *contractual agreement that gives the explicit right of *customer return of a *product.

risk The *probability of the occurrence of an event with negative consequences. The IIA defines risk as "the probability that an event or action, or inaction, may adversely affect the organization or activity under review" (quoted in Hermanson and Rittenberg, 2003, 35). Risk leads to *opportunity costs as well as traditionally understood *costs, and it can be quantified in terms of (i) likelihood of occurrence and (ii) financial or operational outcome. While some risks can be quantified only with difficulty, they can at a minimum be categorized as high, medium, or low, in terms of both likelihood of occurrence and financial or operational outcome.

Risks are often interpreted as potential barriers to the achievement of the objectives or goals of an activity or organization. Typical areas of risk in modern organizations include the following: (i) strategic and *planning risks, (ii) *fraud, (iii) *credit risks, (iv) operational risks (including health and safety concerns), (v) legal matters, (vi) *regulatory risks, (vii) accounting risks, (viii) technological risks (including the *obsolescence of manufactured products), and (ix) *treasury risks. Many of these risks are not stand-alone items, as their interrelations can be complex.

A study by the Institute of Internal Auditors (IIA UK, 1998, section 2.2) identified three underlying primary causes of risk: (i) the random nature of events, (ii) imperfect or incomplete knowledge, and (iii) lack of *control.

See also (in addition to the dictionary's entries that begin with the word risk) *absolute risk, *audit risk, *Control Risk Self Assessment, *credit risk, *enterprise risk management, *interest rate risk, *portfolio risk, *reputation risk, *sampling risk, *systematic risk, *uncertainty, and *unsystematic risk.

Further reading: Bernstein (1996); Doherty (2000); IIA UK (1998)

risk acceptance An informed decision to accept the *risks (and *rewards) of an activity or *market. For example, the risks of operating in high technology markets can be extremely high, owing to the danger of rapid *product *obsolescence, but markets of this type can offer extremely attractive *returns to its *risk-seeking participants. Risk acceptance decisions can also occur on geographical lines. In the period following the Argentine financial crisis that started in late 2001, for example, some *multinational corporations may have been tempted to pull out of the country on the basis of unacceptably high economic and political risks. On the other hand, some *investors justified continued activity in Argentina on the grounds of a long-term view of that country's economic health. Pulling out of a market only to re-enter it later can be a more costly option than remaining throughout a period of crisis. Contrast *risk avoidance.

risk analysis An alternative term for *risk assessment.

risk appetite The willingness of investors to assume *risks in order to achieve *returns. Risk appetites range from *risk-averse to *risk-seeking.

risk assessment The identification, analysis, and measurement of *risks relating to an activity or organization. Risk assessment comprises the initial stages of *risk management, and it is one of the five components of effective *internal control identified in *Internal Control—Integrated Framework* (the *COSO Report*). Risk assessment practices have spread beyond their historic heartlands of the *insurance and financial services sectors to enter the wider organizational mainstream. In turn, the centrality to *corporate governance of both external and internal auditing has resulted in risk assessment becoming central to auditing.

Auditors use risk assessment to prioritize work and to maximize resources. For example, risk assessment techniques can be used to identify suitable areas for review in a large *audit universe, and to identify specific *audit tests for a defined topic. This approach contrasts with the often cyclical nature of *audit planning prior to the 1990s. Some commentators have expressed reservations over the extensive use of risk assessment techniques in auditing: "A worry is that over emphasis on risk assessment may perpetuate the traditional culture of the risk-averse internal auditor, with risk being seen as something to avoid rather than being an opportunity to be exploited" (Vinten, 1996, 93). However, risk assessment is now generally considered to be indispensable to effective auditing.

Risk assessment for both auditing and wider corporate governance purposes can take the form of *quantitative or *qualitative measurements, or a combination of the two. Some commentators make a distinction between risks (quantifiable) and *uncertainties (unquantifiable). The dangers of attempting to place overreliance on quantitative risk assessment techniques has been expressed as follows: "On occasion the calculation of risk assessment 'formulae' seems to provide a veneer of pseudo-scientific clarity to complex matters that cannot be captured purely by numbers... Risks are often difficult (and sometimes impossible) to quantify, and over-reliance on quantified data may reduce the scope for intuitive assessment. The risk assessor who over-relies on numbers often therefore seems to dance around the heart of the risk assessment process, never quite managing to penetrate its core. In extreme cases, over-elaborate risk assessment processes can detach themselves from the organizational realities they purport to represent. A curious scenario then develops, in which risk-assessment becomes a self-referential exercise divorced from the surrounding context. In such cases, the process has as much to do with effective risk assessment as the obsessive polishing of a car has to do with maintaining its engine" (O'Regan, 2003a, 41). In practice, risk assessment often involves a combination of quantitative and qualitative factors.

Further reading: *AS/NZS 4360* (1999); IIA UK (1998); Messier and Austen (2000); Reding et al. (2000); Shelton et al. (2001)

risk aversion Attitudes toward *risk characterized by avoidance or minimization. Risk-averse investors are deemed to have low *risk appetites—they prefer certain but relatively low rates of *return over doubtful but higher rates of return. For example, an individual who chooses to receive $100 with certainty rather than a 50 percent chance of receiving $200 would be classified as risk-averse. Contrast *risk-seeking.

risk avoidance An informed decision not to accept the *risks (and *rewards) of an activity or *market. Refraining from involvement in an activity or a market, or disengaging from existing commitments, can sometimes be a costly strategy, as it can involve significant *opportunity costs. At the end of the Korean War in 1953, for example, South Korea was one of the world's poorest countries, with a *per capita *Gross Domestic Product comparable to India and Central Africa. The devastation of war had destroyed much of the country's infrastructure and industrial base, but over the following decades the country's rapid economic growth was little short of miraculous. By the 1990s, South Korea had become one of the most affluent countries in the world. International *investors who accepted the risks of operating in war-devastated South Korea in its early years were rewarded during the subsequent economic boom, while those who initially avoided South Korea faced expensive entry costs as latecomers to a dynamic Asian "tiger" economy. Contrast *risk acceptance.

risk-based auditing (RBA) Auditing in which *audit objectives and *audit planning are driven by a *risk assessment philosophy.

risk committee A committee of a *board of directors (or similar governing body) that oversees an organization's *risk management policies. Risk committees are a relatively new concept in the early twenty-first century, and are not as widespread as *audit committees. In many organiziations, audit committees take on the duties typically associated with risk committees.

risk elimination The complete removal of a *risk. Unlike *risk avoidance, risk elimination does not necessarily imply nonengagement in (or disengagement from) an activity or *market. Risk elimination techniques can be costly. For example, an organization can eliminate its foreign exchange rate risk by the full *hedging of foreign currency liabilities, but it can find itself locked into *contractual exchange rates that turn out to be unfavorable at transaction *settlement dates. Further, many risks can never be entirely eliminated. The risk of theft in a warehouse can be reduced to acceptable levels, for example, but it can almost never be eradicated. See *risk minimization.

risk event An occurrence that gives rise to a *risk.

risk factor An element of *risk included for consideration in a *risk assessment or *risk management exercise.

risk-free Involving no *risk.

risk identification The process of establishing the existence and nature of *risks. Risk identification is the first stage of a *risk assessment exercise.

risk management The assessment, evaluation, and monitoring of *risks in an activity or organization, with the undertaking of necessary corrective actions. Risk management is a comprehensive process that aims to create a disciplined environment for the achievement of an organization's objectives. The monitoring and corrective actions arising from risk management tend therefore to focus on *procedures and *internal controls that provide reasonable *assurance on the achievement of objectives. Five risk management strategies are *risk acceptance, *risk avoidance, *risk elimination, *risk minimization, and *risk transfer. It is frequently observed that risk management may increase a corporation's *value by reducing risks and, thereby, reducing *cost of capital.

A recent risk management standard defines risk as "the culture, process and structures that are directed towards the effective management of potential opportunities and adverse effects" (*AS/NZS 4360*, 1999). *Risk assessment is the first stage of a *risk management process, which may or may not involve the measurement of risk by formal quantification. Typically, this depends on the nature of the risks to be addressed, as well as on management objectives. Risk management can be performed at an organization-wide level (when it is often called *Enterprise Risk Management) or at the more discrete level of individual departments, processes, or other operational units. Typical risk management functions in organizations include departments or suppliers providing (i) internal auditing, (ii) external auditing, (iii) *insurance, (iv) *quality control, and (v) health and safety monitoring.

Further reading: *AS/NZS 4360* (1999); Crawford and Stein (2002); Doherty (2000); IIA UK (1998); McNamee and Selim (1998)

Risk Management and Governance Board A board of the *Canadian Institute of Chartered Accountants (CICA) that provides guidance on *corporate governance, *internal control, and *risk management. The CICA Web site states the board's mission to be as follows: To "develop and promote guidance and related materials to provide opportunities for...focusing on improving the quality of corporate governance and risk management in organizations." Prior to 2001, the Board was known as the *Criteria for Control (CoCo) Board, and its 1995 *Guidance on Control* has an international reputation as a *control framework of enduring value.

risk minimization A *risk management technique that reduces the likelihood of occurrence of a *risk or reduces the potential impact of a *risk. If a risk has been managed to acceptable levels of *residual risk, the incremental costs of attempting *risk elimination may be unacceptably high. For example, an organization may significantly reduce levels of *inventory *shrinkage by establishing robust security measures around a warehouse. Once an acceptable level of shrinkage has been achieved, it may be too costly to spend more on security measures, as additional investment may result in an unacceptably small benefit.

risk premium An additional *return on a high-*risk *investment required to *reward investors for assuming a high level of risk.

risk ranking The listing of *risks in a *risk register in order of severity. Severity can be measured in terms of: (i) the likelihood of occurrence of a risk, (ii) its potential financial or operational outcome, or (iii) a combination of (i) and (ii).

risk register A list of an organization's *risks identified in a *risk assessment exercise.

risk retention An alternative term for *risk acceptance.

risk-seeking Readiness to assume high rates of *risk in order to achieve opportunities for high *returns. Risk-seeking investors are deemed to have high *risk appetites. In contrast to a *risk-averse individual, for example, a risk-seeker would tend to reject the offer of a certain $100 in favor of a 50 percent chance of receiving $200. Gamblers are classic risk-seekers.

risk sharing A partial or incomplete *risk transfer.

risk transfer A *risk management strategy that involves the moving of a *risk from one individual, activity, or organization to another. Risk transfer can imply the moving of an entire risk elsewhere, but in practice it tends to involve the sharing of risk with another party. *Insurance cover is a classic risk transfer strategy, and it illustrates that risk transfer strategies can be very costly. In 2001, for example, a guerrilla attack on Sri Lanka's Colombo International Airport destroyed a number of commercial airliners, and antiwar insurance *premiums rocketed by over 300 percent for commercial airlines operating to and from that country. Other potential risk transfer parties include *customers, *suppliers, *agents, and *joint venture partners. A transfer of risk does not imply a transfer of *accountability, as an organization's management remains responsible for the results of its risk management strategy.

ritualistic audit An *audit of limited value or ambition that is restricted to the performance of predictable *audit tests. A ritualistic audit can create an impression of the reliability and orderliness of the *auditees' activities, but at worst it does little more than offer a rather dubious legitimacy to the subject matter of an audit.

Further reading: Mills and Bettner (1992)

rollover **1.** A renewal of a *loan or other type of borrowing. **2.** A transfer of *funds between investments following the *maturity of individual investments. **3.** A transfer of *taxation relief between different activities or time periods.

Roth, James (born 1947) A U.S. internal auditing and *corporate governance specialist. Roth is a prolific author on internal auditing topics. He has written numerous articles, many of which have appeared in *Internal Auditor magazine, and his books include *Best Practices: Value-Added Approaches of Four Innovative Internal Auditing Departments* (Roth, 2000) and *Internal Audit's Role in Corporate Governance: Sarbanes-Oxley Compliance* (Roth and Espersen, 2003). President of the consulting firm *AuditTrends, Roth is a prominent public speaker on internal auditing. His areas of interest include *operational auditing, *soft controls, and the *Sarbanes-Oxley Act*.

Further reading: Roth (2000); Roth (2002); Roth (2003); Roth and Espersen (2003)

Web link: *www.audittrends.com / JR.htm*

rounding To restate an amount as a convenient, whole number, rather than as a fraction or decimal.

royalty A payment made for the use of the property of an individual or organization. Examples of royalties include (i) payments by publishers to authors for the latter's intellectual capital as captured in books and (ii) payments for the use of a *brand name under a *franchise agreement.

Rutteman Report A British *corporate governance report of 1994. The report's formal title was *Internal Control and Financial Reporting: Guidance for Directors of Listed Companies Registered in the UK*. The *Rutteman Report* was prepared to give guidance on the internal control provisions of the *Cadbury Report* of 1992. The *Rutteman Report* has been superseded by subsequent corporate governance developments in the United Kingdom, notably the *Hampel Report* of 1998 and the related internal control guidance of the 1999 *Turnbull Report*.

Further reading: *Rutteman Report* (1994)

S

sacred cow A term used to refer to an activity or practice considered immune from change or criticism. The expression derives from the respect given to the cow in Hinduism. It is often used by auditors, who talk of "slaughtering sacred cows" in the sense of challenging received wisdom and inefficient practices. The phrase is best avoided, however, as it is clichéd and potentially offensive to Hindus.

safeguarding The protection of an asset or activity. The safeguarding of assets is often considered to be among the main objectives of *internal controls. In *Internal Control—Integrated Framework* (the *COSO Report*), the safeguarding of assets is included within the *internal control objective of providing reasonable *assurance on the *effectiveness and *efficiency of operations.

safety margin See *margin of safety.

salary Regular *remuneration paid to an employee of an organization. In contrast to *wages, *salaries are usually set at fixed amounts and paid at regular intervals. However, the two terms are often used synonymously.

sale **1.** The exchange of a good or service for *money or for the promise of money. **2.** An offer of the exchange of a good or service for an exceptionally low *price.

sales discount See *discount (definition 1).

sales return An alternative term for *customer return.

sales tax An *indirect tax charged on the sales *prices of goods and services, and collected as *sales are made. See also *consumption tax and *value added tax.

sample **1.** [noun] An item selected from a *population of data. Auditors often test representative samples of data in cases when it is unfeasible to audit large populations. See also *judgmental sampling, *random sampling, and *statistical sampling. **2.** [noun] A representative item or specimen of *merchandise given for review to a customer, in the hope of winning a larger sales *order. **3.** [verb] To test an item before deciding whether to purchase it.

sampling risk The *risk that a *sample of data does not accurately represent the *population from which it has been extracted. In auditing, incorrect conclusions and *audit opinions can result from sampling risk.

sanction 1. A punitive measure taken by one country against another. Often adopted as an alternative to war, sanctions usually take the form of restrictions of economic activity or cultural exchange. Sanctions are often directed at specific economic sectors, in contrast to an *embargo's more general prohibition against all economic links with a country. See also *boycott. 2. A provision for the enforcement of a law or procedure.

Sarbanes-Oxley Act (2002) A U.S. legislative act passed in July 2002. Named for two U.S. senators, the *Sarbanes-Oxley Act* was designed to shore up investor confidence and to reform aspects of *corporate governance and the regulation of listed corporations. Massive frauds and accounting scandals at *Enron and *WorldCom, and the collapse of the *Big Five accounting firm *Arthur Andersen had seriously undermined public confidence in corporate governance by the middle of 2002.

The *Sarbanes-Oxley Act* has been described as "the most sweeping law on securities regulation and corporate governance since the 1930s" (McElveen, 2002, 40). It is complex and wide-ranging: Among other things, it requires *Chief Executive Officers and *Chief Financial Officers to certify quarterly and annual financial reports. This generated significant media attention in late 2002, when it resulted in hundreds of senior executives swearing in front of notaries that "to the best of my knowledge" their latest financial statements contained neither an "untrue statement" nor omitted a "material fact."

The Act also mandated the creation of a *Public Company Accounting Oversight Board, to enhance regulation and supervision of the external auditing process. Another area of particular interest to auditors was a strengthening of the role and responsibilities of *audit committees. The Act's provisions cover (i) the *independence of audit committee members, (ii) the duties of the audit committees in approving *management advisory services (MAS) provided by external auditors, and (iii) the responsibilities of audit committees for dealing with *whistle-blowing. It also restricted certain MAS provided by external auditors.

The *Sarbanes-Oxley Act* set down principles in the above areas, leaving detailed implementation to organizations like the *Securities and Exchange Commission (SEC) and the New York Stock Exchange. For example, in 2003 the SEC issued rules and deadlines for compliance with Section 404 of the *Sarbanes-Oxley Act*, which requires management to file an internal control report with its annual report. The ramifications of the *Sarbanes-Oxley Act* have an international dimension, affecting non-U.S. corporations with secondary listings in the United States, as well as significant overseas subsidiaries of U.S. corporations.

Further reading: McElveen (2002); Roth and Espersen (2003); *Sarbanes-Oxley Act* (2002)

SEC Web link: *www.sec.gov/spotlight/sarbanes-oxley.htm*

IIA corporate governance guidance Web link: *www.theiia.org/ecm/iiaglance. cfm?doc_id=4061*

savoir-faire The French term for *know-how. The term is often dropped into English sentences with the intention of conveying a more elegant or exotic turn of phrase than that associated with its English equivalent.

Sawyer, Laurence B. (1911–2002) A U.S. internal auditing practitioner, educator, and author. Laurence (Larry) B. Sawyer is often referred to as the "grandfather" of modern internal auditing. This respectful title was coined from his *Grandfather Dialogues*, a series of articles in *Internal Auditor magazine in the early 1970s that were gathered in a book collection titled *Modern Internal Auditing—What's It All About?* (Sawyer, 1974). Sawyer was a prolific author, and his output included the seminal internal auditing book *The Practice of Modern Internal Auditing* (1973): An indication of the book's success and status among internal auditors is the renaming of subsequent editions with the eponymous title *Sawyer's Internal Auditing*. With *Gerald Vinten, he also coauthored *The Manager and the Internal Auditor: Partners for Profit* (1996).

Sawyer sought to shift the emphasis of internal auditing from that of a purely compliance function to one of constructive engagement with an organization's management. He insisted that "internal auditors must be equipped and prepared to review and appraise anything under the sun" (quoted in Flesher, 1991, 175). This shift of auditing emphasis involved, as he put it, a move "from the commonplace aspect of mathematical verification to the managerial concept of organization-wide evaluations" (Sawyer, 1998), and it marked the end of "the internal auditor of the classic stereotype, the cold, secretive, finger-pointer" (Sawyer and Vinten, 1996, 339). Sawyer made significant contributions to the development and reform of internal auditing, and the *Institute of Internal Auditors honored him with many awards during his lifetime.

Further reading: Sawyer (1973); Sawyer (1974); Sawyer (1983); Sawyer (1998); Sawyer and Vinten (1996); Sawyer et al. (2003)

Sawyer's Internal Auditing A landmark internal auditing student text. Published by the *Institute of Internal Auditors, the book first appeared in

1973, and is named for the author of its first editions, *Laurence B. Sawyer. Following the author's death the book has been updated by other writers, but the retention of the name Sawyer in its title is a reflection of the book's (and the original author's) prestige. It remains a valued text for the study of internal auditing, for both university curricula and the *Certified Internal Auditor professional examinations.

Further reading: Sawyer et al. (2003)

scam A *fraudulent scheme aimed at improperly extracting *money from *investors or participants. An example of a sophisticated scam is a *pyramid scheme.

scan, to **1.** To read a document quickly, in order to identify its main features. **2.** To convert a document or image into digital format for storage in a computer.

scatter graph A graph that plots the patterns of items in relation to two variables set out along the x and y axes. From a scatter graph, a pattern of *correlation between the plotted points can be estimated by visually drawing a line of best fit among the points, or calculated more precisely by regression analysis. Although easy to prepare and understand, the results of scatter graph analysis should be treated with caution, owing to the subjectivity involved in estimations of a line of best fit.

schedule **1.** A document that sets out calculations and information. **2.** An alternative term for *audit schedule. **3.** A plan, timetable, or list.

scenario planning An assessment of the outcomes of various courses of action in a range of potential settings or circumstances. Scenario planning is a means of assessing alternative actions in decision-making processes, organizational *planning, and *risk assessment. The range of risk scenarios that a *multinational corporation may consider when deciding to establish a remote *branch in a foreign country may include (i) *market risks, (ii) cultural risks, (iii) a change of political regime, (iv) the danger of an economic *recession, (v) the effects of a natural catastrophe (like an earthquake), and (vi) and the impact of changes in local *Generally Accepted Accounting Principles. For each scenario, a review of potential risks and *rewards could lead to either *quantitative or *qualitative risk assessments (or a combination of both) used to determine the corporation's strategies. Scenario planning requires imaginative and wide-ranging thinking, and *brainstorming activities are frequently employed to tease ideas from participants in the process.

Schmalenbach, Eugen (1873–1955) A German accounting and auditing theorist. Schmalenbach was an early pioneer of the importance of external auditing in Germany. In the 1930s extensive German corporate external auditing requirements were established and the profession of *Wirtschaftprüfer* came into being—Schmalenbach played a major role in promoting both developments. His academic writings also contributed significantly to the development of German *charts of accounts.

Further reading: Potthoff and Sieben (1994)

scope limitation A restriction on the performance of an audit. The term is usually used in the context of external auditing, when restrictions on *audit evidence that originate from circumstances or from the behavior of an *auditee prevent the auditor from offering an *unqualified opinion on *financial statements under audit. *Disclaimers are common in such circumstances.

scrap An alternative term for *spoilage.

scrap value The sales value of *spoilage.

seasonal Characteristic of, or fluctuating with, specific time periods. Climate patterns, vacations, and religious festivals are typical causes of seasonal behavior. For example, sales of sunglasses tend to be seasonally related to sunny, summer weather, and sales of Christmas cards are seasonally related to the Christmas period.

secured [of a loan] Guaranteed by the pledge of an asset in case of *default in repayment. See also *collateral.

Securities and Exchange Commission (SEC) The U.S. federal agency responsible for overseeing and regulating security markets and corporate financial reporting. Established in 1934, following the Securities Act of 1933 and the Securities Exchange Act of 1934, the SEC has quasi-judicial powers of enforcement that it uses in hundreds of civil cases every year. The SEC Web site states that its primary mission is "to protect investors and maintain the integrity of the securities markets" and that it "requires public companies to disclose meaningful financial and other information to the public, which provides a common pool of knowledge for all investors to use to judge for themselves if a company's securities are a good investment." The SEC works closely with organizations like the U.S. stock exchanges and the *Financial Accounting Standards Board (FASB). The SEC endorses the FASB's accounting standards, although it has reserved the right to intervene in the FASB's standards-setting procedure (Nobes and Parker, 2002, 168–169). The SEC's interpretations of FASB standards are contained in *Staff Accounting Bulletins*, which are considered to be part of U.S. *Generally Accepted Accounting Principles.

In 2002 the **Sarbanes-Oxley Act* set important new criteria for securities regulation and *corporate governance, and the SEC was charged with introducing many aspects of the new reforms. This included the creation of the *Public Company Accounting Oversight Board.

Web site: *www.sec.gov*

security 1. A *financial instrument traded on a *stock exchange or in a similar market. A security may or may not confer a share of ownership in an organization. Examples include *common stock and some types of *bonds. **2.** *Collateral for a debt or loan. **3.** The condition of safety from danger or theft.

segment reporting In the notes to *financial statements, an analysis of *sales, *employees, *net assets or other items by geographical area, market sector, or *division.

segmental reporting An alternative term for *segment reporting.

segregation of duties The separation of individual employees' duties and responsibilities to enhance an organization's *internal controls. A fundamental aspect of segregation of duties is the notion that "persons having the custody of control of assets should not also be responsible for the accounting in respect of those assets" (Cooper, 1966, 13). In other words, segregation of duties involves the separation of asset *safeguarding from asset-related *transactions. For example, the practice of *lapping (concealing the theft of cash by shifting *cash amounts between *accounts receivable balances) can be made more difficult by segregating the tasks of (i) handling cash receipts from customers, (ii) recording cash receipts in accounts receivable balances, and (iii) preparation of the accounts receivable ledger. In small organizations, low employee numbers can complicate the achievement of a satisfactory segregation of duties.

self-financing With the ability to generate sufficient *money without the need for external *funding or *subsidies.

semi-fixed cost An alternative term for *semi-variable cost.

semi-variable cost An item of expenditure that has elements of both *fixed and *variable costs. For example, the cost of gas supply tends to comprise a fixed charge, irrespective of the level of usage, and a variable element linked to the level of consumption.

service 1. [noun] An activity of economic or social value that involves the use of *labor rather than tangible *goods or *commodities. Examples of services include transportation, haircutting, and professional activity like accounting and auditing. **2.** [noun] Employment in an organization. **3.** [noun] The activity of dealing with *customers. **4.** [verb] To repay an amount on or before a *due date.

service department A *department in an organization that performs services to support *manufacturing and operating activity. Examples include factory canteens and information technology support departments.

service level agreement (SLA) An arrangement in an organization for the performance standards of a specific *service department. An SLA normally involves the use of metrics to monitor performance—for example, an information technology support department may include among its objectives the target of responding to requests for assistance within 24 hours.

settlement 1. The payment of a sum of *money to extinguish a *liability. The term is frequently used in the context of the purchase of *securities. **2.** An agreement or decision to resolve a problem. **3.** A legally binding agreement for the transfer of an asset.

setup cost 1. See *fixed charge (definition 2). **2.** The *costs of establishing a new business or operation.

shadow economy An alternative term for the *underground economy.

share 1. A unit of ownership in a corporation. See also *equity and *common stock. **2.** Part ownership of an asset or activity.

shareholder An alternative term, commonly used in the *United Kingdom, for *stockholder.

Sherman Antitrust Act Landmark *antitrust legislation of 1890. The *Sherman Antitrust Act* made monopoly and the restraint of trade illegal in the United States.

shortage cost An alternative term for *stockout cost.

short term 1. Relating to a period of less than one year. **2.** For some loans and debts, the short term may be defined over a period of three to five years.

short-termism An attitude that places *short-term over long-term gains. The management of a corporation may be tempted to enhance *short-term *earnings to impress investors (and to boost the managers' *remuneration), yet their decisions could cause *long-term damage to the corporation's financial health. For example, reductions in *research and development expenses may boost *net income in the short term, but the reductions may lead to falling revenues in the long term as a result of *obsolete or outdated products.

shrinkage The loss of *inventory or other *short-term, *tangible assets through damage or theft.

significant Important. See also *materiality.

Sikka, Prem Nath (born 1951) A British academic, and specialist in auditing and accounting. Founding joint-editor of the *critical accounting journal *Accountancy, Business, and the Public Interest*, Sikka is Professor of Accounting at the University of Essex in England. He is a trustee of the *Association for Accountancy and Business Affairs, a reformist forum for the critical analysis of auditing and accounting practices. Sikka has contributed significantly to the critical accounting movement in the United Kingdom, with a large body of writing that includes monographs, articles, and journalism.

Sikka is a fearless critic of the external auditing profession, claiming that it is "pre-occupied with fees and client appeasement" (Cousins et al., 1998, 9), and he has memorably referred to the large external auditing firms as "emperors of darkness" (Dunn and Sikka, 1999, 4). He is noted for his challenges to received or "official" notions of external auditing theory. For example, "The social practice of 'audit' does not have a single unambiguous meaning but, rather, numerous competing meanings that exist side by side. Contrary to the profession's preferences, the meaning of audit has been associated with fraud detection, warning of impending bankruptcy, guaranteeing the accuracy of information and financial soundness, etc.... This is not to say that 'audit' is meaningless, but, rather, that its meaning is contingent and negotiable: its fixing within relations of power is precarious and subject to redefinition" (Sikka et al., 1998, 299–304).

Further reading: Cousins et al. (1998); Dunn and Sikka (1999); Mitchell and Sikka (2002); Mitchell et al. (1991); Mitchell et al. (1998); Sikka and Willmott (1997); Sikka et al. (1998)

Web link: *visar.csustan.edu/aaba/aaba.htm*

simple interest The calculation of *interest on a sum of *money by applying an *interest rate to the original sum of money alone (and not to previously accumulated interest). Contrast *compound interest.

simulation modeling An alternative term for *what-if analysis.

single-tier board See *board of *directors.

sinking fund A *fund characterized by the periodic setting aside of amounts of *money to meet obligations. Common purposes of sinking funds include the repayments of loans and the replacement of *property, plant, and equipment.

Six E's An expansion of the traditional *Three E's of *economy, *efficiency, and *effectiveness in *operational or *value-for-money auditing to include (i) *equity (or *corporate social responsibility), (ii) environmental concerns, and (iii) *ethics. Despite this use of Six E's by some commentators (e.g., Chambers and Rand, 1997, 8–9), the term Five E's is also commonly encountered. The five E's are derived by combining equity and ethics into one category.

skewed Unsymmetrical, distorted, or containing bias. A skewed *sample, for example, is one that does not represent the distribution of items in the *population from which it is extracted.

Smith Report A British *corporate governance report of 2003. The report's formal title was *Audit Committees: Combined Code Guidance*, and it was named for Sir Robert Smith, the chairperson of the committee that prepared it. The *Smith Report*'s aim was to provide guidance to *audit committee participants in line with the recommendations of the United Kingdom's *Hampel Report* (or *Combined Code*) of 1998. The *Combined Code* was revised in 2003 to incorporate aspects of the *Smith Report*.

    Further reading: *Smith Report* (2003)

smoothing effect The recording of an accounting item over a number of time periods in a manner that avoids sudden variations. The action of "smoothing" transactions may involve *allocations of revenues and expenses that contravene the *accruals basis of accounting.

smuggling Illegal international trading in goods and services. Smuggling is an aspect of the *underground economy.

social and environmental reporting (SAR) The reporting by organizations of information relevant to *corporate social responsibility.

social audit An *audit of the social impact of an activity or organization. Flint (1988, 175, n.7) describes social auditing as "monitoring the way in which an organisation conducts itself in its various relationships with society—as employer, manufacturer, supplier, member of the community, etc."

soft asset **1.** An alternative term for *intangible asset. **2.** An alternative term for *intellectual capital.

soft control An *internal control based on intangible factors like honesty and ethical standards.

soft currency A *currency that is not widely accepted throughout the world. In contrast to a *hard currency, a soft currency is not freely convertible.

soft loan A *loan at a very low or zero *interest rate.

solvent Able to settle liabilities and debts. Contrast *insolvency.

sort, to 1. [of data] To arrange in a systematic or logical manner. 2. [of a problem] To resolve.

source document 1. A document that records the origin of a transaction. 2. A document that provides *audit evidence.

South, the A collective term for economically *developing countries. The term derives from the fact that most of the world's developing countries (e.g., in South America and sub-Saharan Africa) are located in the southern hemisphere. See also the *North and *Third World.

South African Institute of Chartered Accountants (SAICA) South Africa's main professional accounting and external auditing organization. The SAICA was established in 1980 from pre-existing accounting bodies, and it is headquartered in Johannesburg. It publishes the monthly magazine *Accountancy SA*, which is available in print and online formats. Following British traditions, the organization uses the designatory term *chartered accountant. The SAICA sets both *accounting standards and *auditing standards in South Africa, and its membership in 2003 was approximately 21,000.
Web site: *www.saica.co.za*

spam Unsolicited *e-mails sent in large quantities. The term derives from tinned luncheon meat. See also *junk mail.

special assignment 1. Work undertaken by an auditor that is not strictly of an auditing nature, or which has an unusually narrow scope. An example of a special *audit assignment is the performance of *due diligence and other *acquisition support work. In recent years, definitions of auditing (and, in particular, of *internal auditing) have become so wide as to blur traditional distinctions between audit and nonaudit work. See also *management advisory services in the context of external auditing. 2. An unplanned *audit assignment undertaken at short notice or as a matter of urgency.

Special Purpose Entity (SPE) An organization or entity established as a vehicle for *off-balance sheet financing. The use of SPEs played a major role in the *Enron corporate governance scandal, and as a consequence the topic has attracted the attention of *accounting standards-setters.

Further reading: Hartgraves and Benston (2002)

speculation The making of high-*risk, *short-term investments in anticipation of generous *returns. The term has pejorative undertones, as critics of speculation contend that it is an unproductive practice that can promote market instability. In contrast, defenders of speculation claim that the practice of taking advantage of short-term *price differentials is essential to the smooth running of *free-market economies. They argue that only the rapid buying and selling of items can establish equilibrium prices. Compare *arbitrage.

spoilage *Waste, scrap, and defective goods arising from manufacturing processes. Spoilage is not necessarily without value, as the waste, *by-products, or defective *output of a *production process can sometimes be sold for *scrap value or reworked. A certain amount of spoilage is viewed as inevitable in most manufacturing processes, and is referred to as *normal spoilage. Normal spoilage tends to be considered an element of regular *production costs. In contrast, wastage above anticipated or inherent levels is known as *abnormal spoilage, and is usually expensed as incurred.

spot market A trading system in which items (typically *commodities and *currencies) are purchased for immediate or near-immediate delivery and are paid for at current *market prices.

spreadsheet A computer program that permits *quantitative analysis of *data. Spreadsheet data are arranged in a tabular format, with a grid of *cells that can contain numbers or mathematical formulae. Auditors and accountants often use spreadsheets to analyze accounting and other information, owing to their ease and flexibility of use. Spreadsheets are also commonly used in *what-if analysis: To support decision-making, the formulae in individual spreadsheet cells can be altered to analyze alternative outcomes.

square, to 1. To multiply a number by itself. For example, the number 5 squared is 25. **2.** To *reconcile. For example, "I must square these two accounts." **3.** To settle a *liability. For example, "She squared the hotel bill." **4.** To balance an *account.

Staff Accounting Bulletins The *Securities and Exchange Commission's interpretations of the *accounting standards of the *Financial Accounting

Standards Board.
Web link: *www.sec.gov/interps/account.shtml*

stagflation The simultaneous and persistent occurrence of high levels of *inflation and *unemployment. The term originated in the 1970s from an abbreviated combination of the words stagnation and inflation.

stakeholder An individual or institution, or a group of individuals or institutions, with direct or indirect interest in an organization's activities. Depending on the nature of the organization, stakeholders may include (i) *stockholders, (ii) *debenture holders, (iii) *creditors, (iv) *customers, (v) state and regulatory authorities, (vi) employees, (vii) local communities (especially where an organization is a dominant local employer or a potential polluter), and (viii) the wider public (especially when the organization operates in areas of public safety, such as transport and healthcare). Stakeholder theory contends that an organization's network of rights and responsibilities stretches wider than is the case suggested by the rather simplistic notions of *agency theory. See also *corporate social responsibility.

Stamp, Edward (1928–1986) A British-born accounting academic. A naturalized Canadian, Professor Stamp taught at universities in New Zealand, Scotland, and England. A reformist by nature, one commentator has written that Stamp is remembered "less for the originality of his ideas than for his robust campaigns to raise standards of corporate reporting, auditing, and open administration" (Mumford, 1994, 274). Stamp authored several books, including a coauthored study of the need for international *auditing standards (Stamp and Moonitz, 1978). He was also a major contributor to the United Kingdom's *Corporate Report* of 1975.

Further reading: Mumford (1994); Stamp (1984); Stamp and Moonitz (1979); Tweedie (1993)

standard 1. A rule or guideline. See *accounting standards and *auditing standards. **2.** A defined level of attainment, proficiency, or quality. International, voluntary consensus standards and conformity assessment criteria for an activity or industry sector define specifications to be applied consistently in, among other things, (i) the manufacture and supply of products, (ii) the classification of materials, (iii) the use of terminology, (iv) the provision of services, and (v) testing and analysis. See the *American National Standards Institute and the *International Organization for Standardization. **3.** A mechanism or practice that serves as a quantifiable performance target or as a means of simplifying record keeping. *Standard costs, for example, are used both for *budgetary purposes and to simplify *cost accounting procedures.

standard audit program An *audit program used as a model, *template (definition 2), or basic framework for the undertaking of auditing activity. To enhance the efficiency of *audit planning, auditors often use standard audit programs that address broad topics, adapting them to the circumstances of particular audits. The use of standard audit programs can also encourage a common auditing approach across time and distance barriers.

standard cost A cost established as a target, usually for *budgetary or motivational purposes. *Variances from standard costs are analyzed as either *favorable or *unfavorable. Standard costs also serve to simplify record keeping, as they require only periodic updating.

standard deviation A statistic used in *probability distribution models. In a *normal distribution of a *population of random items, the standard deviation represents the typical distance of an item from the population's *mean value.

standard opinion In external auditing, an *audit opinion that *financial statements conform to *Generally Accepted Accounting Principles in all *material respects.

Standards for the Professional Practice of Internal Auditing Internal auditing standards issued by the *Institute of Internal Auditors (IIA). First issued in 1978, the IIA's standards were the world's first professional standards explicitly designed for internal auditing. Within its current Professional Practices Framework, the IIA designates adherence to the standards as mandatory for its members, though the standards are also frequently followed by internal auditors working outside the IIA's formal structures. The standards are categorized into attribute, performance, and implementation standards, and they are available from the IIA Web site.
Web link: *www.theiia.org/ecm/guidance.cfm?doc_id=1499*

standing data Information that changes infrequently. Standing data can refer to both computerized and manual records, though it is more commonly used to refer to the former. An example of standing data is the recording of customer addresses, trading terms, and *credit limits in the context of *accounts receivable. Standing data excludes the details of individual *transactions.

State Audit Institution (SAI) An alternative term for *Supreme Audit Institution.

statement 1. A verbal utterance that carries a degree of clarity. For example, "The Chief Executive Officer's statement on corporate objectives was crystal clear." 2. A formal, written declaration. For example, "The corporation issued a press statement to clarify its position." **3.** An abbreviated term for *bank statement, *financial statement, or *statement of account.

statement of account A summary of the status of accumulated *transactions between a *creditor and a *debtor. Many trading organizations issue periodic statements of account to their customers, and banks normally summarize their customer's transactions in the form of a *bank statement.

Statement of Responsibilities of the Internal Auditor A document of the *Institute of Internal Auditors that elaborated the responsibilities and functions of internal auditors. The *Statement* was first issued in 1947, and revised several times in the following decades, when it became known as the *Statement of Responsibilities of Internal Auditing*.

Further reading: Flesher (1991)

Statements of Auditing Standards (SAS) British external *auditing standards. British SAS are issued by the *Auditing Practices Board, a subsidiary board of the *Accountancy Foundation, and they comprise the main source of *Generally Accepted Auditing Standards in the United Kingdom and the Republic of Ireland. The standards are available online from the *Accountancy Foundation Web site.

Web link: *www.accountancyfoundation.com/auditing_practices_board/index.cfm?sectionid=3*

Statements of Financial Accounting Standards (SFAS) Accounting and *financial reporting standards issued by the *Financial Accounting Standards Board. The SFAS are the main source of U.S. *Generally Accepted Accounting Principles, and are issued after due process and consultation with interested parties.

Web site: *www.fasb.org/st*

Statements on Auditing Standards (SAS) United States external *auditing standards. Issued by the *Auditing Standards Board of the *American Institute of Certified Public Accountants, SAS comprise the main source of *Generally Accepted Auditing Standards in the United States. They numbered more than 100 in 2003.

Web link: *www.aicpa.org/members/div/auditstd/index.htm*

Statements on Internal Auditing Standards (SIAS) Historical amendments to the *Standards for the Professional Practice of Internal Auditing* of the *Institute of Internal Auditors (IIA). The SIAS were issued by the IIA prior to the formal updating of its standards, but were discontinued following the introduction of the IIA's Professional Practices Framework in 1999. The SIAS have been subsumed into the IIA's standards and its other advisory materials.

static budget A *budget that provides information for only one level of activity. In contrast to a *flexible budget, a static budget cannot be readily adapted to changes in operational circumstances.

statistical sampling The selection of a *sample of data from a *population using objective, statistical methodologies. *Probability theory and *random selection techniques are commonly used in statistical sampling, and properly designed statistical samples identify likely margins of error and *sample risk. Auditors often rely on statistical sampling techniques to reach conclusions about a larger population of items. See also *judgmental sampling and *stratified sampling.

statutory audit 1. An *external audit of a government institution or activity, in accordance with government-established criteria. 2. An *external audit that is required by *legislation. In most developed economies, corporations above a defined size are required to have an annual, external audit.

step cost A cost that is fixed (or that is only slightly variable) over relatively small ranges of activity, but which increases at intervals by significant amounts. For example, a manufacturing process may require additional floor space at various levels of production volume, with rental costs increasing significantly as each of the critical production volumes is exceeded. When plotted graphically, this variation of rental cost with activity levels resembles a series of steps. See also *semi-variable cost.

stewardship The act of exercising responsibility for the supervision or management of an asset or activity. A steward acts in a capacity as an *agent.

stock 1. An investment in a corporation, usually in the form of a *security. See *common stock. 2. An alternative term for *inventory. This use of the term is particularly common in the United Kingdom and in other countries with significant British influence.

stockcount The British term for *physical inventory.

stockholder An investor who holds a share of a corporation's *common stock.

stock option A *right to purchase a specified quantity of a corporation's *common stock within a specified time period at a specified *price.

stockout cost A cost that results from the absence of an item from *inventory. Stockout costs may include the loss of a *sale and the costs of disruption to a *manufacturing process, depending on the nature of the item absent from inventory.

stock warrant An *option to purchase a specified number of *securities or *bonds at a specified *price for a specified time period.

straddle, to To extend over both sides of a physical divide or a point of time. Accounting *cutoff is complicated by *transactions that straddle two or more *financial reporting periods.

straight-line basis A cost or revenue *allocation method that provides for equal amounts in each period of time. The rationale for using a straight-line basis is that the economic activity of the underlying assets or circumstances occurs at a constant level over time. For example, under straight-line *amortization the cost of a fixed asset is expensed in equal annual amounts over the asset's *useful economic life, in circumstances where the asset is deemed to provide constant benefits over the relevant period.

Strategic Finance Magazine A U.S. accounting and finance magazine. Published monthly by the *Institute of Management Accountants, the magazine is available in both print and online formats. Its notes state that its editorial focus is "directed toward leadership strategies in accounting, finance, and information management." Its primary coverage is of news and professional developments in the United States.
   Web link: *www.strategicfinancemag.com*

stratified sampling The selection of a *sample of data from a *population that has been arranged into groups according to a defined trait or attribute. See also *judgmental sampling, *random sampling, and *statistical sampling.

subledger An abbreviated form of *subsidiary ledger.

subscription **1.** The periodic purchase of items by means of payment at regular intervals. For example, "I took out a subscription to a monthly finance magazine." **2.** A commitment to contribute money to, or to participate in, an activity or cause. **3.** A commitment or application to purchase newly-issued *securities. **4.** An archaic term for a signature on a legal document.

subsequent event An alternative term for *event after the balance sheet date.

subsidiary An organization whose management, operating policies, or *common stock voting rights are controlled by a *holding company or *parent organization.

Under most systems of *Generally Accepted Accounting Principles, subsidiaries are accounted for using *consolidation accounting techniques. See also *sub-subsidiary.

subsidiary ledger A group of *accounts used to support a main *general ledger account. Typically, *transaction-intensive accounts like *accounts receivable, *accounts payable, and *petty cash expenses are recorded in subsidiary ledgers, the totals of which are transferred to general ledger *control accounts. See also *journal.

subsidy A sum of *money used to support an organization or activity. The term is often used in the context of financial support given by a government or government agency. The nature of subsidies can be wide, but they often aim to reduce the sales *prices of *commodities or other items. See also *grant.

substance over form The notion that the economic substance of a *transaction, *asset, or *liability takes precedence over its legal and technical form. The exploitation of narrow legal and technical interpretations of items is a typical *creative accounting mechanism to overstate *earnings and understate liabilities (e.g., through *off-balance sheet financing). Consequently, systems of *Generally Accepted Accounting Principles around the world are increasingly emphasizing the importance of substance over form.

substantive testing Auditing procedures that evaluate the accuracy, completeness, and existence of amounts stated in *general ledger accounts and financial statements. Substantive testing involves the auditing of quantifiable amounts (individual *transactions as well as accumulated balances). The substantive testing of the purchase of a *long-term asset, for example, may include the following: (i) *physical inspection of the asset, (ii) reference to a *vendor's invoice, (iii) verification of delivery documentation, (iv) tracing of related disbursement records, and (v) ascertaining that the asset is recorded in an appropriate general ledger account. Substantive testing also includes *analytical review procedures, in which general ledger or financial statement items are evaluated for reasonableness, and the logical nature of their interrelations over time is assessed.

Analytical review procedures apart, detailed substantive testing can be time-consuming, and for most audits only a sample of items in an *auditing population can usually be tested. Auditors therefore rely on either *statistical or *judgmental sampling techniques, or a combination of the two, to test items substantively. Auditors tend to extrapolate their findings from sample testing to the auditing population as a whole. Further, auditors undertake *compliance testing of internal controls, on the assumption that satisfactory controls and procedures reduce the risk of incorrectly extrapolating the findings of tests on sampled items. In practice, therefore, auditing often comprises a combination of substantive and compliance tests: the balance between the two types of testing is determined by factors like the volume of transactions to be tested, and the sophistication and reliability of an entity's internal controls.

sub-subsidiary A *subsidiary organization whose *parent organization is in turn a subsidiary of another entity.

subvention An alternative term for *subsidy.

sum of the digits A method of *allocating costs to time periods based on the formula $n (n + 1) / 2$, where n represents the number of years to which the cost is to be allocated. In *amortization methodologies, the sum of the digits approach results in an *accelerated method that amortizes the cost of a *long-term asset more heavily in the early years of its *useful economic life. For example, for an asset with a useful economic life of 5 years, the sum of the digits is 15, which is calculated as $5 (5 + 1) / 2$. In the first year, the cost of the asset is amortized by 5/15, in the second year by 4/15, and so on, until the final year's amortization of 1/15.

sunk cost An unavoidable item of expenditure incurred because of a past decision. In contrast to an *avoidable cost, a sunk cost cannot be changed by a further decision (without avoiding penalties). For example, an organization that enters a binding agreement for the *long-term rental of warehousing space incurs the rental expense as a sunk cost. See also *unavoidable cost.

supervision The oversight, review, and correction of a matter. In auditing, supervision of audit staff is a fundamental control to ensure the quality of audit work and to ensure that a correct *audit opinion is reached: "Failure to comply with accepted *standards by any [audit] staff member can jeopardize the credibility of the entire audit effort" (Lee, 1993, 120).

supplier A seller of goods or services. See also *vendor.

supply The willingness of participants in a *market to make a good or service available for purchase. In unregulated markets, *prices are (in theory) established by the "invisible hand" of buyers' and sellers' *demand and supply decisions.

supply chain The activities, organizations, and individuals that participate in the supply of an item. Supply chain management is a means of enhancing the *Three E's of supply through enhanced collaboration between parts of the "chain" of activities.

Supreme Audit Institution (SAI) A country's main body for *public sector auditing. The *International Organization of Supreme Audit Institutions is a global SAI forum.

surplus 1. An excess of *income over a level required to pay expenses or satisfy *investor expectations. **2.** An alternative term for *retained earnings. **3.** In *not-for-profit organizations, an alternative term for *net income or profit.

suspense account A *general ledger account used to temporarily record *transactions. By nature, a suspense account should be regularly cleared of its contents, as it is merely a resting place for items awaiting analysis or investigation. See also *transit account.

sustainability The pursuit of economic growth without excessive degradation of the physical and social environment. Sustainability aims to protect resources so that they can extend as far as possible into the future. For example, restrained fishing practices can be undertaken to avoid dangerous depletion of fish stocks. See also *corporate social responsibility, *AccountAbility, and the *World Business Council for Sustainable Development.

sweatshop A factory characterized by poor working conditions, low wages, and the exploitation and intimidation of employees.

SWOT (strengths, weaknesses, opportunities, and threats) analysis An approach to *risk assessment and organizational planning that aims to identify the strong and weak aspects (actual and potential) of an activity or organization.

syndicate A group of individuals or organizations working in combination for a common purpose. For example, investment bankers create temporary syndicates to promote the sale of *securities.

systematic risk The part of an asset's risk that cannot be eliminated through *diversification. This type of risk can be measured by a *beta coefficient.

T

T-account In *double entry bookkeeping, a diagrammatic depiction of an *account in the form of the letter "T." The T-shape is created by attaching to a horizontal line a vertical line that extends down the page. The left side of the account records *debit entries, and the right side records *credit entries.

takeover An alternative term for *acquisition (definition 2).

tangible asset A *long-term *asset that possesses physical substance. Examples include *property, plant, and equipment.

tariff A *customs *duty levied on the *exportation or *importation of goods or services. A tariff may be imposed by a government purely for revenue-generating *taxation purposes, or it can serve more political ends. Examples of the latter include (i) trade *protectionism, (ii) *barriers to entry to a *market, (iii) anti-*dumping measures, (iv) a form of retaliation against the tariffs of another country, and (v) protection of a nation's cultural heritage (by discouraging the export of works of art and items of national treasure).

tax **1.** An abbreviated term for *taxation. **2.** An individual category of *taxation. Examples include *sales tax and *value added tax.

taxation A compulsory contribution to government finances. Taxation falls on both individuals and organizations, and its revenues are used by a government (i) to fund *public sector expenditure and (ii) to pursue political policies (like the redistribution of wealth). See also *ad valorem tax, *consumption tax, *direct taxation, *indirect taxation, *progressive tax, *regressive tax, *sales tax, *value added tax, and *windfall tax.

tax avoidance An arrangement, within the law, of the affairs of an individual or organization to minimize *taxation liabilities. Contrast *tax evasion.

tax break A *taxation concession or exemption given by a government to an individual or organization.

tax effect The *taxation consequences of an event or course of action. The term is often used to differentiate between the treatment of an accounting *transaction under *Generally Accepted Accounting Principles and its comparative treatment in the preparation of taxation calculations.

tax evasion The criminal practice of avoiding or underpaying *taxation liabilities. Contrast *tax avoidance.

tax haven A country or territory that offers low *tax rates or *tax avoidance benefits to individuals or organizations. The economic impact of tax havens tends to be wildly disproportionate to their size. Tax havens are often small island nations or tiny territories at the geographical fringes of major economies, but it is estimated that as much as one-third of the world's Gross Domestic Product passes through them at some point (Mitchell et al., 2002). The *Organization for Economic Co-operation and Development (OECD) has brought pressure on territories it suspects of facilitating *tax evasion or *money laundering. In 2000, for example, the OECD drafted a list of thirty-five "unco-operative" countries and territories it criticized for allegedly poor standards of financial *transparency, tax *regulation, and exchange of information. Most of the territories subsequently committed to improvements in regulation and transparency, but by the end of 2003 the OECD still identified five jurisdictions on its list.
Further reading: Mitchell et al. (2002)
Web site: *www.oecd.org*

tax holiday A period in which, by agreement with the relevant government authorities, no *taxation is paid.

tax rate The rate of *taxation applied to the income or other taxable resources of an individual or organization.

tax return A document used to declare information to *taxation authorities.

tax shelter An *investment mechanism that offers low *taxation liabilities.

Teachers Insurance and Annuity Association College Retirement Equities Fund (TIAA-CREF) A major *institutional investor. Based in New York, TIAA-CREF was founded in the early twentieth century. It offers a range of financial products, including retirement plans and life and health *insurance. Like *CalPERS, another major US institutional investor, TIAA-CREF has contributed to debates on *corporate governance, and its *Policy Statement on Corporate Governance* was first published in 1997. Available online and periodically updated, matters covered by the *Policy Statement* include the responsibilities of *boards of directors to *executive remuneration.
Further reading: TIAA-CREF (2002)
Web site: *www.tiaa-cref.org*

teeming and lading A British term for *lapping.

telegraphic transfer An alternative term for *wire transfer.

template **1.** A shaped or patterned item used as an aid in drawing, designing, cutting, and similar activities. Templates are often used in the manual preparation of *flowcharts. **2.** An item that serves as a *standard (definition 2) or model. **3.** A pre-prepared document or computer program used for the periodic recording of *data of a recurring nature. For example, *spreadsheets can be prepared as templates for the periodic analysis of budgetary accounting information.

temporary difference A transitory difference between *income (definition 2) calculated under *Generally Accepted Accounting Principles and income calculated according to *taxation rules. Temporary differences originate in one *fiscal year and reverse in another. Contrast *permanent difference.

tender **1.** A formal offer, communication, or presentation. For example, "He tendered his resignation last week." **2.** A competitive process of bidding for a *contract to perform work or to supply goods or services at a defined *price. For example, "The corporation invited tenders for its annual external audit."

test See *audit test.

test data **1.** A *sample of *data used in an *audit test. **2.** Simulated *data and *transactions used in the *compliance testing of computer *application controls. See also *computer assisted auditing techniques.

third party An individual or organization not directly involved in a transaction or contract. In auditing, *audit evidence gathered from third parties (e.g., through the *circularization of an organization's customers) is generally considered to provide strong *audit evidence.

Third World An alternative, slightly archaic term for a *developing country. The term was coined during the Cold War as part of the classification of the world's nations into three groups: (i) communist countries, (ii) economically advanced capitalist countries, and (iii) economically underdeveloped nations that did not fall into either of the preceding categories. The term entered English by translation from the French phrase *tiers monde*, but following the collapse of the Soviet bloc in the late twentieth century the notion of the threefold division of nations lost much of its significance. The term has a somewhat old-fashioned ring today.

Three E's The term used in *operational or *value-for-money auditing to denote the *economy, *efficiency, and *effectiveness of operations under audit. Operational audits frequently use these three criteria, which have been summarized succinctly as follows (Sawyer and Vinten, 1996, 66-67):

- Economy is doing things cheap
- Efficiency is doing them right
- Effectiveness is doing the right things.

In recent years some commentators have expanded the list of criteria from three to six, to create the *Six E's.

threshold **1.** A quantifiable limit beyond which the nature of an item changes. For example, a taxation threshold is a point at which a *tax rate changes. **2.** A quantifiable limit used in the establishment of *internal controls over *authorization procedures. For example, the authorization of disbursements in an organization may require the written approval of a number of individuals. Disbursement value thresholds can define individual employees' authorization powers in line with their organizational responsibilities and status.

Thurston, John B. (1908–1951) A U.S. internal auditing pioneer. Thurston was one of three "founding fathers" of the *Institute of Internal Auditors (IIA), along with *Victor Z. Brink and *Robert B. Milne. He was the first president of the IIA on its founding in 1941. It has been suggested that "[w]ithout question, John B. Thurston deserves to be called the 'father of the Institute of Internal Auditors'. It was clearly through his efforts that the creation and development of the Institute was accelerated by many years" (Brink, 1977, 9). Following his death, the IIA established the Thurston Award in his honor. The award is given for outstanding articles in the IIA magazine *Internal Auditor*.
    Further reading: Brink (1977); Flesher (1991)

TIAA-CREF See *Teachers Insurance and Annuity Association College Retirement Equities Fund.

ticking The making of a small mark on a document to indicate the performance of an *audit test. Tick marks are common in manual audit *work papers, where different marks can represent different aspects of testing. The interpretation of tick marks is usually facilitated by a glossary or key to the audit work performed. See also *box-ticking approach.

time and motion study A formal *evaluation of the *efficiency and *effectiveness of operational activity in an organization. Time and motion studies typically look at the physical procedures and time taken to perform defined activities, with a view to simplifying and speeding up the activities reviewed.

time value of money The notion that a unit of *money is worth more at present than in the future, owing to the erosion of its value by *inflation. The concept is central to *discounted cash flow analysis.

timing difference **1.** An inconsistency between the timing of the accounting of an item and the timing of its underlying circumstances. **2.** A difference between *income (definition 2) calculated under *Generally Accepted Accounting Principles and income calculated according to *taxation rules. See *permanent difference and *temporary difference.

token **1.** [adjective] Small, insignificant. For example, "They were offered just a token payment as compensation." **2.** [adjective] Symbolic or representative. For example, "Please except this award as a token of our esteem." **3.** [noun] A *coupon or *voucher that can be exchanged for a good or service. For example, "He gave her a book token as a birthday gift."

tolerable rate **1.** In external auditing, the extent to which the *misstatement of an accounting balance does not *materially misstate *financial statements. Assessments of tolerable rates are a fundamental aspect of *audit risk assessment for external auditors. **2.** In *budgeting, an acceptable divergence of actual results from budgeted amounts.

tone at the top A phrase denoting the attitudes of an organization's *board of directors and senior managers toward *corporate governance, *ethics, *risk management, and *internal controls. The tone at the top is often considered to establish the atmosphere of the entire organization. Acceptance by a board of directors of good ethical and governance standards is therefore deemed to be a prerequisite for good corporate governance in the organization as a whole. It has been suggested that boards of directors "have the dual role of framing codes of conduct and of living by them" (Cadbury, 2002, 38).

Major corporate scandals and misconduct have often derived from a weak governance culture at an organization's highest echelons, For example, the attitudes of senior officials at *Enron, *WorldCom, and *Arthur Andersen are widely considered to have been major contributory factors to the demise of those organizations. "A fish rots from its head," as an old proverb says.

Tone at the Top A U.S. internal auditing and *corporate governance newsletter. Published quarterly by the *Institute of Internal Auditors, the newsletter is available in print and online formats. Its Web page states its aim to be as follows: To "provide executive management, boards of directors, and audit committees with concise, leading-edge information on such issues as risk, internal control, governance, ethics, and the changing role of internal auditing; and guidance relative to their roles in, and responsibilities for the internal audit process."

Web link: *www.theiia.org/ecm/newsletters.cfm?doc_id=739*

top table An alternative, informal term for a corporation's main *board of directors or an organization's similar governing body.

total quality management (TQM) A *management philosophy that stresses the responsibilities of all employees in an organization in contributing to the achievement of the organization's objectives. Total quality management exhibits some or all of the following characteristics: (i) a commitment to *continuous improvement, (ii) the minimization or elimination of *waste, (iii) the minimization or elimination of defects in *products or services, and (iv) a commitment to satisfying (and preferably exceeding) customer expectations.
Further reading: Hawkes and Adams (1994)

trace, to 1. To find something, or the origin of something, through investigation. For example, "He traced the source of the *fraud to a warehouse employee." **2.** To describe something in outline form. For example, "He traced an outline to the *audit committee of how the fraud was perpetrated."

traceable cost A *cost that can be related directly to a particular activity or item. For example, the costs of a manufactured product can be traced to *cost centers or purchases of specific *raw materials, and the costs of a business trip can be traced to supporting invoices and receipts.

trade 1. The activity of buying and selling goods and services. **2.** Individuals and organizations operating in a defined sector of economic activity. For example, "She was well known in the furniture trade." **3.** Work or related activity that requires skills and training, but which does not enjoy the high social status of a *profession.

trade barrier An impediment to a *free market in the *trade of goods or services. See also *protectionism and *tariff.

trade credit See *credit.

trade creditors A British term for *accounts payable.

trade debtors A British term for *accounts receivable.

trade discount See *discount.

trademark 1. The registering of a name or design to obtain legal protection over its exclusive use. See also *patent. **2.** A characteristic or distinctive aspect of an individual, item, or activity. For example, "He won the argument through his trademark charm and eloquence."

trade receivables A British term for *accounts receivable.

trafficking Trading and dealing in an *underground economy.

trail See *audit trail.

tranche An installment or portion of *money. For example, "The first *tranche* of the loan is payable next month." The word is taken from the French word for slice.

transaction An event or interaction between individuals or organizations that has economic consequences. A common example of a transaction is the buying or selling of a good or service.

transfer price The *price of a good or service used in *transactions between parts of a decentralized organization. The transfer pricing arrangements of *multinational corporations can be used to shift taxable *income to low tax countries, but regulatory authorities in recent years have started to closely monitor the international transfer pricing practices of *multinational corporations.

transit account An alternative term for *suspense account. However, the terms transit account and suspense account are sometimes differentiated as follows: (i) a suspense account is used for items awaiting analysis or investigation and (ii) a transit account is used for items whose proper general ledger classification is subject to an underlying time restriction (such as the receipt of a customer *statement of account).

translation 1. The process of converting financial data from one *currency to another. 2. The process of converting written text from one language to another.

transnational corporation (TNC) An alternative term for *multinational corporation.

transparency Openness to public scrutiny. Transparency is widely considered to be central to best practice in *corporate governance and *corporate social responsibility.

Transparency International (TI) An international anti*corruption organization. Transparency International is headquartered in Berlin, Germany, and its mission (as stated on its Web site) is to bring "civil society, business, and governments together in a powerful global [anti-corruption] coalition." The organization's activities include policy statements, compliance monitoring, and research. It also produces well-publicized "league tables" of countries ranked by measures of corruption.
Web site: *www.transparency.org*

traveling auditor An alternative term for *field auditor.

Treadway Commission Report An abbreviated name for the 1987 report of the United States' National Commission on Fraudulent Financial Reporting. Named for its chairperson, James C. Treadway (a former commissioner of the *Securities and Exchange Commission), the establishment of the National Commission in 1985 was a reaction against the corporate accounting scandals of the early 1980s. The report stressed the important role of *audit committees and internal auditors in reducing *financial reporting fraud, and it emphasized the importance of *ethical organizational policies. The sponsors of the Treadway Commission are known as the *Committee of Sponsoring Organizations (COSO), and they have followed up the 1987 report with further *corporate governance initiatives, including *Internal Control–Integrated Framework* (1992). The *Treadway Commission Report* is available online on the COSO Web site.
   Further reading: Phillips et al. (1987); Treadway Commission (1987)
   Web site: *www.coso.org*

treasury 1. The administration and management of the financial assets of an organization. In modern corporations the responsibilities of treasury departments cover, among other things, (i) banking, (ii) investments, and (iii) foreign exchange management. **2.** The finances of a government.

Treasury bill (T-bill) A *short-term, U.S. federal government debt instrument. T-bills are considered to be virtually *risk-free, and they carry low *yields. See also *Treasury bond.

Treasury bond 1. [upper-case initial letter] A *long-term, U.S. federal government bond. Compare *Treasury bill. **2.** [lower-case initial letter] A *bond issued by a corporation and subsequently repurchased. See also *treasury stock.

treasury stock 1. *Common stock issued by a corporation and subsequently repurchased. See also *Treasury bond. **2.** The British equivalent of a *Treasury bond (definition 1 only).

trend analysis An alternative term for *horizontal analysis.

trial balance (TB) A listing of all *accounts in a *general ledger. Under the conventions of *double entry bookkeeping, *transactions are recorded through corresponding *debit and *credit entries of equal value. A trial balance is a means of establishing the accuracy of the *accounting equation, under which the total of debit entries equals the total of credit entries. However, while the trial balance indicates the arithmetical balancing of the general ledger's debit and credit entries, it does not indicate whether individual accounting entries have been *posted to correct accounts. Financial statements can be prepared from an *extended trial balance, which records adjustments and reclassifications made to a basic trial balance.

True and Fair A newsletter of the audit and assurance faculty of the *Institute of Chartered Accountants in England and Wales (ICAEW). Published ten times annually, the newsletter's title is based on the standard wording of British external audit reports—*true and fair. The newsletter focuses on external auditing, but it also occasionally covers internal auditing topics.
  Web link: *www.icaew.co.uk/auditassfac*

true and fair view A British term for the *fair presentation of financial statements. In the United Kingdom, expressions used prior to the adoption of the phrase "true and fair" included (i) full and fair and (ii) true and correct.

trust **1.** A legal agreement whereby a *trustee holds or manages assets on behalf of a beneficiary. Trusts involve a division in the title to property between trustees and beneficiaries: The beneficiary of a trust is the true owner of the trust's assets, though the trustee holds formal legal title. The concept of trusts is encountered most commonly in countries with legal traditions influenced by English common law. See also *fiduciary. **2.** A rather archaic term for a group of corporations with the characteristics of *monopolies or *cartels. See *antitrust laws.

trustee A party to a *trustee agreement who holds legal title to assets, but who also holds or manages the assets on behalf of a beneficiary.

Turnbull Report A British *corporate governance report of 1999. The report's formal title was *Internal Control—Guidance to Directors on the Combined Code*. The *Turnbull Report* was prepared by a committee chaired by Nigel Turnbull, and the report itself has come to be popularly named for the chairperson. The report's aim was to provide guidance to directors on implementation of the internal control recommendations of the United Kingdom's *Hampel Report* (or *Combined Code*) of 1998.
  Further reading: *Turnbull Report* (1999)

turnover **1.** The frequency with which an *asset is used or replaced during a period of time. For example, inventory turnover can be calculated as the total value of items of inventory sold in a defined period divided by the average value of inventory held. The term is also used to designate the frequency of employee changes in an organization. **2.** A British term for *sales or sales volume.

two-bin inventory procedure An *inventory control procedure in which two bins, or locations, are used to store quantities of a *raw material or product. The first bin is used for day-to-day use, and the second bin serves as a backup of buffer stock to avoid *stockouts in periods when the first bin awaits replenishment.

two-tier board See *board of directors.

U

ultra vires A Latin expression that means "beyond the powers." The term is used to refer to actions of an individual or organization that exceed the scope of defined, legal authority.

unadjusted trial balance A *trial balance that simply lists all *accounts in a *general ledger, before the making of adjustments and reclassifications. Compare *extended trial balance.

unauditable See *auditability.

unaudited **1.** Not subjected to an audit. **2.** Not subjected to an audit conducted in accordance with *Generally Accepted Auditing Standards.

unavoidable cost An expense that is incurred irrespective of the discretion of an organization's managers. Compare *avoidable cost, *controllable cost, and *sunk cost.

uncertainty The condition of being unknown or incompletely known. In auditing and *corporate governance, uncertainty is sometimes distinguished from *risk on the following basis: (i) Uncertainty is a situation in which the outcomes of various courses of action are either unknown or cannot be estimated, while (ii) risk is a situation where outcomes can be estimated using *probability theory. This differentiation of uncertainty and risk has the advantage of separating the *quantitative from the *qualitative. However, in practice, many individuals collapse both meanings into the term "risk." Contrast *certainty.

unconsolidated [of the financial statements of business combinations] Not yet subjected to *consolidation accounting.

underground economy Economic activity undertaken outside official channels. Transactions in the informal economy are usually illegal, and they are designed to circumvent laws, *regulations, and *taxation. They also tend to be settled in *cash. For obvious reasons, activities in an underground economy are normally excluded from a country's *Gross Domestic Product statistics. However, attempts at estimating the value of underground economies are frequently attempted. The term "black market" is sometimes used to distinguish *smuggling and *tax evasion activities from other aspects of the underground economy, but the two terms are often used interchangeably.

understandability The comprehension of a matter. Understandability is central to auditing in two senses: (i) An auditor is unable to perform satisfactory auditing duties in relation to an organization, activity, or asset if it is beyond his or her comprehension; and (ii) the significance of *audit evidence must be open to objective perception. Understandability is also central to the *fair presentation of *financial statements.

understatement The inadequate quantification or description of an item. The term is often used in the context of incorrectly stated accounting *balances. Contrast *overstatement.

undertaking **1.** A *profit-seeking *enterprise or activity. **2.** A commitment or promise to perform an action.

underwrite, to **1.** To accept the potential liabilities arising from an *insurance policy or *guarantee. **2.** To agree to purchase all unsold *securities arising from a new issuance of *securities.

unearned income An alternative term for *unearned revenue.

unearned revenue Revenue not yet earned in a *financial reporting period, but for which cash has already been received. In line with the *accruals basis of accounting, unearned revenue is recorded in *current or *long-term deferred revenue accounts (classified among liabilities) in the *balance sheet, and released to the *income statement in the accounting periods to which it relates. Typical examples of unearned revenue are rental and *subscription income.

unemployment The existence of individuals who are available for work yet who are unable or unwilling to obtain fixed employment.

unfavorable variance In *budgeting, the incurring of larger than anticipated costs or the earning of lower than anticipated revenues. An unfavorable variance indicates that actual performance is worse than expected. The term is also used in *standard costing. Contrast *favorable variance.

unfunded Not receiving *funds or *money to achieve a defined purpose.

uniformity Without variation or differences. Both *Generally Accepted Accounting Principles and *Generally Accepted Auditing Standards encourage uniform bases for the preparation of *financial statements between organizations and between *financial reporting periods.

unit An individual item that is not further divided in smaller elements for analytical or operational purposes. In production processes, for example, manufactured items are counted in units (which typically represent a finished *consumer good) and production unit volumes drive *absorption costing methodologies. In auditing, an *audit universe tends to be analyzed into *auditable units for *risk assessment and planning purposes.

unitary board See *board of *directors.

unit cost Total production costs attributable to *individual units of production output. See *absorption costing.

unit trust A British term for *mutual fund.

unqualified opinion An external auditor's opinion that an entity's *financial statements conform with *Generally Accepted Accounting Principles, and offer a *fair representation of the entity's financial position, the results of its operations, and changes in cash flows. External auditors can issue an *adverse or *qualified opinion if they are unsatisfied with a *material aspect of the financial statements. See also *disclaimer.

unsecured [of a loan] Not guaranteed against a *default (definition 2) in repayments by the pledge of an asset. Contrast *secured.

unsystematic risk The part of an asset's risk that can be controlled or eliminated through *diversification.

Urgent Issues Task Force (UITF) A committee of the British *Accounting Standards Board. Established in 1990, the UITF is charged with reviewing the implications of urgent accounting issues. It is modeled on the United States' *Emerging Issues Task Force.

useful (economic) life The period of time over which an asset can provide economic benefits to its owner. The costs of *long-term assets are *amortized over their useful lives. See also *wasting asset.

usury The charging of excessive *interest for the lending of *money. In traditional Christian and Islamic jurisprudence, usury has sometimes been defined as simply the charging of interest, irrespective of the "unjustness" of the *interest rate applied.

utility 1. The benefit, pleasure, or satisfaction obtained by consuming a product or service. See also *diminishing returns and *value. 2. The practical usefulness of an item. 3. An abbreviation for *public utility.

validate, to **1.** To confirm the *validity of something. External auditors confirm the validity of items in *financial statements through the gathering of appropriate *audit evidence. **2.** To make or to declare a *contract or other arrangement legally binding.

validity **1.** The state of being relevant. *Audit evidence is valid only if it relates directly to the supporting or refuting of an *audit objective. **2.** The state of being compliant with *regulations or the law.

value **1.** The monetary worth of an item. See also *book value, *market value, *price, and *wealth. **2.** The *qualitative worth of an item, activity, or individual. For example: "Her experience makes her of great value to the audit department." See also *utility. **3.** An ethical principle or standard of behavior. For example, "He is a man of impeccable values."

value added See *add value.

value added tax (VAT) An *indirect tax on goods or services collected at incremental stages of *production and distribution. See also *consumption tax and *sales tax.

value-at-risk (VAR) Models used by financial institutions to measure the *risks of complex *derivatives.

value-for-money auditing (VFM) An alternative term for *operational auditing. The term is frequently used in the United Kingdom and countries with a history of British influence, in the context of *public sector auditing, for audits that assess the Three E's of the *economy, *efficiency, and *effectiveness.
   Further reading: Flesher et al. (2003)

value in use The *present value of an *asset. Value in use is calculated by discounting future cash flows attributable to the use (and, ultimately, the disposal proceeds) of the asset.

variable budget An alternative term for *flexible budget.

variable cost An item of expenditure that is linked closely to levels of activity. For example, the cost of *raw materials in the manufacture of a product tends to be related closely to production levels. Contrast *fixed cost.

variance 1. In *budgeting and *standard costing, the difference between actual and anticipated costs or revenues. Variances are often categorized as *favorable or *unfavorable. 2. A measure of the dispersion of a *probability distribution. The variance is calculated as the square of the *standard deviation.

vendor A seller or *supplier of goods or services. Organizations manage their *credit transactions with vendors through *accounts payable records.

venture capital Sources of finance for new business ventures that carry high *risks and potentially high *rewards.

verifiable The state of being capable of confirmation and objective assessment. *Audit evidence should be verifiable in the sense of being capable of review by different auditors who may reach similar conclusions on the basis of the evidence. However, *verification does not necessary imply complete objectivity, as there can still be scope for subjective assessment and variety of interpretation.

verification An *examination of an activity or asset in order to obtain evidence of its existence, condition, or truth. Verification is an important *substantive test to obtain *audit evidence: "Depending on the...circumstances, verification takes place intuitively or by instruction; instantly or over time; expertly or crudely; explicitly or implicitly; and formal or informal. Whatever the mechanism, however, verification can be described as a form of auditing which is conducted with the objective of establishing the degree of correspondence between [an] object of doubt and some acceptable criteria by which it can be judged" (Lee, 1993, 20). See also *physical verification.

Verschoor, Curtis C. (born 1931) A U.S. accounting and auditing academic. A Professor of Accountancy at DePaul University, Chicago, IL, Verschoor's areas of specialism include *audit committees, international accounting, internal auditing, and business ethics. Before entering DePaul in 1974, he held a series of senior accounting and accounting posts in public practice and at major corporations. His writings include the book *Audit Committee Briefing: Understanding the 21st Century Audit Committee and its Governance Roles* (2000).
  Further reading: Verschoor (2000); Verschoor (2001)
  Web link: *http://fac.comtech.depaul.edu/bios/cverscho.html*

vertical analysis The use of one item in *financial statements as a base amount for comparative purposes. For example, if the value of *gross sales in an *income statement is set at 100 percent, the various expenses within the income statement can be expressed as a percentage of gross sales. Compare *horizontal analysis.

vertical integration A *business combination of an organization with its suppliers. For example, a corporation that acquires its suppliers of *raw materials and components can control and simplify its *supply chain.

Viénot Report A French *corporate governance report of 1995. Prepared by a committee chaired by Marc Viénot, the report was the French equivalent of the 1992 British *Cadbury Report*. The *Rapport Viénot* (*Viénot Report*) has had considerable influence in continental Europe and in the wider francophone community, and a second *Viénot Report* was issued in 1999.
    Further reading: *Viénot Report* (1995)

Vinten, Gerald (born 1948) A British academic, author, and *internal auditing specialist. Editor of *Managerial Auditing Journal*, and Head of Business as the European Business School in London, Professor Vinten's written output is vast. He has authored more than 300 articles on various aspects of auditing and management, including a number of contributions to the journal he edits. He has also produced several monographs, and was the contributing editor of the essay collection *Whistle-blowing: Subversion or Corporate Citizenship?* (Vinten, 1994). With *Laurence B. Sawyer, he coauthored *The Manager and the Internal Auditor: Partners for Profit* (Vinten, 1996).
    An indefatigable promoter of internal auditing, Vinten is a former president of the *Institute of Internal Auditors in the United Kingdom and Ireland. He has shared Laurence B. Sawyer's mission to lift internal auditing from a compliance-focused accounting role into a wider managerial function: "Professional internal auditors are equipped . . . to evaluate any activity in the organization, both financial and operational. Virtually nothing is immune from their review" (Sawyer and Vinten, 1996, 3). Vinten has not been eager to embrace every innovation in internal auditing theory, however, as indicated by this caution against overemphasis on *risk assessment techniques: "A worry is that over emphasis on risk assessment may perpetuate the traditional culture of the risk-averse internal auditor, with risk being seen as something to avoid rather than being an opportunity to be exploited" (Vinten, 1996, 93). His other areas of interest include *chaos theory, internal auditing research, *whistle-blowing, and (beyond the field of auditing) theological matters.
    Further reading: Sawyer and Vinten (1996); Vinten (1991); Vinten (1992); Vinten (1994); Vinten (1996); Vinten (2003)

virus 1. An organism, typically comprised of nucleic acid coated in protein, that causes infection or disease. The spread of viruses can present a serious operational *risk to organizations—in 2003, for example, the Severe Acute Respiratory Syndrome (SARS) virus caused massive economic disruption in Hong Kong and Toronto, among other places. **2.** A program defect or code that corrupts computer software programs. The potentially devastating effects of computer viruses can be controlled through antivirus programs, and through the adequate *backup of data. See also *bug.

visible asset An alternative term for *tangible asset.

volatility The state of being subjected to rapid and unpredictable changes, with resulting high *risks. For example: "The volatility of Middle East oil markets is legendary."

volume 1. The quantity of an item, or the amount of space occupied by an item. **2.** The degree of loudness of a noise. **3.** [of books and magazines] One of a series or sequence of publications.

voucher 1. A document that confers an economic benefit of some type. For example, a retail organization may give its customers vouchers that entitle them to *discounts. See also *coupon and *token. **2.** A document used as part of an *internal control system. For example, an organization may control its *disbursements by attaching to vendor *invoices supporting, sequentially-numbered vouchers that record written authorization of the payments. **3.** An alternative term for *receipt.

wage *Remuneration paid to an employee of an organization. Wages can be differentiated from *salaries in several ways: (i) wages tend to vary in accordance with the amount of work performed, while salaries tend to be fixed amounts, (ii) wages tend to be paid in *cash rather than by *check or *wire transfer, and (iii) wages are often paid daily or weekly, in contrast to monthly salaries. However, the terms wages and salaries are frequently used interchangeably.

walk-through test An audit *compliance test of procedures and *internal controls. Walk-through testing involves the tracing of a sample *transaction (or a *sample of transactions) through accounting and *internal control processes. Through analysis of the *audit trail, the auditor attempts to obtain *audit evidence of the satisfactory operation of controls and procedures.

warehouse A storage facility for *inventory. The application of the so-called *Three E's of *economy, *efficiency, and *effectiveness to warehousing facilities is often addressed in *operational auditing.

warrant 1. An abbreviated term for *stock warrant. **2.** A document that authorizes police or other law enforcement agents to arrest an individual, search a building, or seize assets. **3.** A legally binding *guarantee to support an activity or transaction. **4.** In some *public sector organizations, an instruction that authorizes a *disbursement to a specified individual or organization.

warranty An undertaking or *guarantee (definition 2) made by the seller of a good or service to compensate a customer for any deficiencies or unsatisfactory performance within a specified time period.

waste 1. An alternative term for *spoilage arising from production processes. The term is sometimes restricted to the designation of spoilage with no resale value, but the words spoilage and waste are often used synonymously. **2.** An alternative term for the *shrinkage of inventory or other *short-term, *tangible assets.

wasting asset A *fixed asset with a limited *useful economic life. Wasting assets are normally subjected to *amortization charges.

wealth **1.** Possession of riches and resources. Wealth covers items like *money and *tangible assets as well as *intangible assets like *intellectual capital. **2.** The qualitative *value (definition 2) of something. **3.** An abundant or generous amount of something. For example, "She has a wealth of experience in internal auditing."

wear and tear A reduction in the value of a *fixed asset owing to its normal use. Wear and tear is a major contributory factor in *amortization.

WebCPA™ A U.S. online accounting resource center. *WebCPA* is published by the Accountants Media Group, a division of Thomson. It was established in 1997 as the *Electronic Accountant*. Initially on CD-Rom, it migrated to the Internet and adopted its current name in 2003. *WebCPA* provides daily updated news on accounting issues, and its subscribers have access to online editions of the magazines *Accounting Today*, *Accounting Technology*, and *Practical Accountant*. In addition to accounting, it has frequent coverage of taxation and external auditing topics.
    Web site: *www.webcpa.com*

weight, to **1.** To calculate the amounts of various items in proportion to their importance. See *weighted average. **2.** To regard or treat with importance or preference. For example, "The organization weighted its purchases toward European suppliers."

weighted average The *mean of a number of items that has been calculated to reflect the items' relative importance. For example, a corporation that purchases *inventory of the same *raw material on two separate dates, 100 units at $10 per unit and 50 units at $5 per unit, calculates the weighted average of the inventory as $8.33. This represents [(100 x 10) + (50 x 5)] / 150.

weighted average cost of capital (WACC) A corporation's *costs of capital derived from—and *weighted in proportion to—the capital structure of its *equity and *debt finance.

weighted mean An alternative term for *weighted average.

what-if analysis A form of *quantitative analysis in which assumptions are changed and the resulting outcomes compared. For example, an analysis of the potential profitability of a manufactured product can be analyzed under a range of sales scenarios—sales levels can be changed in order to illustrate the resulting effects on income. What-if analysis is a common decision-making tool, and it has been facilitated from the late twentieth century by the increasing sophistication of *spreadsheets and other computer programs.

whistle-blowing The bringing to public attention of improper or illegal activities within an organization. It has been suggested that whistle-blowing "is a new name for an ancient practice. Alternative terms may be conscientious objector, ethical resister, mole or informer, or licensed spy" (Vinten, 1992, 1).

This quotation hints at the ambiguities and moral dilemmas facing whistle-blowers: They are often praised for identifying matters of great importance, but equally often they face accusations of organizational disloyalty and breaches of confidentiality. In the age of the so-called *organization man or woman, it can take great bravery to blow the whistle on improper activities. Social ostracism or even dismissal can be the consequences. The internal auditing activities of *Cynthia Cooper at *WorldCom were frequently described in the popular media as whistle-blowing.

Further reading: Figg (2000a); Jubb (2000); Reed and Rama (2003); Vinten (1992); Vinten (1994)

white-collar crime The undertaking of *fraudulent or other illegal activity by individuals engaged in clerical or other nonmanual occupations. The term is often used in the context of nonviolent yet serious financial crime like (i) *false accounting, (ii) *tax evasion, (iii) *insurance fraud, and (iii) *money laundering.

widget A term, often used humorously, to describe a small, manufactured product of small size or low value. For example, "She made a fortune from manufacturing millions of widgets in her factory."

windfall profit Large-scale *income (definition 2) of an unexpected, exceptional, and sudden nature.

windfall tax An exceptional *taxation charge on *corporations that are deemed by a government to have made *windfall (or excessive) profits owing to unusual circumstances. *Private sector *monopoly suppliers of *public utilities, for example, are subjected to periodic windfall taxes in some countries. In the United States, the 1980 Crude Oil Windfall Profits Tax was imposed on oil corporations that had benefited from exceptional increases in the *price of oil in the 1970s.

winding up The orderly closure of an organization or completion of an activity. See also *liquidation.

window dressing A *creative accounting technique that manipulates transactions around a *cutoff date to improve the appearance of a *balance sheet. For example, an organization may delay some payments until after a sensitive financial reporting date to boost *cash balances and *liquidity ratios. Around the world, systems of *Generally Accepted Accounting Principles are increasingly reducing the scope for permitted window dressing techniques.

wire transfer A disbursement of *money directly from one bank account to another, without the intermediary of a *check or the physical movement of *cash.

Wirtschaftprüfer A German term that approximates to *Certified Public Accountant. The term is used in Germany, Austria, and Switzerland.

withholding tax 1. Deductions of *taxation made by an employer from an employee's *salary or *wage and paid to taxation authorities. 2. Deductions of *taxation on income from *dividends and *interest that are paid to an individual resident outside a country.

working capital 1. *Short-term assets used for day-to-day trading and operational purposes. Working capital comprises *cash, *accounts receivable, *inventory, and *prepaid expenses. 2. A measure of *liquidity calculated by deducting *current liabilities from *current assets.

working papers 1. An alternative term for *work papers. 2. A document that shows detailed calculations to support a *general ledger balance or similar item.

work-in-process (WIP) 1. The partially completed goods of a *manufacturing process. Compare *raw materials and *finished goods. 2. A partially completed, *long-term *contract.

work-in-progress (WIP) An alternative term for *work-in-process, used in the United Kingdom and other countries with a history of British influence.

work papers Documents that record *audit evidence and *audit tests. Work papers are important records of the conduct of an audit. In external auditing, they can be used as court evidence in cases of claims of *negligent or unsatisfactory audit work. In internal auditing, the Professional Practices Framework of the *Institute of Internal Auditors requires adequate documentation of auditing work. See also *ticking.

World Bank A specialized agency of the United Nations. Headquartered in Washington, DC, the World Bank Group consists of five divisions: the International Bank for Reconstruction and Development (established in 1945, a year after the Bretton Woods conference), the International Finance Corporation (1956), the International Development Association (1960), the International Center for the Settlement of Investment Disputes (1966), and the Multilateral Investment Guarantee Agency (1988). The World Bank operates under the coordinating machinery of the United Nation's Economic and Social Council. At its Web site, the World Bank states that its "primary focus is on helping the poorest people and the poorest countries," and that it aims to "help developing countries onto paths of stable, *sustainable, and equitable growth."

In addition to its economic and development activities, the World Bank also takes an interest in the theory and practice of global *corporate governance. It assists individual countries by assessing their corporate governance institutional frameworks, using the Principles of Corporate Governance of the *Organization for Economic Co-operation and Development as a benchmark. The World Bank also publishes a wide range of guidance, statistics, and research on international corporate governance and financial accountability, an inventory of which is available from the organization's Web site. It also participates in the *International Forum on Accountancy Development.

Web site: *www.worldbank.org*

World Business Council for Sustainable Development (WBCSD) An international organization dedicated to the promotion of environmental and social *sustainability. Based in Geneva, Switzerland, the WBCSD was established in 1991 by a Swiss industrialist, Stephan Schmidheiny. In 1995 the organization merged with the Paris-based World Industry Council for the Environment. The WBCSD Web site describes the organization as a coalition of international corporations "united by a shared commitment to sustainable development via the three pillars of economic growth, ecological balance and social progress" and it describes its mission as follows: "To provide business leadership as a catalyst for change toward sustainable development, and to promote the role of eco-efficiency, innovation and *corporate social responsibility." The WBCSD's activities include publications, research, and sustainability-related projects.

Web site: *www.wbcsd.ch*

WorldCom® A U.S. *multinational telecommunications corporation that filed for Chapter 11 bankruptcy reorganization in 2002. The importance of WorldCom in the history of auditing arose not only from the magnitude of the corporation's accounting scandal that led to adjustments of more than $7 billion to its *financial statements. It was also the timing of events—the WorldCom scandal broke as the business and auditing worlds were still reeling from the aftershocks of the *Enron affair. (WorldCom and Enron shared the same external auditing firm, *Arthur Andersen.)

Among mechanisms used to boost its *earnings, WorldCom had *capitalized billions of dollars of *operating expenses and exploited the use of *cookie jar reserves. Essentially, the corporation appears to have overstretched itself through a series of poorly integrated *acquisitions, and it tried to meet market expectations by *cooking the books. Some sections of the media started to use the term "WorldCon" (Jeter, 2003, 176). Tenacious internal auditor *Cynthia Cooper played a key role in uncovering the accounting *fraud, and she was nominated by Time magazine as one of its "Persons of the Year 2002." Her role in the WorldCom affair brought the importance of internal auditing to public attention.

Further reading: Jeter (2003); Piper (2003); Toffler and Reingold (2003)

World Trade Organization (WTO) An organization that promotes international free trade. Established in 1995 to replace the *General Agreement on Tariffs and Trade, the WTO is based in Geneva, Switzerland. Its activities include the promotion of free trade through negotiated agreements between its member countries, and the provision of mechanisms for resolving trade disputes.

Web site: *www.wto.org*

write-down The recording in *financial statements or a *general ledger of a reduction of the *book value of an *asset. Contrast *write-off and *write-up.

write-off The elimination of a *balance sheet item by direct transfer to an *income statement. For example, an irrecoverable *accounts receivable balance from a *bankrupt customer is normally eliminated by writing off the item to expenses. (In contrast, the existence of a customer receivable balance with doubtful yet possible recovery is normally reflected in the creation of an *allowance for doubtful debts.)

write-up The recording in *financial statements or a *general ledger of an increase in the *book value of an *asset. Contrast *write-down and *write-off.

X, Y, Z

yardstick A comparative measurement used to assess an organization or activity. Yardsticks are used in *benchmarking exercises: For example, an industry average of employee costs as a proportion of sales may be used as a yardstick to measure the reasonableness of an organization's payroll expenses.

year-end **1.** The end of the calendar year: 31 December. **2.** The end of a *financial reporting period of 12 month's duration.

Yellow Book, the A common name for *Government Auditing Standards.

yield **1.** The *return from an investment in an *asset or activity. **2.** The *return from a *bond adjusted for *interest rates and *market prices. A yield to maturity also takes account of a bond's *maturity date. **3.** The output from an agricultural or industrial process.

zero-base budgeting (ZBB) A *budgeting methodology based on the recalculation of costs for each budgetary period. In contrast to traditional budgeting, which is based on historical assumptions and incremental changes in relation to prior years, ZBB requires new cost estimations for each budgeting period, irrespective of historic performance. ZBB also frequently uses *cost-benefit analysis to determine optimal resource allocation in an organization.

zero-sum game A branch of *game theory for the systematic analysis, in competitive conditions, of strategies for the optimal selection of alternative courses of action. The participants in a zero-sum game have conflicting interests: One participant's gain is another participant's loss, and there is no basis or rationale for cooperation.

Sources

The following texts are the sources of quotations in the dictionary and suggested further reading.

Abbott, Andrew (1988), *The System of the Professions: An Essay on the Division of Expert Labor*. Chicago: University of Chicago Press.

Accounting Standards Committee (1975), *The Corporate Report*. London: Accounting Standards Steering Committee.

AICPA (American Institute of Certified Public Accountants) (1997), *Serving the Public Interest: A New Conceptual Framework for Auditor Independence*. New York: AICPA.

AICPA (American Institute of Certified Public Accountants) (2000), *SAS90: Audit Committee Communications*. New York: AICPA.

Allen, David Grayson (1993), *Accounting for Success: A History of Price Waterhouse in America, 1890–1990*. Cambridge, MA: Harvard Business School Press.

American Accounting Association (1973), *A Statement of Basic Accounting Concepts*. Sarasota, FL: American Accounting Association.

Anderson, Urton (1983), *Quality Assurance for Internal Auditing* (Research Report 26). Altamonte Springs, FL: Institute of Internal Auditors.

Anderson, Urton (2003), "Assurance and Consulting Services." In Bailey et al. (2003), pp. 97–127.

Applegate, Dennis (2001), "Controlling Joint Venture Risk." *Internal Auditor* (June), pp. 44–49.

Applegate, Dennis, and Ted Wills (1999), "Integrating COSO." *Internal Auditor* (December), pp. 60–66

Apostolou, Barbara A., John M. Hassell, Sally A. Webber, and Glenn E. Sumners (2001), "The Relative Importance of Management Fraud Risk Factors." *Behavioral Research in Accounting*, Vol. 13.

AS/NZS 4360 (Joint Standards Australia/Standards New Zealand Committee Standard on Risk Management) (1999), Strathfield, New South Wales: Standards Association of Australia.

Bailey, Andrew D., Jr., Audrey A. Gramling, and Sridhar Ramamoorti (eds.) (2003), *Research Opportunities in Internal Auditing*. Altamonte Springs, FL: Institute of Internal Auditors.

Baker, C. Richard (2003), "Investigating Enron as a Public Private Partnership." *Accounting, Auditing & Accountability Journal*, Vol. 16, No. 3, pp. 446–466.

Balkaran, Lal (2002), "Curbing Corruption." *Internal Auditor* (February), pp. 40–47.

Banks, David G. (2001), *Auditing Accounts Payable for Fraud.* Altamonte Springs, FL: Institute of Internal Auditors.

Barrier, Michael (2003), "Cynthia Cooper: One Right Path." *Internal Auditor*(December), pp. 52–57.

Beasley, M.S., J.V. Carcello, and D.R. Hermanson (1999), *Fraudulent Financial Reporting, 1987–1997: An Analysis of U.S. Public Companies.* New York: COSO.

Beattie, Vivien, Stella Fearnley, and Richard Brandt (2001), *Behind Closed Doors: What Company Audit Is Really About.* London and New York: Palgrave.

Béjoint, Henri (2000), *Modern Lexicography.* Oxford and New York: Oxford University Press.

Berle, Adolf Augustus, and G.C. Means (1932, reprinted 1997), *The Modern Corporation and Private Property.* New Brunswick, NJ: Transaction Publishers.

Bernstein, Peter L. (1996), *Against the Gods: The Remarkable Story of Risk.* Hoboken, NJ: John Wiley & Sons.

Blank, Dennis (2003), "A Matter of Ethics." *Internal Auditor* (February), pp. 26–31.

Brief, Richard P. (1980), *Dicksee's Contribution to Accounting Theory and Practice.* New York: Arno Press.

Brink, Victor Z. (1941), *Internal Auditing.* New York: Ronald Press.

Brink, Victor Z. (1977), *Foundations for Unlimited Horizons: The Institute of Internal Auditors, 1941–1976.* Altamonte Springs, FL: Institute of Internal Auditors.

Brink, Victor Z., and Mortimer A. Dittenhofer (1986), *Case Studies in Internal Auditing.* Altamonte Springs, FL: Institute of Internal Auditors.

Brink, Victor Z., Robert R. Moeller, and Herbert N. Witt (1999), *Brink's Modern Internal Auditing,* 5th ed. Hoboken, NJ: John Wiley & Sons.

Brown, R. Gene (1984), *Pacioli on Accounting.* New York: Garland.

Bruntland Report (United Nations World Commission on Environment and Development) (1997). New York: United Nations.

Bryce, Robert (2002), *Pipe Dreams: Greed, Ego, and the Death of Enron.* New York: Public Affairs.

Cadbury, Adrian (2002), *Corporate Governance and Chairmanship: A Personal View.* Oxford and New York: Oxford University Press.

Cadbury Report (*Report of the Committee on the Financial Aspects of Corporate Governance*) (1992). London: Gee Publishing.

Cadmus, Bradford (1962), "Research Activities in the Institute of Internal Auditors." *Internal Auditor* (Fall).

Cadmus, Bradford (1964), *Operational Auditing Handbook.* New York: Institute of Internal Auditors.

CAGC Guidelines (*Principles for Corporate Governance in the Commonwealth: Towards Global Competitiveness and Economic Accountability*)(1999). London: Commonwealth Business Council.

CalPERS (1998), *Corporate Governance Core Principles and Guidelines*. Sacramento, CA: CalPERS.

Camfferman, Kees, and Stephen A. Zeff (1994), "The Contributions of Theodore Limpberg. Jr. (1879–1961) to Dutch Accounting and Auditing." In Edwards (1994), pp. 112–141.

Carsberg, Bryan (1996), "The Role and Future Plans of the International Accounting Standards Committee," in Lapsley (1996), pp. 68–84.

Caswell, Allen T. (1999), "Does the Provision of Non-audit Services Impair Auditor Independence?" *International Journal of Auditing*, Vol. 3, No. 1, pp. 29–40

Chambers, Andrew (1997), *Effective Internal Audits: How to Plan and Implement*, rev. ed. Spilsby, UK: Management Audit.

Chambers, Andrew (1998), *Internal Control*, No. 9 (March).

Chambers, Andrew (2002), *Tolley's Corporate Governance Handbook*. Croydon, UK: Tolley Publishing.

Chambers, Andrew, and Graham Rand (1997), *The Operational Auditing Handbook: Auditing Business Processes*. Chichester, UK, and Hoboken, NJ: John Wiley & Sons.

Chambers, Raymond John (1966), *Accounting, Evaluation and Economic Behavior*. Hemel Hempstead, UK: Prentice Hall.

Chambers, Raymond John (1995), *An Accounting Thesaurus: 500 Years of Accounting*. Oxford, UK: Pergamon.

Chapman, Christy (2001), "The Big Picture." *Internal Auditor* (June), pp. 30–37.

Chapman, Christy (2003), "Sir Adrian Cadbury: Let There Be Light." *Internal Auditor* (February), pp. 38–45.

Chapman, Christy, and Urton Anderson (2002), *Implementing the Professional Practices Framework*. Altamonte Springs, FL: Institute of Internal Auditors.

Chau, Chak-Tong (1996a), "Game Theory and Strategic Auditing, Part I: Introduction." *Managerial Auditing Journal*, Vol. 11, No. 4, pp. 21–25.

Chau, Chak-Tong (1996b), "Game Theory and Strategic Auditing, Part II: Advanced Applications." *Managerial Auditing Journal*, Vol. 11, No. 4, pp. 26–31.

Chiba, Junichi (1994), "Kiyoshi Kurosawa (1902–1990): An Intellectual Portrait." In Edwards (1994), pp. 181–197.

Chwastiak, Michele (1999), "Deconstructing the Principal-Agent Model: A View from the Bottom." *Critical Perspectives on Accounting*, Vol. 10, No. 4, pp. 425–441.

CoCo (Criteria for Control Board) (1995), *Guidance on Control*. Toronto: Canadian Institute of Chartered Accountants.

Cohen Commission (1978), *Report, Conclusions, and Recommendations of the Commission on Auditors' Responsibilities*. New York: American Institute of Certified Public Accountants.

Cohen, Jeffrey, Ganesh Krishnamoorthy, and Arnold M. Wright (2002), "Corporate Governance and the Audit Process." *Contemporary Accounting Research*, Vol. 19, No. 4, pp. 573–594.

Colasse, Bernard, and Romain Durand (1994), "French Accounting Theorists of the Twentieth Century." In Edwards (1994), pp. 41–59.

Cooper, Christine (1997), "Against Postmodernism: Class Orientated Questions for Critical Accounting." *Critical Perspectives on Accounting*, Vol. 8, Nos. 1/2, pp. 15–41.

Cooper, Vivian R.V. (1966), *Manual of Auditing*. London: Gee.

COSO (Committee of Sponsoring Organizations of the Treadway Commission) (1992), *Internal Control: Integrated Framework*. New Jersey: COSO.

Cousins, Jim, Austin Mitchell, Prem Nath Sikka, and Hugh Willmott (1998), *Auditors: Holding the Public to Ransom*. Basildon, UK: Association for Accountancy and Business Affairs.

Crawford, Margaret, and William Stein (2002), "Auditing Risk Management: Fine in Theory But Who Can Do It in Practice?" *International Journal of Auditing*, Vol. 6, No. 2, pp. 119–131.

Crumbley, Larry D., Douglas E. Ziegenfuss, and John J. O'Shaughnessy (2000), *The Big "R": An Internal Auditing Action Adventure*. Durham, NC: Carolina Academic Press.

Davis, Keith (1975), "Five Propositions for Social Responsibility." *Business Horizons* (June), p. 20.

Davison, Barbara (2001), *Understanding the Merger and Acquisition Process*. Altamonte Springs, FL: Institute of Internal Auditors.

Debreceny, Roger, Glen L. Gray, Wai-Lum Tham, Kay-Yiong Goh, and Puay-Ling Tang (2003), "The Development of Embedded Audit Modules to Support Continuous Monitoring in the Electronic Commerce Environment." *International Journal of Auditing*, Vol. 7, No. 2, pp. 169–185.

Deegan, Craig (2002), "The Legitimising Effect of Social and Environmental Disclosures: A Theoretical Foundation." *Accounting, Auditing & Accountability Journal*, Vol. 15, No. 3, pp. 282–311.

Dicksee, Lawrence Robert (1893, and subsequent editions), *Auditing: A Practical Manual for Auditors*. London: Gee.

Dicksee, Lawrence Robert (1927), *Published Balance Sheets and Window Dressing*. London: Gee.

Dittenhofer, Mortimer A. (1983), *Ethics and the Internal Auditor*. Altamonte Springs, FL: Institute of Internal Auditors.

Dittenhofer, Mortimer A. (2001), "Performance Auditing in Government." *Managerial Auditing Journal*, Vol. 16, No. 8, pp. 438–442.

Dittenhofer, Mortimer A., and John T. Sennetti (1994), *Ethics and the Internal Auditor: Ten Years Ago*. Altamonte Springs, FL: Institute of Internal Auditors.

Doherty, Neil (2000), *Integrated Risk Management: Techniques and Strategies for Managing Corporate Risk*. New York: McGraw-Hill.

Dunn, John, and Prem Nath Sikka (1999), *Auditors: Keeping the Public in the Dark*. Basildon, UK: Association for Accountancy & Business Affairs.

Figg, Jonathan (2000a), "Whistleblowing." *Internal Auditor* (April), pp. 30–37.

Figg, Jonathan (2000b), "Outsourcing: A Runaway Train." *Internal Auditor* (June), pp. 48–55.

Flesher, Dale L. (1976), *Operations Auditing in Hospitals.* New York: Lexington Books.

Flesher, Dale L. (1982), *Independent Auditor's Guide to Operational Auditing.* Hoboken, NJ: John Wiley & Sons.

Flesher, Dale L. (1991), *50 Years of Progress through Sharing.* Altamonte Springs, FL: Institute of Internal Auditors.

Flesher, Dale L., and Elaine R. McIntosh (2002), *60 Years of Progress through Sharing* (10-year Supplement to *50 Years of Progress through Sharing*). Altamonte Springs, FL: Institute of Internal Auditors.

Flesher, Dale L., William D. Samson, and Gary John Previts (2003), "The Origins of Value-for-Money Auditing: The Baltimore and Ohio Railroad, 1827–1830." *Managerial Auditing Journal*, Vol. 18, No. 5, pp. 374–386.

Flint, David (1988), *Philosophy and Principles of Auditing: An Introduction.* London: Macmillan.

Fonfeder, Robert, Mark P. Holtzman, and Eugene Maccarrone (2003), "Internal Controls in the Talmud: The Jerusalem Temple." *Accounting Historians Journal*, Vol. 30, No. 1, pp. 73–93.

Fox, Loren (2003), *Enron: The Rise and Fall.* Hoboken, NJ: John Wiley & Sons.

Frecknall Hughes, Jane, Christopher Humphrey, and Stuart Turley (1998), "Learning from Mistakes? Using Corporate Scandals to Enhance Audit Teaching." *International Journal of Auditing*, Vol. 2, No. 2 (July), pp. 89–101.

Friedlob, George T., Frank J. Plewa Jr., Lydia L. F. Schleifer, and Corey D. Schou (1997), *An Auditor's Guide to Encryption.* Altamonte Springs, FL: Institute of Internal Auditors.

Friedman, Milton (1982), *Capitalism and Freedom.* Chicago: University of Chicago Press.

Friedson, Eliot (1986), *Professional Powers: A Study of the Institutionalization of Formal Knowledge.* Chicago: University of Chicago Press.

Frigo, Mark L., George W. Krull, and Stephen V.N. Yates (1995), *The Impact of Business Process Reengineering on Internal Auditing.* Altamonte Springs, FL: Institute of Internal Auditors.

Fullerton, Rosemary R., and Cheryl S. McWatters (2002), "The Role of Performance Measures and Incentive Systems in Relation to the Degree of JIT Implementation." *Accounting, Organizations and Society*, Vol. 27, No. 8, pp. 711–735.

Funston, Rick (2003), "Creating a Risk-Intelligent Organization." *Internal Auditor* (April), pp. 59–63.

Gaffikin, Michael (1994), "Raymond Chambers: Determined Seeker of Truth and Fairness," in John Richard Edwards (ed.) (1994), *Twentieth-Century Accounting Thinkers.* London and New York: Routledge.

Genaldi, Allen J. (2002), "Fraud in Foreign Operations." *Internal Auditor* (August), pp. 61–65.

Glover, Steven M., James Jiambalvo, and Jane Kennedy (2000), "Analytical Procedures and Audit Planning Decisions." *Auditing: A Journal of Practice and Theory,* Vol. 19, No. 2.

Graham, Lynford, and Jean C. Bedard (2003), "Fraud Risk and Audit Planning." *International Journal of Auditing,* Vol. 7, No. 1, pp. 55–70.

Gray, Glen L., and Maryann Jacobi Gray (2000), *Assurance Services within the Audit Profession.* Altamonte Springs, FL: Institute of Internal Auditors.

Greenbury Report (Directors' Remuneration: Report of a Study Group Chaired by Sir Richard Greenbury) (1995). London: Confederation of British Industry.

Groot, Tom, and Kenneth A. Merchant (2000), "Control of International Joint Ventures." *Accounting, Organizations and Society,* Vol. 25, No. 6, pp. 579–607.

Gugler, Klaus (ed.) (2001), *Corporate Governance and Economic Performance.* Oxford and New York: Oxford University Press.

Gunasekaran, A. (1999), "A Framework for the Design and Audit of an Activity-Based Costing System." *Managerial Auditing Journal,* Vol. 14, Nos. 4/5, pp. 161–261.

Habgood, Wendy (ed.) (1994), *Chartered Accountants in England and Wales: A Guide to Historical Records.* Manchester, UK: Manchester University Press.

Hala, Nancy (2003), "If Capitalists Were Angels." *Internal Auditor* (April), pp. 38–43.

Hampel Report (Final Report: The Committee on Corporate Governance) (1998). London: Gee Publishing.

Hartgraves, Al L., and George J. Benston (2002), "The Evolving Accounting Standards for Special Purpose Entities and Consolidations." *Accounting Horizons,* Vol. 16, No. 3.

Hawkes, Lindsay C., and Michael B. Adams (1994), "Total Quality Management: Implications for Internal Audit." *Managerial Auditing Journal,* Vol. 9, No. 4, pp. 11–18.

Henderson, David (2001), *Misguided Virtue: False Notions of Corporate Social Responsibility.* London: Institute of Economic Affairs.

Hermanson, Dana R., and Larry E. Rittenberg (2003), "Internal Audit and Organizational Governance." In Bailey et al. (2003), pp. 25–71.

Higgs Report (Review of the Role and Effectiveness of Non-Executive Directors) (2003). London: Department of Trade and Industry.

Hillary, Ruth (1998), "Environmental Auditing: Concepts, Methods and Developments." *International Journal of Auditing,* Vol. 2, No. 1, pp. 71–85.

Hillison, William, Carl Pacini, and David Sinason (1999), "The Internal Auditor as Fraud-buster." *Managerial Auditing Journal,* Vol. 14, No. 7, pp. 351–363.

Hopwood, Anthony G., and Peter Miller (eds.) (1994), *Accounting as Social and Institutional Practice.* Cambridge, UK: Cambridge University Press.

Hubbard, Larry (2000), *Control Self-Assessment: A Practical Guide.* Altamonte Springs, FL: Institute of Internal Auditors.

Hubbard, Larry (2003), "CSA by Any Name." *Internal Auditor* (December), pp. 22–23.

Humphrey, C. (1991), "Audit Expectations." In Sherer and Turley (1991), pp. 3–21.

IIA (Institute of Internal Auditors) (1999), *A Vision for the Future: Professional Practices Framework for Internal Auditing.* Altamonte Springs, FL: Institute of Internal Auditors.

IIA UK (Institute of Internal Auditors—United Kingdom and Ireland) (1998), *Managing Risk* (Professional Briefing Note 13). London: IIA UK.

Izzard, Harold J.M. (1988), "The Impact of the Standards Outside North America." *Internal Auditor* (June), pp. 36–38.

Jensen, Michael C., and William H. Meckling (1976), "Theory of the Firm: Managerial Behavior, Agency Costs and Ownership Structure." *Journal of Financial Economics,* Vol. 3 (October).

Jeter, Lynne W. (2003), *Disconnected: Deceit and Betrayal at WorldCom.* Hoboken, NJ: John Wiley & Sons.

Jones, Edgar (1995), *True and Fair: A History of Price Waterhouse.* London: Hamish Hamilton.

Jubb, Peter B. (2000), "Auditors as Whistleblowers." *International Journal of Auditing,* Vol. 4, No. 2, pp. 153–167.

Keasey, Kevin, and Mike Wright (eds.) (1999), *Corporate Governance: Responsibilities, Risks, and Remuneration.* Chichester, UK, and Hoboken, NJ: John Wiley & Sons.

Keller, Joyce (1997), *Activity-Based Costing and Management in Government.* Altamonte Springs, FL: Institute of Internal Auditors.

King Report I (Report of the King Committee on Corporate Governance) (1994). Johannesburg: Institute of Directors in Southern Africa.

King Report II (The King Report on Corporate Governance for South Africa, 2002) (2002). Johannesburg,: Institute of Directors in Southern Africa.

Kitchen, Jack, and Robert H. Parker (1994), "Lawrence Robert Dicksee (1864–1932)." In Edwards (1994), pp. 206–224.

Klein, April (2002), "Audit Committee, Board of Director Characteristics, and Earnings Management." *Journal of Accounting and Economics,* Vol. 33, No. 3, pp. 375–400.

Lapsley, Irvine (ed.) (1996), *Essays in Accounting Thought: A Tribute to W.T. Baxter.* Edinburgh: Institute of Chartered Accountants of Scotland.

Larson, Magali Sarfatti (1977), *The Rise of Professionalism: A Sociological Analysis.* Berkeley and Los Angeles: University of California Press.

Lee, Tom A. (1972), *Company Auditing.* Edinburgh: Institute of Chartered Accountants of Scotland.

Lee, Tom A. (ed.) (1988), *The Evolution of Auditing Thought and Practice.* New York: Garland.

Lee, Tom A. (1993), *Corporate Audit Theory.* London and New York: Chapman and Hall.

Lee, Tom A. (1998), "A Stakeholder Approach to Auditing." *Critical Perspectives on Accounting,* Vol. 9, No. 2 (April), pp. 217–226.

Lee, Tom A. (2001), "A Crisis of Confidence: US Auditing in the 21st Century." *International Journal of Auditing*, Vol. 5, No. 1, pp. 1–2.

Lee, Tom A. (2002), "The Shame of Auditing." *International Journal of Auditing*, Vol. 6, No. 3, pp. 211–214.

Lee, Tom A., A. Bishop, and R.H. Parker (1996), *Accounting History from the Renaissance to the Present: A Remembrance of Luca Pacioli.* New York: Garland.

Lehman, Glen (2001), "Reclaiming the Public Sphere: Problems and Prospects for Corporate Social and Environmental Accounting." *Critical Perspectives on Accounting*, Vol. 12, No. 6, pp. 1–21.

Limpberg, Theodore (1985), *The Social Responsibility of the Auditor.* Amsterdam: Limpberg Institute.

Lin, Kenny Z., Ian A.M. Fraser, and David J. Hatherly (2003), "Auditor Analytical Review Judgement: A Performance Evaluation." *British Accounting Review*, Vol. 35, No. 1, pp. 19–34.

Lipton, Martin, and Jay W. Lorsch (1992), "A Modest Proposal for Improved Corporate Governance." *Business Lawyer*, Vol. 48.

Makkhawi, Bilal, and Allen Schick (2003), "Are Auditors Sensitive Enough to Fraud?" *Managerial Auditing Journal*, Vol. 18, Nos. 6/7, pp. 591–598.

Marcella, Albert J., Jr. (1998), *Electronic Commerce: Control Issues for Securing Virtual Enterprises.* Altamonte Springs, FL: Institute of Internal Auditors.

Maroney, James J., and Jean C. Bedard (1997), "Auditors' Use of Inconsistent Evidence." *International Journal of Auditing*, Vol. 1, No. 3, pp. 187–204.

Matthews, Derek, Malcolm Anderson, and John Richard Edwards (1998), *The Priesthood of Industry: The Rise of the Professional Accountant in British Management.* Oxford and New York: Oxford University Press.

Mautz, Robert Khun (1954), *Fundamentals of Auditing.* Hoboken, NJ: John Wiley & Sons.

Mautz, Robert Khun, and Hussein A. Sharaf (1961 and subsequent editions), *The Philosophy of Auditing.* Sarasota, FL: American Accounting Association.

McBarnet, Doreen, and Christopher Whelan (1999), *Creative Accounting and the Cross-Eyed Javelin Thrower.* Chichester, UK, and Hoboken, NJ: John Wiley & Sons.

McCall, Sam M. (2003), "The Auditor as Consultant." *Internal Auditor* (December), pp. 35–39.

McElveen, Mary (2002), "New Rules, New Challenges." *Internal Auditor* (December), pp. 40–47.

McKesson and Robbins, Inc. (1982), *United States of America Before the Securities and Exchange Commission in the Matter of McKesson & Robbins, Inc.: Report on Investigation.* New York: Garland.

McNamee, David (1998), *Business Risk Assessment.* Altamonte Springs, FL: Institute of Internal Auditors.

McNamee, David, and Georges M. Selim (1998), *Risk Management: Changing the Internal Auditor's Paradigm.* Altamonte Springs, FL: Institute of Internal Auditors.

Messier, William F., Jr., and Lizabeth A. Austen (2000), "Inherent Risk and Control Risk Assessments: Evidence on the Effect of Pervasive and Specific Risk Factors." *Auditing: A Journal of Practice and Theory*, Vol. 19, No. 2.

Micklethwait, John, and Adrian Wooldridge (2003), *A Future Perfect: The Challenge and Hidden Promise of Globalization*, 2nd ed. New York: Random House.

Miller, Norman C. (1965), *The Great Salad Oil Swindle*. New York: Howard McCann.

Mills, S.K., and M.S. Bettner (1992), "Ritual and Conflict in the Audit Profession." *Critical Perspectives on Accounting*, Vol. 3, No. 2, pp. 185–200.

Mints, Frederic E. (1954), "Operational Auditing." *The Internal Auditor* (June), p. 32.

Mints, Frederic E. (1972), *Behavioural Patterns in Internal Auditing Relationships*. Altamonte Springs, FL: Institute of Internal Auditors.

Mitchell, Austin, Anthony Puxty, Prem Nath Sikka, and Hugh Willmott (1991), *Accounting for Change: Proposals for Reform of Audit and Accounting*. London: Fabian Society.

Mitchell, Austin, and Prem Nath Sikka (2002), *Dirty Business: The Unchecked Power of Major Accountancy Firms*. Basildon, UK: Association for Accountancy and Business Affairs.

Mitchell, Austin, Prem Nath Sikka, and Hugh Willmott (1998), *The Accountants' Laundromat*. Basildon, UK: Association for Accountancy and Business Affairs.

Mitchell, Austin, Prem Nath Sikka, John Christensen, Philip Morris, and Steven Filling (2002), *No Accounting for Tax Havens*. Basildon, UK: Association for Accountancy and Business Affairs.

Montgomery, Robert Hiester (1912), *Auditing Theory and Practice*. New York: Ronald Press.

Morgan, Stephen L., and Ronell B. Raaum (2001), *Performance Auditing: A Measurement Approach*. Altamonte Springs, FL: Institute of Internal Auditors.

Morita, Tetsuya (1994), "Iwao Iwata (1905–1955)." In Edwards (1994), pp. 166–180.

Mouritsan, Jan (2003), "Intellectual Capital and the Capital Market: The Circulability of Intellectual Capital." *Accounting, Auditing & Accountability Journal*, Vol. 16, No. 1, pp. 18–30.

Mumford, Michael J. (1994), "Edward Stamp (1928–1986): A Crusader for Standards." In Edwards (1994), pp. 274–292.

Mumford, Michael J., and Ken V. Peasnell (1993), *Philosophical Perspectives on Accounting: Essays in Honour of Edward Stamp*. London: Routledge.

Murphy, Ruth, and Margaret Bruce (2003), "Strategy, Accountability, e-Commerce and the Consumer." *Managerial Auditing Journal*, Vol. 18, No. 3, pp. 193–201.

Mutchler, Jane, Stanley Chang, and Douglas Prawitt (2001), *Independence and Objectivity: A Framework for Internal Auditors*. Altamonte Springs, FL: Institute of Internal Auditors.

Myers, Patricia M., and Audrey A. Gramling (1997), "The Perceived Benefits of Certified Internal Auditor Designation." *Managerial Auditing Journal*, Vol. 12, No. 2, pp. 70–79.

NACD (National Association of Corporate Directors) (1996), *The Role of the Board in the Public Company.* Washington, DC: NACD.

NACD (National Association of Corporate Directors) (2000), *Report of the NACD Blue Ribbon Commission on Audit Committees.* Washington, DC: NACD.

NACD (National Association of Corporate Directors) (2001), *Report of the NACD Blue Ribbon Commission on Director Professionalism.* Washington, DC: NACD.

Newman, Benjamin (1964), *Auditing: A CPA Review Text.* Hoboken, NJ: John Wiley & Sons.

Nobes, Christopher, and Robert Parker (2002), *Comparative International Accounting,* 7th ed. London and New York: Pearson.

Nolan Principles (Report of the Committee on Standards in Public Life) (1995). London: Her Majesty's Stationary Office.

Norberg, Johan (2003), *In Defence of Global Capitalism.* Washington, DC: Cato Institute.

Normanton, E.L. (1966), *The Accountability and Audit of Governments.* Manchester, UK: Manchester University Press/New York: Prager.

OECD (Organization for Economic Co-operation and Development) (1999), *OECD Principals of Corporate Governance.* Paris: OECD. Available from *www.oecd.org*

O'Regan, David (2001), "Genesis of a Profession: Towards Professional Status for Internal Auditing." *Managerial Auditing Journal,* Vol. 16, No. 4, pp. 215–226.

O'Regan, David (2003a), *International Auditing: Practical Resource Guide.* Hoboken, NJ: John Wiley & Sons.

O'Regan, David (2003b), "Reflections on the Critical Accounting Movement." *Accountancy, Business and the Public Interest,* Vol. 2, No. 2. Available from: *visar.csustan.edu/ aaba/aaba.htm*

O'Reilly, Vincent M., Patrick J. McDonnell, Barry N. Winograd, James S. Gerson, and Henry R. Jaenicke (1998), *Montgomery's Auditing,* 12th ed. Hoboken, NJ: John Wiley & Sons.

Pacini, Carl, Judyth Swingen, and Hudson Rogers (2002), "The OECD Convention and Bribery in International Business Transactions: Implications for Auditors." *Managerial Auditing Journal,* Vol. 17, No. 4, pp. 205–215.

Percy, J.P. (1997), "Auditing and Corporate Governance: A Look Forward into the 21st Century." *International Journal of Auditing,* Vol. 1, No. 1 (July), pp. 1–12.

Peters, Edgar E. (1994), *Fractional Analysis: Applying Chaos Theory to Investment and Economics.* Hoboken, NJ: John Wiley & Sons.

Phillips, Thomas J., Barry T. Lewis, and Tom Agee (1987), "The Treadway Commission: Implications for Internal Auditors." *Internal Auditor* (October), pp. 24–28.

Pickett, K.H. Spencer (2001), *Internal Control: A Manager's Journey.* Hoboken, NJ: John Wiley & Sons.

Pickett, K.H. Spencer (2003), *The Internal Auditing Handbook,* 2nd ed. Hoboken, NJ: John Wiley & Sons.

Piper, Arthur (2003), "Where WorldCom Went Wrong." *Internal Auditing & Business Risk* (August), pp. 24–27.

Pixley, F.W. (1888), *Auditors: Their Duties and Responsibilities.* London: Effingham Wilson.

Porter, Brenda, Jon Simon, and David Hatherly (2003), *Principles of External Auditing,* 2nd ed. Chicester, UK, and Hoboken, NJ: John Wiley & Sons.

Potthoff, Erich, and Günter Sieben (1994), "Eugen Schmalenbach (1873–1955)." In Edwards (1994), pp. 79–94.

Power, Michael (ed.) (1994a), *Accounting and Science: Natural Enquiry and Commercial Reason.* Cambridge, UK: Cambridge University Press.

Power, Michael (1994b), *The Audit Explosion.* London: Demos.

Power, Michael (1994c), "The Audit Society." In Hopwood and Miller (1994), pp. 299–316.

Power, Michael (1997), *The Audit Society: Rituals of Verification.* Oxford and New York: Oxford University Press.

Power, Michael (2000), "The Audit Society: Second Thoughts." *International Journal of Auditing,* Vol. 4, No. 1, pp. 111–119.

Power, Michael (2003), "Auditing and the Production of Legitimacy." *Accounting, Organizations and Society,* Vol. 28, No. 4, pp. 379–394.

Preuss, Lutz (1998), "On Ethical Theory in Auditing." *Managerial Auditing Journal,* Vol. 13, No. 9, pp. 500–508.

Quinn, Lawrence Richter (2002), "Following the Money Trail." *Internal Auditor* (December), pp. 49–55.

Radcliffe, Vaughan S. (1999), "Knowing Efficiency: The Enactment of Efficiency in Efficiency Auditing." *Accounting, Organizations and Society,* Vol. 24, No. 4, pp. 333–362.

Radde, Leon R. (1982), "Reaching Out: Mark of a Professional." *Internal Auditor* (August), p. 12.

Radebaugh, Lee H., and Sidney J. Gray (1997), *International Accounting and Multinational Enterprises,* 4th ed. Hoboken, NJ: John Wiley & Sons.

Raghunandan, K., William J. Read, and Dasaratha V. Rama (2001), "Audit Committee Composition, "Gray Directors," and Interaction with Internal Auditing." *Accounting Horizons* (June), pp. 105–118.

Ramamoorti, Sridhar (2003), "Internal Auditing: History, Evolution, and Prospects." In Bailey et al. (2003), pp. 1–23.

Ratliff, Richard L., and I. Richard Johnson (1998), "Evidence." *Internal Auditor* (August), pp. 56–61.

Reding, Kurt F., Craig H. Barber, and Kristine K. Digirolamo (2000), "Creating a Business Risk Inventory." *Internal Auditor* (February), pp. 47–51.

Reed, William J., and D.V. Rama (2003), "Whistle-blowing to Internal Aditors." *Managerial Auditing Journal,* Vol. 18, No. 5, pp. 354–362.

Rezaee, Zabihollah, Rick Elam, and Ahmad Sharbatoghlie (2001), "Continuous Auditing: The Audit of the Future." *Managerial Auditing Journal,* Vol. 16, No. 3, pp. 150–158.

Rezaee, Zabihollah, Kingsley O. Olibe, and George Minmier (2003), "Improving Corporate Governance: The Role of Audit Committee Disclosures." *Managerial Auditing Journal*, Vol. 18, Nos. 6/7, pp. 530–537.

Ridley, Jeffrey, and Kystyna Stephens (1996), *International Quality Standards: Implications for Internal Auditing.* Altamonte Springs, FL: Institute of Internal Auditors.

Ridley, Jeffrey, and Andrew Chambers (1998), *Leading Edge Internal Auditing.* London and New York: ICSA Publishing/Prentice Hall.

Ripley, Amanda (2002), "The Night Detective." Available from the Web link: *www.time.com/ time/personoftheyear/2002/poycooper.html*

Rittenberg, Larry E. (1997), *The Outsourcing Dilemma: What Works Best for Internal Auditing.* Altamonte Springs, FL: Institute of Internal Auditors.

Rittenberg, Larry E., and Mark A. Covalski (2001), "Internalization versus Externalization of the Internal Audit Function: An Examination of Professional and Organizational Imperatives." *Accounting, Organizations and Society*, Vol. 26, Nos. 7/8, pp. 617–641.

Root, Steven J. (1998), *Beyond COSO: Internal Control to Enhance Corporate Governance.* Hoboken, NJ: John Wiley & Sons.

Roth, James (2000), *Best Practices: Value-Added Approaches of Four Innovative Internal Auditing Departments.* Altamonte Springs, FL: Institute of Internal Auditors.

Roth, James (2002), *Adding Value: Seven Roads to Success.* Altamonte Springs, FL: Institute of Internal Auditors.

Roth, James (2003), "How Do Internal Auditors Add Value?" *Internal Auditor* (February), pp. 33–37.

Roth, James, and Donald Espersen (2003), *Internal Audit's Role in Corporate Governance: Sarbanes-Oxley Compliance.* Altamonte Springs, FL: Institute of Internal Auditors.

Roussey, Robert S. (2000), "The Case for Global Corporate Governance Rules: An Auditor's Perspective." *International Journal of Auditing*, Vol. 4, No. 3, pp. 203–211.

Rutteman Report (*Internal Control and Financial Reporting: Guidance for Directors of Listed Companies Registered in the UK*) (1994). London: Institute of Chartered Accountants in England and Wales,

Sarbanes-Oxley Act of 2002, H.R. Rep. No. 107–610, July 25, 2002. Title 1 of Pulic Law No. 107–204, July 30, 2002.

Sawyer, Laurence B. (1973), *The Practice of Modern Internal Auditing.* Altamonte Springs, FL: Institute of Internal Auditors.

Sawyer, Laurence B. (1974), *Modern Internal Auditing: What's It All About?* Altamonte Springs, FL: Institute of Internal Auditors.

Sawyer, Laurence B. (1983), *Elements of Management-Oriented Auditing.* Altamonte Springs, FL: Institute of Internal Auditors.

Sawyer, Laurence B. (1998), "Performance Evaluators?" *Internal Auditor* (February), p. 112.

Sawyer, Laurence B., and Gerald Vinten (1996), *The Manager and the Internal Auditor: Partners for Profit.* Hoboken, NJ: John Wiley & Sons.

Sawyer, Laurence B., Mortimer A. Dittenhofer, and James H. Scheiner (2003), *Sawyer's Internal Auditing: The Practice of Modern Internal Auditing,* 5th ed. Altamonte Springs, FL: Institute of Internal Auditors.

Schandl, Charles W. (1978), *Theory of Auditing: Evaluation, Investigation, and Judgment* Houston, TX: Scholars Book Co.

Schilit, Howard (2002), *Financial Shenanigans: How to Detect Accounting Gimmicks and Fraud in Financial Reports.* New York: McGraw-Hill.

Schwartz, Mimi, and Sherron Watkins (2003), *Power Failure: The Inside Story of the Collapse of Enron.* New York: Doubleday.

Scruton, Roger (2002), *The West and the Rest: Globalization and the Terrorist Threat.* New York: Continuum.

Selim, Georges M., Sudi Sudarsanam, and Michael K. Lavine (2002), *Mergers, Acquisitions, and Divestitures: Control and Audit Best Practices.* Altamonte Springs, FL: Institute of Internal Auditors.

Shafer, William E., Roselyn E. Morris, and Alice A. Ketchand (2001), "Effects of Personal Values on Auditors' Ethical Decisions." *Accounting, Auditing & Accountability Journal,* Vol. 14, No. 3, pp. 254–277.

Shelton, Sandra Waller, O. Ray Whittington, and David Landsittel (2001), "Auditing Firms' Fraud Risk Assessment Practices." *Accounting Horizons,* Vol. 15, No. 1.

Sherer, M., and S. Turley (eds.) (1991), *Current Issues in Auditing.* London and New York: Paul Chapman.

Sikka, Prem Nath, and Hugh Willmott (1997), "Practising Critical Accounting." *Critical Perspectives on Accounting,* Vol. 8, Nos. 1/2, pp. 149–165.

Sikka, Prem Nath, Anthony Puxty, Hugh Willmott, and Christine Cooper (1998), "The Impossibility of Eliminating the Expectations Gap: Some Theory and Evidence." *Critical Perspectives on Accounting,* Vol. 9, No. 3, pp. 299–330.

Sikka, Prem Nath, Bob Wearing, B. and Ajit Nayak (1999), *No Accounting for Exploitation.* Basildon, UK: Association for Accountancy & Business Affairs.

Smith Report (Audit Committees: Combined Code Guidance) (2003). London: Financial Reporting Council.

Smith, James E. (1975), *An Evaluation of Selected Internal Auditing Terms* (IIA Research Report 19). Altamonte Springs, FL: Institute of Internal Auditors.

Smith, Terry (1996), *Accounting for Growth,* 2nd ed. London: Century Business Books.

Spacek, Leonard (1989), *The Growth of Arthur Andersen & Co., 1928–1973: An Oral History.* New York: Garland.

Spira, Laura (2002), *The Audit Committee: Performing Corporate Governance.* New York: Kluwer Academic Publishers.

Stamp, Edward (1984), *Selected Papers on Accounting, Auditing, and Professional Problems.* New York: Garland.

Stamp, Edward, and Maurice Moonitz (1979), *International Auditing Standards*. London: Prentice Hall.

Stephens, John (1990), *The Italian Renaissance: The Origins of Intellectual and Artistic Change before the Reformation*. London and New York: Longman.

Stevenson, Joanna E. (2002), "Auditor Independence: A Comparative Descriptive Study of the UK, France and Italy." *International Journal of Auditing*, Vol. 6, No. 2, pp. 155–182.

TIAA-CREF (Teachers Insurance and Annuity Association College Retirement Equities Fund] (2002), *Policy Statement on Corporate Governance*. Available from: *www.tiaa-cref.org/libra/governance*

Toffler, Barbara Ley, and Jennifer Reingold (2003), *Final Accounting: Ambition, Greed, and the Fall of Arthur Andersen*. New York: Broadway Books.

Treadway Commission (1987), *Report of the National Commission on Fraudulent Financial Reporting*. Washington, DC: National Commission on Fraudulent Financial Reporting.

Turnbull Report (Internal Control: Guidance to Directors on the Combined Code) (1999). London: Institute of Chartered Accountants in England and Wales.

Tweedie, David (1993), "The Accountant: A Tradesman or a Professional?" In Mumford and Peasnell (1993), pp. *x–xxv*.

Usoff, Catherine A., Jay C. Thibodeau, and Priscilla Burnaby (2002), "The Importance of Intellectual Capital and Its Effect on Performance Measurement Systems." *Managerial Auditing Journal*, Vol. 17, Nos. 1/2, pp. 9–15.

Vanasco, Rocco R. (1998), "Fraud Auditing." *Managerial Auditing Journal*, Vol. 13, No. 1, pp. 4–71.

Vanasco, Rocco R. (1999), "The Foreign Corrupt Practices Act: An International Perspective." *Managerial Auditing Journal*, Vol. 14, Nos. 4/5, pp. 161–261.

Verschoor, Curtis C. (2000), *Audit Committee Briefing: Understanding the 21st Century Audit Committee and Its Governance Roles*. Altamonte Springs, FL: Institute of Internal Auditors.

Verschoor, Curtis C. (2002), "Reflections on the Audit Committee's Role." *Internal Auditor* (April), pp. 26–35.

Viénot Report (1995). Paris: Conseil d'Administration des Sociétés Cotées.

Vinten, Gerald (1991), "Teaching Chaos: How to Manage Operational Audits." *Managerial Auditing Journal*, Vol. 6, No. 2.

Vinten, Gerald (1992), *Whistleblowing Auditors: A Contradiction in Terms?* London: Chartered Association of Certified Accountants.

Vinten, Gerald (ed.) (1994), *Whistleblowing: Subversion or Corporate Citizenship?* New York: St. Martin's Press.

Vinten, Gerald (1996), *Internal Audit Research: The First Half Century*. London: Certified Accountants Educational Trust.

Vinten, Gerald (2003), "Enronitis: Dispelling the Disease." *Managerial Auditing Journal*, Vol. 18, Nos. 6/7, pp. 448–455.

Walker, David (1997), "Internal Audit Reports: Keeping Them on Target." *Managerial Auditing Journal*, Vol. 11, No. 4, pp. 11–20.

Whyte, William H. (2002, originally published 1956), *The Organization Man*. Philadelphia, PA: University of Pennsylvania Press.

Wilks, T. Jeffrey (2002), "Predecisional Distortion of Evidence as a Consequence of Real-Time Audit Review." *The Accounting Review*, Vol. 77, No. 1.

Williams, Russell (2003), "Consultobabble and the Client-Consultant Relationship." *Managerial Auditing Journal*, Vol. 18, No. 2, pp. 134–139.

Windsor, Carolyn A., and Neal M. Ashkenasy (1995), "The Effect of Client Management Bargaining Power, Moral Reasoning Development, and Belief in a Just World on Auditor Independence." *Accounting, Organizations and Society*, Vol. 20, Nos. 7/8, pp. 701–720.

Wolf, Fran M., James A. Tackett, and Gregory A. Claypool (1999), "Audit Disaster Futures: Antidotes for the Expectation Gap?" *Managerial Auditing Journal*, Vol. 14, No. 9, pp. 468–478.

Wolnizer, Peter W. (1987), *Auditing as Independent Verification*. Sydney, Australia: Sydney University Press.

Woodward, David, Pam Edwards, and Frank Birkin (2001), "Some Evidence on Executives' Views of Corporate Social Responsibility." *British Accounting Review*, Vol. 33, No. 3, pp. 357–397.

Youkins, E.W. (1983), "A History of Auditors' Independence in the US." *Accounting Historians Notebook* (Spring), pp. 22–27.

Ziegenfuss, Douglas (1994), *Challenges and Opportunities of Small Internal Auditing Organizations*. Altamonte Springs, FL: Institute of Internal Auditors.

Abbreviations

The following abbreviations have dictionary entries under their full format:

AA	Arthur Andersen
AAA	American Accounting Association
AABA	Association for Accountancy and Business Affairs
AAOIFI	Accounting and Auditing Organization for Islamic Financial Institutions
AAT	Association of Accounting Technicians
ABB	Activity Based Budgeting
ABC	Activity Based Costing
ABO	Accounting, Behavior and Organizations (Section of the AAA)
ACAUS	Association of Chartered Accountants in the United States
ACCA	Association of Chartered Certified Accountants
ACFE	Association of Certified Fraud Examiners
ACL	Audit Command Language
ACUA	Association of College and University Auditors
ADB	Asian Development Bank
ADBG	African Development Bank Group
AFC	*Association Francophone de Comptabilité*
AGA	Association of Government Accountants
AIA	Association of International Accountants
AICPA	American Institute of Certified Public Accountants
AIMR	Association for Investment Management and Research
ANSI	American National Standards Institute

APB	Accounting Principles Board *also* Auditing Practices Board
ASB	Auditing Standards Board
ASCA	Arab Society for Certified Accountants
ASCII	American Standard Code for Information Interchange
ASWA	American Society of Women Accountants
BAA	British Accounting Association
BAP	Beta Alpha Psi
BEAC	Board of Environmental, Health & Safety Auditor Certifications
BOM	bill of materials
BPR	business process re-engineering
CA	chartered accountant
CAAA	Canadian Academic Accounting Association
CAATs	computer assisted audit techniques
CAE	Chief Audit Executive
CAGC	Commonwealth Association for Corporate Governance
CalPERS	California Public Employees' Retirement System
CAPA	Confederation of Asian and Pacific Accountants
CAPM	capital asset pricing model
CCAB	Consultative Committee of Accountancy Bodies
CCSA	Certification in Control Self-Assessment
CERES	Coalition for Environmentally Responsible Economies
CEO	Chief Executive Officer
CFO	Chief Financial Officer
CFSA	Certified Financial Services Auditor
CGAP	Certified Government Auditing Professional
CI	continuous improvement
CIA	Certified Internal Auditor *also* Chief Internal Auditor
CICA	Canadian Institute of Chartered Accountants

CICPA	Chinese Institute of Certified Public Accountants
CIAO	Critical Infrastructure Assurance Office
CIMA	Chartered Institute of Management Accountants
CIPFA	Chartered Institute of Public Finance and Accountancy
CISA	Certified Information Systems Auditor
CNCC	*Compagnie Nationale des Commissaires aux Comptes*
CoCo	Criteria of Control (Board)
COGS	cost of goods sold
COS	cost of sales
COSO	Committee of Sponsoring Organizations (of the Treadway Commission)
CPA	Certified Public Accountant *also* critical path analysis
CPEA	Certified Professional Environmental Auditor
CRSA	Control Risk Self Assessment
CSA	Control Self Assessment
CSR	corporate social reporting *also* corporate social responsibility
DBMS	database management system
DCF	discounted cash flow
EAA	European Accounting Association
ECGI	European Corporate Governance Institute
ECSAFA	Eastern, Central and Southern African Federation of Accountants
EDI	electronic data interchange
EITF	Emerging Issues Task Force
EMH	efficient markets hypothesis
EOQ	economic order quantity
EPS	earnings per share
ERM	enterprise risk management
EV	expected value

FAF	Financial Accounting Foundation
FASAC	Financial Accounting Standards Advisory Council
FASB	Financial Accounting Standards Board
FCPA	*Foreign Corrupt Practices Act*
FEE	*Fédération des Experts Comptables Européens*
FEI	Financial Executives International
FIFO	first-in first-out
FLA	Fair Labor Association
FMCG	fast moving consumer goods
FRC	Financial Reporting Council
FV	future value
FY	fiscal year *also* financial year
GAAP	Generally Accepted Accounting Principles
GAAS	Generally Accepted Auditing Standards
GAGAS	Generally Accepted Government Auditing Standards
GASAC	Government Accounting Standards Advisory Council
GASB	Governmental Accounting Standards Board
GAIN	Global Auditing Information Network
GAO	General Accounting Office
GATT	General Agreement on Tariffs and Trade
GCGF	Global Corporate Governance Forum
GDP	Gross Domestic Product
GL	general ledger *also grand livre*
GRI	Global Reporting Initiative
HP	hire purchase
IAAER	International Association for Accounting Education and Research
IAAIA	International Association of Airline Internal Auditors
IAASB	International Auditing and Assurance Standards Board

IAF	internal audit function
IAPC	International Auditing Practices Committee
IAPS	International Auditing Practice Statements
IAS	International Accounting Standards
IASB	International Accounting Standards Board *also* Internal Auditing Standards Board
IASC	International Accounting Standards Committee
IASCF	IASC Foundation
IAWWW	Internal Auditors World Wide Web
IBRACON	*Instituto dos Auditores Independentes do Brasil*
ICAA	Institute of Chartered Accountants in Australia
ICAEW	Institute of Chartered Accountants in England and Wales
ICAB	Institute of Chartered Accountants of Bangladesh
ICAI	Institute of Chartered Accountants in Ireland *also* Institute of Chartered Accountants of India
ICAN	Institute of Chartered Accountants of Nigeria
ICANZ	Institute of Chartered Accountants of New Zealand
ICAP	Institute of Chartered Accountants of Pakistan
ICAS	Institute of Chartered Accountants of Scotland
ICASL	Institute of Chartered Accountants of Sri Lanka
ICGN	International Corporate Governance Network
ICPAK	Institute of Certified Public Accountants of Kenya
IFAC	International Federation of Accountants
IFAD	International Forum on Accountancy Development
IFRS	International Financial Reporting Standards
IIA	Institute of Internal Auditors
IMA	Institute of Management Accountants
IMF	International Monetary Fund
INTOSAI	International Organization of Supreme Audit Institutions
IOSCO	International Organization of Securities Commissions

IRR	internal rate of return
IRS	Internal Revenue Service
ISA	International Standards on Auditing
ISACA	Information Systems Audit and Control Association
ISO	International Organization for Standardization
JICPA	Japanese Institute of Certified Public Accountants
JIT	just-in-time
KICPA	Korean Institute of Certified Public Accountants
KPI	Key Performance Indicator
KPMG	Klynveld, Peat, Marwick, and Goerdeler
LAN	local area network
L/C	letter of credit
LDC	less developed country
LIFO	last-in first-out
LP	linear programming
MAS	management advisory services
MIA	Malaysian Institute of Accountants
MICPA	Malaysian Institute of Certified Public Accountants
MIS	management information system
MNC	multinational corporation
MNE	multinational enterprise
NACD	National Association of Corporate Directors
NALGA	National Association of Local Government Auditors
NAO	National Audit Office
NAS	nonaudit services
NASBA	National Association of State Boards of Accountancy
NED	nonexecutive director
NIFO	next-in first-out
(Royal) NIVRA	*Koninklijk Nederlands Instituut van Registeraccountants*

NGO	nongovernmental organization
NMIA	(Association of) News Media Internal Auditors
NPV	net present value
NRV	net realizable value
OBS	off-balance sheet
OECD	Organization for Economic Co-operation and Development
OIOS	Office of Internal Oversight Services
OTC	over-the-counter (market)
PCAOB	Public Company Accounting Oversight Board
PCG	plan comptable général
P/E ratio	price/earnings ratio
PERT	program evaluation and review techniques
PI	perpetual inventory
PICPA	Philippine Institute of Certified Public Accountants
PPF	Professional Practices Framework (of the Institute of Internal Auditors)
POS	point of sale
PwC	PricewaterhouseCoopers
R&D	research and development
RBA	risk-based auditing
RQB	Recognised Qualifying Body
SAI	State Audit Institution *also* Supreme Audit Institution
SAICA	South African Institute of Chartered Accountants
SAR	social and environmental reporting
SAS	Statements on Auditing Standards [U.S.] *also* Statements of Auditing Standards [U.K.]
SEC	Securities and Exchange Commission
SFAS	Statements of Financial Accounting Standards
SIAS	Statements on Internal Auditing Standards

SLA	service level agreement
SPE	Special Purpose Entity
SWOT	strengths, weaknesses, opportunities, threats
TB	trial balance
T-bill	Treasury bill
TI	Transparency International
TIAA-CREF	Teachers Insurance and Annuity Association College Retirement Equities Fund
TNC	transnational corporation
TQM	total quality management
UITF	Urgent Issues Task Force
VAT	value added tax
VAR	value-at-risk
VFM	value-for-money
WACC	weighted average cost of capital
WBCSD	World Business Council for Sustainable Development
WIP	work-in-process *also* work-in-progress
WTO	World Trade Organization
ZBB	zero-base budgeting

Appendix 1
List of Institutions

The following institutions and organizations appear as separate entries in the dictionary.

Academy of Accounting Historians

Accenture

AccountAbility

Accountancy Foundation

Accounting and Auditing Organization for Islamic Financial Institutions (AAOIFI)

Accounting Foundation

Accounting Hall of Fame

Accounting Principles Board (APB)

African Development Bank Group (ADBG)

Allied Crude Vegetable Oil Refining Corporation

American Accounting Association (AAA)

American Institute of Certified Public Accountants (AICPA)

American National Standards Institute (ANSI)

American Society of Women Accountants (ASWA)

Arab Society for Certified Accountants (ASCA)

Arthur Andersen (AA)

Asian Development Bank (ADB)

Association for Accountancy and Business Affairs (AABA)

Association for Investment Management and Research (AIMR)

Association Francophone de Comptabilité (AFC)

Association of Accounting Technicians (AAT)

Association of Certified Fraud Examiners (ACFE)

Association of Chartered Accountants in the United States (ACAUS)

Association of Chartered Certified Accountants (ACCA)

Association of College and University Auditors (ACUA)

Association of Government Accountants (AGA)

Association of International Accountants (AIA)

Association of News Media Internal Auditors (NMIA)

Audit and Attest Standards Team

Auditing Practices Board (APB)

Auditing Roundtable

Auditing Standards Board (ASB)

AuditNet

Audit Trends

Beta Alpha Psi (BAP)

Big Five, The

Big Four, The

Blue Ribbon Commissions

Board of Environmental, Health & Safety Auditor Certifications (BEAC)

British Accounting Association (BAA)

California Public Employees' Retirement System (CalPERS)

Canadian Academic Accounting Association (CAAA)

Canadian Institute of Chartered Accountants (CICA)

Chartered Institute of Management Accountants (CIMA)

Chartered Institute of Public Finance and Accountancy (CIPFA)

Chinese Institute of Certified Public Accountants (CICPA)

Coalition for Environmentally Responsible Economies (CERES)

Committee of Sponsoring Organizations of the Treadway Commission (COSO)

Commonwealth Association for Corporate Governance (CAGC)

Compagnie Nationale des Commissaires aux Comptes (CNCC)

Confederation of Asian and Pacific Accountants (CAPA)

Consiglio Nazionale dei Dottori Commercialisti

Consultative Committee of Accountancy Bodies (CCAB)

Corporate Library, The

CPA Australia

CPA Ireland

Criteria for Control (CoCo) Board

Critical Infrastructure Assurance Office (CIAO)

Deloitte Touche Tohmatsu

Eastern, Central and Southern African Federation of Accountants (ECSAFA)

Emerging Issues Task Force (EITF)

Enron

Ernst & Young

European Accounting Association (EAA)

European Corporate Governance Institute (ECGI)

European Federation of Accountants

Fair Labor Association (FLA)

Fédération des Experts Comptables Européens (FEE)

Financial Accounting Foundation (FAF)

Financial Accounting Standards Advisory Council (FASAC)

Financial Accounting Standards Board (FASB)

Financial Executives International (FEI)

Financial Reporting Council (FRC)

General Accounting Office (GAO)

General Agreement on Tariffs and Trade (GATT)

Global Auditing Information Network (GAIN)

Global Corporate Governance Forum (GCGF)

Global Reporting Initiative (GRI)

Governmental Accounting Standards Advisory Council (GASAC)

Governmental Accounting Standards Board (GASB)

IASC Foundation

Information Systems Audit and Control Association (ISACA)

Institut der Wirtschaftprüfer in Deutschland e.V.

Institute of Certified Public Accountants in Ireland

Institute of Certified Public Accountants in Israel

Institute of Certified Public Accountants of Kenya (ICPAK)

Institute of Chartered Accountants in Australia (ICAA)

Institute of Chartered Accountants in England and Wales (ICAEW)

Institute of Chartered Accountants in Ireland (ICAI)

Institute of Chartered Accountants of Bangladesh (ICAB)

Institute of Chartered Accountants of India (ICAI)

Institute of Chartered Accountants of New Zealand (ICANZ)

Institute of Chartered Accountants of Nigeria (ICAN)

Institute of Chartered Accountants of Pakistan (ICAP)

Institute of Chartered Accountants of Scotland (ICAS)

Institute of Chartered Accountants of Sri Lanka (ICASL)

Institute of Internal Auditors (IIA)

Institute of Internal Auditors UK and Ireland

Institute of Management Accountants (IMA)

Institute of Social and Ethical Accountability

Instituto dos Auditores Independentes do Brasil (IBRACON)

Internal Auditing Standards Board (IASB)

Internal Revenue Service (IRS)

International Accounting Standards Board (IASB)

International Accounting Standards Committee (IASC)

International Association for Accounting Education and Research (IAAER)

International Association of Airline Internal Auditors (IAAIA)

International Auditing and Assurance Standards Board (IAASB)

International Auditing Practices Committee (IPAC)

International Corporate Governance Network (ICGN)

International Federation of Accountants (IFAC)

International Forum on Accountancy Development (IFAD)

International Monetary Fund (IMF)

International Organization for Standardization (ISO)

International Organization of Securities Commissions (IOSCO)

International Organization of Supreme Audit Institutions (INTOSAI)

IT Governance Institute

Japanese Institute of Certified Public Accountants (JICPA)

Jefferson Wells International

Koninklijk Nederlands Instituut van Registeraccountants (Royal NIVRA)

Korean Institute of Certified Public Accountants (KICPA)

KPMG International

Malaysian Institute of Accountants (MIA)

Malaysian Institute of Certified Public Accountants (MICPA)

Management Audit Ltd

Mc2 Management Consulting

McKesson and Robbins Inc.

National Association of Corporate Directors (NACD)

National Association of Local Government Auditors (NALGA)

National Association of State Boards of Accountancy

National Audit Office (NAO)

Office of Internal Oversight Services (OIOS)

Ordre des Experts-Comptables

Organization for Economic Co-operation and Development (OECD)

Pacioli Society

Philippine Institute of Certified Public Accountants (PICPA)

PricewaterhouseCoopers (PwC)

Protiviti

Public Company Accounting Oversight Board (PCAOB)

Recognised Qualifying Body (RQB)

Risk Management and Governance Board

Securities Exchange Commission (SEC)

South African Institute of Chartered Accountants (SAICA)

Teachers Insurance and Annuity Association College Retirement Equities Fund (TIAA-CREF)

Transparency International (TI)

Urgent Issues Task Force (UITF)

World Bank

World Business Council for Sustainable Development (WBCSD)

WorldCom

World Trade Organization (WTO)

Appendix 2
List of Publications, Texts, and Legislation

The following publications, texts, and legislative acts appear as separate entries in the dictionary. To follow the format of the entries, all these items have been rendered in italics.

Abacus: A Journal of Accounting, Finance and Business Studies

ABO Reporter

ACCA Internal Audit Bulletin

Accountancy

Accountancy, Business, and the Public Interest

Accountancy Ireland

Accountancy S.A.

Accountant, The

Accounting & Business

Accounting & Business Research

Accounting, Auditing and Accountability Journal

Accounting, Business, and Financial History

Accounting Education: An International Journal

Accounting Historians Journal

Accounting History

Accounting Horizons

Accounting, Organizations and Society

Accounting Review, The

Accounting Technology

Accounting Today

Advances in Accounting

Advances in International Accounting

AS/NZS 4360

Auditing: A Journal of Practice and Theory

Audit News

Auditor's Report, The

Audit Vision

Auditwire

Behavioral Research in Accounting

Big "R," The

British Accounting Review

Cadbury Report

CAE Bulletin

CAGC Guidelines

CA Magazine (Canada)

CA Magazine (Scotland)

Cohen Commission Report

Combined Code

Comptabilité, Contrôle, Audit

Contemporary Accounting Research

Control & Governance Series

Corporate Governance Site, The

Corporate Report, The

COSO Report

CPA Journal

CPA Letter

Critical Perspectives on Accounting

CSA Sentinel

Electronic Accountant

European Accounting Review

Financial Accountability and Management

Financial Executive Magazine

Foreign Corrupt Practices Act (FCPA)

Fraudulent Financial Reporting: 1987–1997

Gaming Auditorium

Governance

Government Auditing Standards

Greenbury Report

Guidance on Control

Guidelines for Internal Control Standards

Hampel Report

Head 2 Head

Higgs Report

Information Systems Control Journal

In Our Opinion

Internal Auditing & Business Risk

Internal Auditor

Internal Auditors World Wide Web (IAWWW)

Internal Control–Integrated Framework

Internal Control Newsletter

International Accountant

International Accounting Bulletin

International Accounting Standards (IAS)

International Auditing Practice Statements (IAPS)

International Financial Reporting Standards (IFRS)

International Journal of Auditing

International Journal of Government Auditing

International Standards on Auditing (ISA)

Journal of Accountancy

Journal of Accounting and Economics

Journal of Accounting Literature

Journal of Accounting Research

Journal of International Financial Management and Accounting

King Reports

Kingston Cotton Mill

Local Government Auditing Quarterly

Managerial Auditing Journal

Nolan Principles

Petroleum Accounting and Financial Management Journal

Philosophy of Auditing, The

Practical Accountant

Practicing CPA, The

Rapport Viénot

Revue Française de la Comptabilité

Rutteman Report

Sarbanes-Oxley Act

Sawyer's Internal Auditing

Sherman Antitrust Act

Smith Report

Staff Accounting Bulletin

Standards for the Professional Practice of Internal Auditing

Statement of Responsibilities of the Internal Auditor

Statements of Auditing Standards (SAS)

Statements of Financial Accounting Standards (SFAS)

Statements on Auditing Standards (SAS)

Statements on Internal Auditing Standards (SIAS)

Strategic Finance Magazine

Tone at the Top

Treadway Commission Report

True and Fair

Turnbull Report

Viénot Report

WebCPA

Yellow Book, The

Appendix 3
Biographical Names

The following individuals have been included as entries in the dictionary:

Anderson, Urton L. (born 1951)

Brink, Victor Z. (1906–1992)

Cadmus, Bradford (d. 1964)

Chambers, Andrew (born 1943)

Chambers, Raymond John (born 1917)

Cooper, Cynthia (born c.1964)

Dicksee, Lawrence Robert (1864–1932)

Flesher, Dale L. (born 1945)

Iwata, Iwao (1905–1955)

Kurosawa, Kiyoshi (1902–1990)

Lee, Tom A. (born 1941)

Limpberg, Theodore (1879–1961)

Mautz, Robert Khun (born 1915)

McNamee, David (born 1945)

Milne, Robert B. (d. 1964)

Mitchell, Austin (born 1934)

Montgomery, Robert Hiester (1872–1953)

Pacioli, Luca (1445–1517)

Power, Michael (born 1957)

Radde, Leon (d. 1986)

Ridley, Jeffrey (born 1930)

Roth, James (born 1947)

Sawyer, Laurence B. (1911–2002)

Schmalenbach, Eugen (1873–1955)

Sikka, Prem Nath (born 1951)

Stamp, Edward (1928–1986)

Thurston, John B. (1908–1951)

Verschoor, Curtis C. (born 1931)

Vinten, Gerald (born 1948)

Appendix 4
Non-English Terms

The following non-English terms appear as entries in the dictionary. Although some of the terms have been fairly acclimatized into English, all recognizably non-English words (other than the names of organizations or publications) have been included here for the sake of completeness. To follow the format of the entries, all these items have been rendered in italics.

ad valorem (Latin)

caveat emptor (Latin)

comptroller (Anglo-Norman French)

contra (Latin)

crore (Hindi)

dottore commercialista (Italian)

ex gratia (Latin)

expert-comptable (French)

grand livre (French)

gratis (Latin)

inter alia (Latin)

kaizen (Japanese)

kanban (Japanese)

lakh (Hindi)

lex (Latin)

lien (French)

pari passu (Latin)

per annum (Latin)

per capita (Latin)

per diem (Latin)

plan comptable général (French)

prima facie (Latin)

pro forma (Latin)

pro rata (Latin)

quasi (Latin)

savoir-faire (French)

tranche (French)

ultra vires (Latin)